XML-BASED CONTENT MANAGEMENT

XML-BASED CONTENT MANAGEMENT

Integration, Methodologies, and Tools

RICARDO EITO-BRUN

Chandos Publishing is an imprint of Elsevier
50 Hampshire Street, 5th Floor, Cambridge, MA 02139, United States
The Boulevard, Langford Lane, Kidlington, OX5 1GB, United Kingdom

British Library Cataloguing-in-Publication Data
A catalogue record for this book is available from the British Library

Library of Congress Cataloging-in-Publication Data
A catalog record for this book is available from the Library of Congress

ISBN: 978-0-08-100204-9 (print)
ISBN: 978-0-08-100241-4 (online)

For information on all Chandos Publishing publications
visit our website at https://www.elsevier.com/books-and-journals

Publisher: Glyn Jones
Acquisition Editor: Glyn Jones
Editorial Project Manager: Ashlie M. Jackman
Production Project Manager: Debasish Ghosh
Cover Designer: Victoria Pearson

Typeset by MPS Limited, Chennai, India

CONTENTS

INTRODUCTION

The book discusses the standards, tools, and techniques for managing the life cycle of XML-based content. XML has become a consolidated standard in different industries and activity sectors for encoding and exchanging of information.

The design and deployment of XML-based solutions requires knowledge of specific tools and a methodological approach that differs from the one used to design and deploy traditional document management solutions. The adoption of tools and the identification of integration requirements between them need to be based on a well-defined methodology. This methodology should cover the different phases of the content and metadata management life cycle, from generation to archiving, and demonstrate compliance with existing content management and archiving standards like OAIS or ISO standards for trusted repositories.

This book describes different scenarios where XML can be used for content and metadata management and the tools needed to support the deployment of these solutions and obtain competitive advantages. Although the book provides descriptions of the functionalities characteristics of XML tools, the description of specific tools is out of the scope of this book. References to tools are made only to support and illustrate the description of the typical functionalities and integration capabilities they offer.

The reader will find an updated view of consolidated technologies for structured data management, with a link between technologies, reference models, tools and standards, and the necessary conceptual and practical information to start working with different schemas for data encoding and exchange: EAD, DITA, TEI, etc.

The book is structured as follows: Chapter 1, XML: The Basis of the Language, provides an introduction to XML and structured markup. Chapter 2, Scenarios for Structured Data Management, describes different scenarios for structured data management: archival description, exchange of digital objects, cultural heritage or technical documentation. Chapter 3, XML Authoring and Presentation Tools, introduces the tools for authoring and publishing XML content. Chapter 4, Databases for XML Data, focuses on the tools to store and index XML content, with references to Solr, native XML database, and NoSQL. This chapter also provides a description of the XQuery query language. Chapter 5, Life Cycle of XML Publication, discusses the life cycle of XML data and provides a description of related standards such as ISO/IEC 26531 or content delivery formats and protocols like OAI-PMH, RSS, EPUB, and RDF, and the OAIS reference model for archiving.

Finally, Chapter 6, Case Study and Methodology, describes an initiative where the different tools and standards described in the previous chapters were successfully applied in the deployment of an XML-based portal for managing and publishing content.

CHAPTER 1

XML: The Basis of the Language

1.1 INTRODUCTION

Markup languages and XML (*eXtensible Markup Language*) in particular, have become a widely used tool to support the exchange and transfer of data in electronic format. The origin of XML dates back to 1996, with the publication of the first draft of the specification by the W3C. Two years later, on February 10, 1998, the draft reached recommendation status, which corresponds to a formal, released standard in W3C terminology.

Since the publication of XML 1.0 in 1998, the language has been reviewed and some revisions have been released by W3C with minor corrections. Now, 20 years after the publication of the first draft of XML, the XML language is present in many different areas. Computing systems make extensive use of this language to exchange data between software applications through public and private networks; a large amount of content repositories are using XML to keep and store both content and metadata, and linked open data (LOD) initiatives heavily depend on this format to encode and share metadata. It is possible to say that XML has become the most relevant standard to support data encoding and exchange and the integration of heterogeneous software systems.

XML should be understood as a family of related standards. Although there is one specific W3C recommendation that specifies key characteristics of the language, W3C has also published a set of additional, complementary, specifications related to XML. The set of XML-related recommendations include XHTML (*Hypertext Markup Language*), XSLT (*XML Stylesheet Language*), XSLT-FO, XQuery, and the XML schemas, among others. In addition, there are other W3C recommendations that make use of XML and define what are called XML vocabularies. They include those specifications related to the Semantic Web languages, like OWL (*Ontology Web Language*), RDF (*Resource Description Format*), RDF-S, and SPARQL.

The success of XML is due to many factors, but the most relevant is the favorable context that was created with the appearance of the World Wide Web in the 1990s: an open network that made feasible an unlimited

XML-based Content Management
DOI: http://dx.doi.org/10.1016/B978-0-08-100204-9.00001-9

exchange of information between computing platforms. But XML characteristics also played a significant role in achieving this unexpected success. Compared with other previous similar initiatives, XML is characterized by its simplicity. XML documents are plain text files that include tags to distinguish the documents' structural components and the data embedded within their text. The inclusion of tags and markup makes possible the processing and extraction of the documents' information and process those data with context-specific purposes.

The following sections describe the evolution and characteristics of XML, its relationships with other markup languages like SGML (*Structured Generalized Markup Language*) and HTML, and the related specifications published by the W3C to process and manage XML content.

1.2 CHARACTERISTICS OF XML DOCUMENTS

XML development started in 1996 at the W3C with the aim of designing a markup language suitable to the characteristics of the web. Up to that moment, the basic language for publishing content in the web was the HTML (Hyper Text Markup Language), but it did not offer all the necessary features to design complex applications focused on data processing, exchange, and integration.

The list of agents involved in the development of XML included large IT companies like Microsoft®, IBM®, Sun Microsystems®, Novell®, and Hewlett-Packard®. Since its inception, XML has been the result of the consensus reached by different parties under the coordination of the W3C. This ensured the independence of the language from specific companies. The first draft describing the language was presented at the WWW6 Conference on April 1997, and the first version of the W3C recommendation appeared on February 1998. XML is a markup language that is used to encode the content of the documents. This means that:

- the documents based on this standard will include tags,
- the set of tags to be used is not initially restricted, and it is possible to define the tags needed for encoding different document types in response to different information management problems,
- the documents do not contain any information regarding the expected visualization or presentation of their content, and
- the language offers improved hypertext capabilities.

1.2.1 Markup and Tags

XML documents are plain text documents that include tags or markup with the aim of distinguishing their data and structure. Tags in XML documents are written in between the special characters < and >. These special characters make a clear distinction between the textual content of the documents and the tags used to indicate the purpose and meaning of specific text fragments. XML also uses another special type of markup, the entity references, which are written between the reserved characters & and ;. As we will see later, entity references are used with different purposes: as text shortcuts, to use an abbreviation instead of a name not known in advance, or to refer to binary files embedded within the XML document.

Fig. 1.1 shows an XML document edited with a text editor. Tags are highlighted in a different color by the browser, and all of the tags are written within the reserved characters < and >.

It can be noted that the document contains different tags: `<gcapaper>`, `<front>`, `<title>`, `</title>` `<acronym>`, `</acronym>`, etc.

The document's sections, subsections, or specific data that need to be explicitly differentiated are always written in between a start and an end

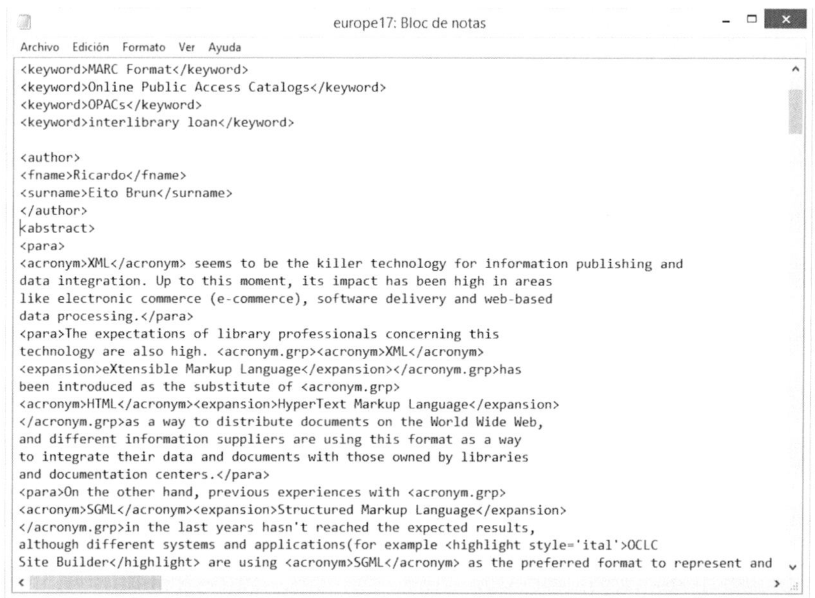


```
<keyword>MARC Format</keyword>
<keyword>Online Public Access Catalogs</keyword>
<keyword>OPACs</keyword>
<keyword>interlibrary loan</keyword>

<author>
<fname>Ricardo</fname>
<surname>Eito Brun</surname>
</author>
<abstract>
<para>
<acronym>XML</acronym> seems to be the killer technology for information publishing and
data integration. Up to this moment, its impact has been high in areas
like electronic commerce (e-commerce), software delivery and web-based
data processing.</para>
<para>The expectations of library professionals concerning this
technology are also high. <acronym.grp><acronym>XML</acronym>
<expansion>eXtensible Markup Language</expansion></acronym.grp>has
been introduced as the substitute of <acronym.grp>
<acronym>HTML</acronym><expansion>HyperText Markup Language</expansion>
</acronym.grp>as a way to distribute documents on the World Wide Web,
and different information suppliers are using this format as a way
to integrate their data and documents with those owned by libraries
and documentation centers.</para>
<para>On the other hand, previous experiences with <acronym.grp>
<acronym>SGML</acronym><expansion>Structured Markup Language</expansion>
</acronym.grp>in the last years hasn't reached the expected results,
although different systems and applications(for example <highlight style='ital'>OCLC
Site Builder</highlight> are using <acronym>SGML</acronym> as the preferred format to represent and
```

Figure 1.1 XML document.

tag. End tags always include the / character after the < character. Start tags do not include the / character. For example, there are several keywords enclosed within the <keyword> and </keyword> tags. The text fragment within these tags contain a specific keyword assigned to the document with the aim of indicating its subject or topic. The <author> and </author> tags are used to enclose the details about the document author. In this case, <author> and </author> contain in turn additional tags: <firstname> and </firstname> for the author's first name and <lastname> and </lastname> for their family name. In a similar way, each paragraph in the document is tagged with the pairs of tags <para> and </para>.

XML documents must start with a special line called the *XML declaration*:

```
<?xml version="1.0"?>
```

This is a mandatory line used to indicate that the document is an XML document.

1.2.2 Open Set of Tags and User Defined Markup

Readers familiar with HTML will find that the method used in XML to encode the content with the use of tags is similar to the approach used in HTML for creating web pages. This is true concerning the syntax and the special characters used to include the tags. But there is a relevant difference between the approaches used in both languages. In HTML documents, users must use a predefined set of tags defined for that language in the specification also published by the W3C. But in XML, users can define the tags to be used in the documents. In other words, you are not limited to the use of a predefined set of tags, but you can define the tags that you want to use when encoding a particular type of document. This gives XML an important flexibility because users and user communities can define multiple tag sets for different document types and applications.

A document type refers to an abstraction or model for all the documents that share a common purpose and structure. The documents having the same "document type" will share common characteristics and will encode the same type of information or data. For example, a purchase order, an invoice, a medical record, or a bibliographic description are examples of document types. In the XML world, all the documents of the same type would be encoded or tagged using the same tag set or schema.

To establish and define the specific tags to be applied when encoding a particular type of document, XML offers different alternatives. In the early days of XML, a method inherited from the SGML language was used: the *Document Type Definition* or DTD. Later on, the W3C defined a new method, the XML schemas. Today, users can rely on both XML schemas and on a more recent method designed by OASIS called Relax NG (See http://relaxng.org/spec-20011203.html). In all three cases, DTDs, XML schemas, and Relax NG are files that define the tags that can be used when creating and editing XML documents. These methods also indicate rules regarding the allowed order of the tags, how they can be nested, whether they can be repeated or not, whether they are mandatory or optional, etc. Users of the XML language can define the set of tags to be used in the creation of specific document types by applying any of these methods. This feature gives XML users great flexibility to solve different requirements and information processing needs. Of course, one of the issues derived from this flexibility is the potential conflicts between organizations using different tag sets or vocabularies to encode documents of the same type. To handle this derived complexity, organizations may:

- Agree on the use of a common set of tags or vocabulary when exchanging their documents. It is important to note that today the community of users has, at their disposal, a large number of XML schemas (including DTD and Relax NG schemas) that can be reused.
- Establish the equivalence or mapping between the tags in the tag sets or vocabularies they are using. Once this mapping is created, the documents from one organization can be "translated" or "converted" to the tag set used by the second organization. To support these kinds of translations or conversions between tags, the W3C published a dedicated language called XSLT (*XML Stylesheet Language—Transformation*).

1.2.3 Distinction Between Structure and Presentation

XML is not the only document encoding language that makes use of tags and markup. In fact, this characteristic is common in most of the formats used by text processing tools like Microsoft Word®, Adobe FrameMaker®, etc. When the users edit the documents using these tools, they make use of the *wysiwyg* (*what you see is what you get*) interface, that hides the internal tags that are added by the tool to the documents. The user interfaces of the document processing tools show the content as it will be displayed to the final reader on screen or print.

If most of the document formats currently in use make use of tags and markup, you might ask, "what is the main difference with the XML approach?" The main difference is the purpose of the tags that are added to the documents. In word processing tools, tags are added to the documents to indicate how the document must be displayed on screen or printed. Tags in these documents contain information about the font, font size, margins, line spacing, etc. The term *procedural markup* is used to refer to this kind of markup. The document formats based on procedural markup include Microsoft RTF (*Rich Text Format*), *Adobe Frame Maker* MIF (*Maker Interchange Format)* or *TeX*.

But tags in procedural markup do not provide any information about the internal structure of the documents or the data they contain. In XML, tags will never be used to indicate how the document must be printed or displayed on screen. The purpose of XML markup is entirely to indicate the document structure and its constituent parts (sections, subsections, etc.) and to distinguish the data it contains. This markup is called *descriptive* or *generalized*.

If we compare two documents encoding the same information, one encoded in a procedural markup language like RTF and another one in a generalized markup language like XML as shown in Fig. 1.2 and Fig. 1.3, it is possible to see the differences between both approaches:

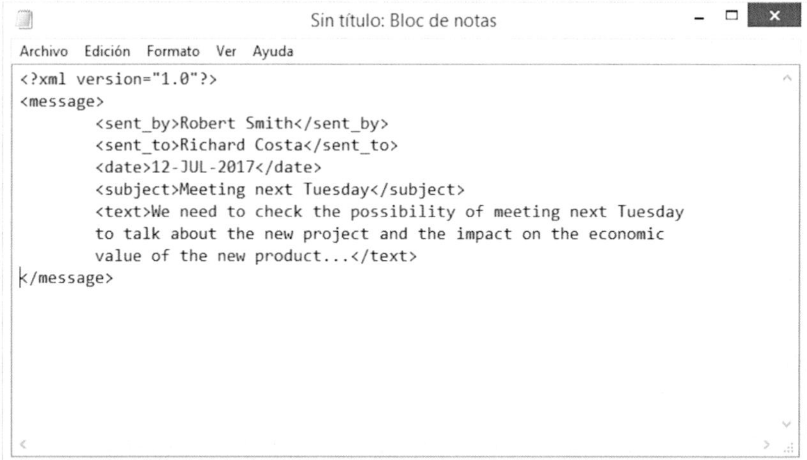


```
<?xml version="1.0"?>
<message>
        <sent_by>Robert Smith</sent_by>
        <sent_to>Richard Costa</sent_to>
        <date>12-JUL-2017</date>
        <subject>Meeting next Tuesday</subject>
        <text>We need to check the possibility of meeting next Tuesday
        to talk about the new project and the impact on the economic
        value of the new product...</text>
</message>
```

Figure 1.2 Descriptive markup—Example.

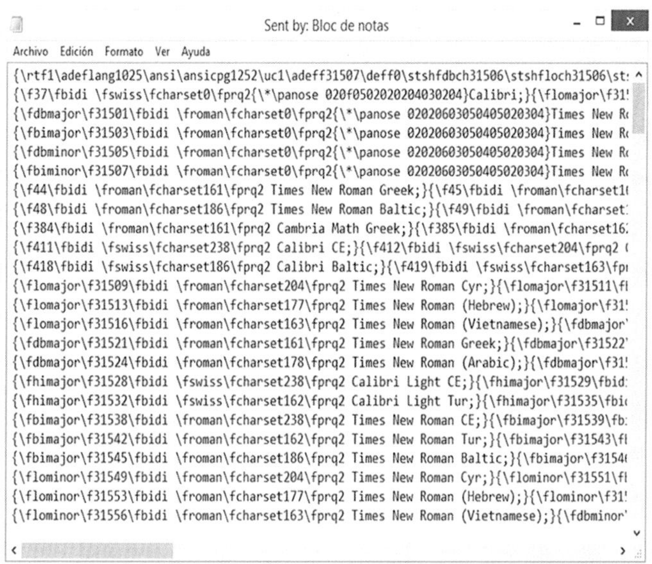

Figure 1.3 Procedural markup—Example.

It can be seen that, although the content of the documents is the same, the RTF document based on procedural markup is more complex and difficult to understand. In addition, the XML document allows you to distinguish data such as the message author and subject. The equivalent RTF document does not include any tag that allows for the identification of these data, as the procedural markup just indicates information about the fonts, font size, and margins.

The use of generalized markup offers more capabilities for the automated processing of documents. One application based on XML can easily identify and extract data from the documents and process these data with multiple purposes. In documents based on procedural markup like RTF, data extraction would be extremely complex.

The distinction between the structure, content, and presentation that characterizes XML makes it necessary to use an additional component to support the display and printing of the XML documents. These components are the stylesheets, which consist of separate, independent files that contain the instructions on how the different data items of the XML documents should be presented. For the different data elements of a specific document type, the stylesheet file will include instructions for their formatting.

1.2.4 Hypertext Capabilities

HTML and the web made popular the use of hypertext links to establish relationships between web pages hosted on different computers. Using dedicated tags, authors of HTML documents are able to link local and remote pages, creating a network of content that can be later explored by end-users. XML also supports the creation of hyperlinks, although the model behind XML is more complex and extends the possibilities offered by HTML.

The W3C published two specifications for the creation of hyperlinks in XML documents: *XLink (XML Linking Language)* and *XPointer (XML Pointer Language)*, the latest version of which was released on May 6 2010 (XLink v1.1).

The XLink hypertext model enriched the model of HTML with additional features:

- In XLink, links can connect more than two resources (in HTML you could only link the source page with the target page).
- XLink links can be stored separate from the source document, which gives the possibility of editing or updating the links without modifying the source document.
- Any element in the XML document can be used as the source or the target of a link (in HTML the links must be created using a dedicated element <a>, and the link target must be either one document or a special element <a name> within the target document).
- It is possible to indicate, as part of the XLink link, how the target item must be shown (e.g. in a new window, in the same window as the source document, or embedded in the content of the target item within the content of the source item).
- Finally, in XLink you can create links to intermediate positions of the target document without the need to add specific tags to the target document, as is needed in the HTML model.

1.3 THE EVOLUTION TO XML

XML is the result of the evolution of one existing language, SGML, in response to the constraints of the HTML language. Because of this, it may be said that XML is the result of the potential of SGML and the restrictions of HTML.

1.3.1 SGML

SGML was, until the creation of XML, the most relevant language for the creation of electronic documents based on the descriptive or generalized markup. The origin of SGML dates back to 1969, with the creation of the *GML (Generalized Markup Language)* by Charles Goldfarb, Edward Mosher, and Raymond Lorie. These three men created it when they were working for IBM and developing an integration between a content creation tool and an information retrieval system for legal information (Goldfarb and Prescod, 2004).

The basic features of SGML were those described in previous sections of this chapter: inclusion of tags to make explicit the structure, organization and data in the documents, formal definition of *document types* by means of DTD files, the possibility of defining specific tag sets for different types of documents, no initial constraint on the use of a predefined set of tags, and/or the distinction between the document content and structure and its presentation (managed with stylesheets).

SGML defined:

1. the syntax of the files indicating the set of tags valid for a specific document type (that is to say, the syntax for the DTD or *Document Type Definition*), and
2. the method used to add tags and markup to the documents, using the special characters < and >.

SGML became an international ISO standard in 1986: *ISO 8879:1986 "Information processing—Text and Offices systems—standard generalized markup language"*. Although SGML never reached the popularity and acceptance of XML, there were two events that contributed to extend the knowledge on SGML: the development of the CALS program, and the creation of HTML (Travis and Waldt, 1996).

- CALS (*Computer-aided Acquisition and Logistic Support*) was an initiative led by the US *Department of Defense (DoD)* to improve the supply chain between the US Army and its suppliers. This initiative paid special attention to the technical documentation that was delivered with the products. CALS adopted SGML for the creation of textual information, and this decision forced suppliers to create their technical documents using this format.
- Later on, the development of the HTML language at the beginning of the 1990s reactivated the interest in SGML. In fact, HTML was designed as an application of SGML aimed to support the creation of web pages. Application is the name used in the SGML world to refer

to the different document types or DTDs that are created according to the SGML standard. The creators of HTML created a DTD for the set of tags that are allowed in HTML documents.

The advantages of SGML included:

- Nonproprietary standard. The language did not depend on a specific manufacturer or company (although the language was created within IBM, it became an ISO international standard).
- Strictly controlled structure of the documents. This supported the notion of "valid documents", that is to say, documents whose structure and content could be automatically checked to ensure that they met the requirements imposed in their DTD and that the right set of tags were applied.
- Distinction between the structure and content of the documents and their presentation. In SGML the word "composition" was used to refer to the automatic generation of user-friendly presentations of the SGML documents that hid the tags and applied the styles defined in a separate stylesheet. Two different types of stylesheets were developed for SGML: *FOSI (Format Output Specification Instance)* and *dsssl* (*document style semantics and specification language*). The second one was published as international standard ISO 10179:1996 "*Information technology—Processing languages—Document Style Semantics and Specification Language (DSSSL)*", and it supported not only the composition process, but also the translation of the documents' tags to other tags from a different set.

But the generalization of the web and HTML did not result in a positive outcome for the development and adoption of additional applications of SGML. Some tools were created to support the deployment of SGML documents in the web (for example the Panorama plugin for the Netscape Navigator browser developed by Softquad). But the use of SGML was limited to those organizations that worked on industries with specific requirements for the use of that standard (defense, aerospace, etc.), due to the high costs derived from the use of the generalized markup (tagging effort and the need of investment in expensive, dedicated tools).

XML was created as a simplified version of SGML. Authors of the XML specification removed some complex characteristics of SGML. These simplifications contributed to the current success of the XML language because it maintains the advantages of SGML and, at the same time, its adoption is easier and there is no need to invest in expensive, complex tools to start using the language.

1.3.2 HTML

The origin and evolution of XML cannot be understood without a quick reference to HTML. This language, designed by *Tim Berners Lee at the* CERN *(Conseil* Europ*éen pour la* R*echerche* N*ucléaire)* in the 1990s, was an application of SGML that had the aim of creating web pages.

HTML, along with its predecessor SGML, is independent of hardware and software platforms, is managed by the W3C, and does not depend on any specific manufacturer. The W3C defined a limited set of tags for aspects related to the presentation of the documents in the browsers. This can be seen as a contradiction with the spirit of SGML: although HTML is an SGML application, its tags indicate aspects related to the visual display of the document, and not with its structure and data. HTML includes tags for the markup of paragraphs, tables, list, fragments in bold, and italics, but it does not contain tags to distinguish the information contained in the documents. As an example, an HTML page containing the description of a bibliographic resource will show all the book data, but it will not be possible to distinguish the author, title or publication year. As a result, HTML is well suited for creating documents to be read by human beings, but it lacks important features as a language to create documents addressed to computers and software applications.

During its evolution, HTML incorporated additional features, but most of these improvements were related to presentation aspects and the interactivity between the user and the documents. Dynamic HTML or *dHTML* was the term coined to refer to additional specifications developed to provide HTML with more attractive displays of data. These specifications included *CSS* (*Cascading Stylesheets*), *JavaScript* language, or the *Document Object Model* (*DOM*). Using these specifications, authors of HTML content could control certain aspects like the positioning of the elements on the screen or implementing behaviors in response to the actions completed by the readers. However, these improvements were limited to the presentation of the content and visual effects, and the HTML language still presented constraints when representing the document's structure and data.

Some years later, in 2000, after the publication of XML, the W3C published an updated version of HTML under the name XHTML. This specification redefined the HTML language: although the available tags existed in the previous versions of HTML, the XHTML documents would be compliant with the XML syntax (*XHTML™ 1.0: The Extensible HyperText Markup*

Language: A Reformulation of HTML 4 in XML 1.0. W3C Recommendation 26 January 2000. Available at: http://www.w3.org/TR/2000/REC-xhtml1-20000126/). For example, all the elements would have a start and end tag, the attribute values would be written within quotes, element and attribute names had to be written in lowercase, and the empty elements were required to include the / character (e.g., <hr/> would be written instead of <hr>). XHTML documents would include the XML declaration at the beginning, as shown in the example below:

```
<?xml version="1.0" encoding="UTF-8"?>
<!DOCTYPE html PUBLIC "-//W3C//DTD XHTML 1.0 Strict//EN"
"http://www.w3.org/TR/xhtml1/DTD/xhtml1-strict.dtd">
<html xmlns="http://www.w3.org/1999/xhtml">
    <head>
        <title>Ejemplo</title>
    </head>
    <body>
        <h1>Titulo primero</h1>
        <p>Este es el primer párrafo.</p>
        <p>Este es el segundo</p>
        <img src="imagen.gif" />
    </body>
</html>
```

The purpose of XHTML was to reinforce some basic syntactic rules to ensure the usage of html on different devices. The language tags were grouped in modules (`xhtml1-tables.mod`, `xhtml1-form.mod`, etc.) and supported the creation of different versions of HTML tailored to the characteristics of different devices. The flexibility to set up different versions of HTML was a reason to avoid the proliferation of markup languages designed for specific devices, a situation that had happened in the past with languages like the WML (*Wireless Markup Language*), cHTML, etc.

In the early days of XML, some people thought that XML was going to replace HTML as the language for creating content for the web. Today, XML and HTML are complementary, not rival languages, that serve different purposes and that can be used together. HTML is the preferred choice for distributing content on the web aimed at human readers and XML is the preferred choice for encoding content in a way that makes it easily reusable. Content storage and exchange for data processing purposes are the main areas of application for XML. In numerous cases, organizations are creating content in XML format to repurpose later using different formats including HTML and PDF. Each language fulfills specific requirements in the content lifecycle.

1.4 STRUCTURE OF XML DOCUMENTS

XML documents are made up of several, hierarchically arranged, elements. Elements may have attributes. In XML documents we can also find *entity references*, *comments*, and XML documents will always contain one special line, the *XML declaration*.

1.4.1 Elements

XML documents contain elements. These elements are delimited by a star and ending tag, and elements are hierarchically arranged. The fragment below shows an XML document open in a web browser. The document contains different elements: `title`, `abstract`, etc. All these elements have start and end tags (`<title>`, `</title>`, `<abstract>`, and `</abstract>`).

End tags can be easily identified because they include the / character just after the < character that starts the tag. As an example, the `author` element starts with the `<author>` tag and finishes with the `</author>` tag; the `abstract` element starts with the `<abstract>` tag and finishes with `</abstract>` tag, etc.

XML elements include the start and end tags, as well as the content within them. Elements can contain text, and they can also include other elements. We can talk about child or descendants. Child elements are those that directly depends on the element. Descendants are the elements that depends on one element or on any of its children. In the previous example the `abstract` element contains two child elements with name `par`. Both `par` and `abstract` are descendants of the `reference` element.

The use of markup gives the possibility of tagging sequences of charts or text fragments with a special meaning or purpose, applying different levels of detail or granularity when tagging the content. One element called `author` may contain the full name of the author, or may be divided into the child elements `firstName` and `lastName`. The greater the level of detail in the markup, the greater the granularity. A more detailed markup gives the choice of doing a more accurate processing of the data, but of course the effort needed to create the documents will also be higher.

Because XML elements can include other elements, the XML document results in a hierarchy. Nesting elements within other elements are a way of keeping the relationships between the data in the document (that is to say, if several elements are nested under that same parent element, there will exist some kind of relationship between their data). All the XML documents have a root element, which contains all the other elements in the document, and is not included within any other element.

In the document in Fig. 1.4, the root element is `reference`; its start tag `<reference>` is at the beginning of the document after the XML declaration, and its end tag `</reference>` is the last line of the document. All the other elements are nested within `reference`.

The possible ways to enclose or nest elements is defined in the schema or DTD that establish the documents' structure.

1.4.2 Attributes

XML elements may have attributes. The purpose of the attributes is to add some additional meaning or information to the element content. Attributes have a name and a value, which is written within quotes. The attributes always appear in the start tag of the elements, after the element name. The attribute name and its value are separated by the equal character (=).

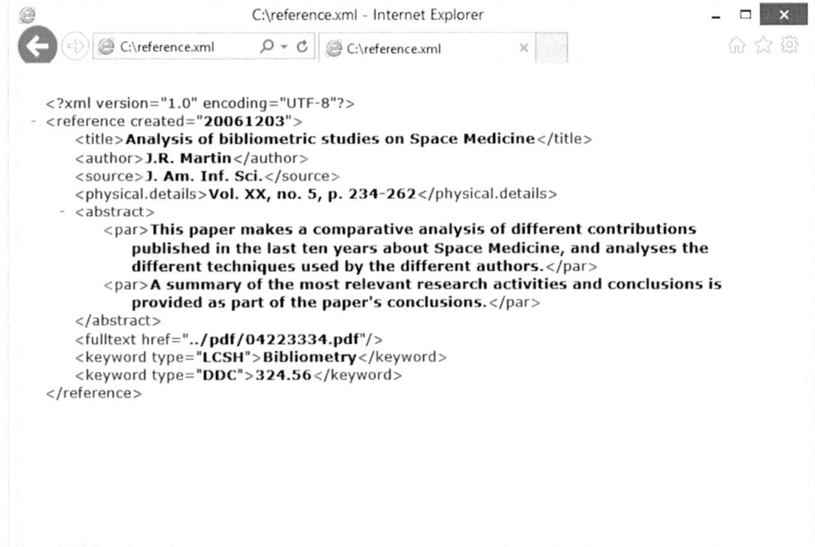


```
<?xml version="1.0" encoding="UTF-8"?>
- <reference created="20061203">
    <title>Analysis of bibliometric studies on Space Medicine</title>
    <author>J.R. Martin</author>
    <source>J. Am. Inf. Sci.</source>
    <physical.details>Vol. XX, no. 5, p. 234-262</physical.details>
  - <abstract>
      <par>This paper makes a comparative analysis of different contributions
        published in the last ten years about Space Medicine, and analyses the
        different techniques used by the different authors.</par>
      <par>A summary of the most relevant research activities and conclusions is
        provided as part of the paper's conclusions.</par>
    </abstract>
    <fulltext href="../pdf/04223334.pdf"/>
    <keyword type="LCSH">Bibliometry</keyword>
    <keyword type="DDC">324.56</keyword>
  </reference>
```

Figure 1.4 XML Document.

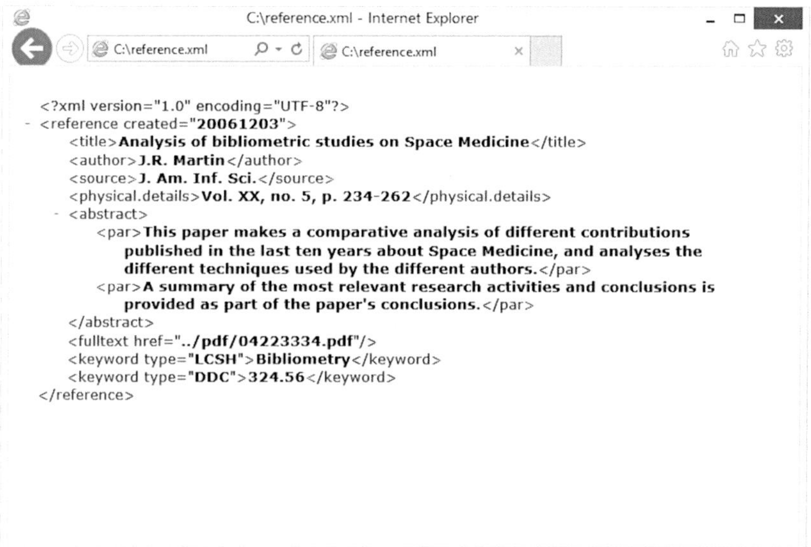


```
<?xml version="1.0" encoding="UTF-8"?>
- <reference created="20061203">
     <title>Analysis of bibliometric studies on Space Medicine</title>
     <author>J.R. Martin</author>
     <source>J. Am. Inf. Sci.</source>
     <physical.details>Vol. XX, no. 5, p. 234-262</physical.details>
   - <abstract>
        <par>This paper makes a comparative analysis of different contributions
           published in the last ten years about Space Medicine, and analyses the
           different techniques used by the different authors.</par>
        <par>A summary of the most relevant research activities and conclusions is
           provided as part of the paper's conclusions.</par>
     </abstract>
     <fulltext href="../pdf/04223334.pdf"/>
     <keyword type="LCSH">Bibliometry</keyword>
     <keyword type="DDC">324.56</keyword>
  </reference>
```

Figure 1.5 Document XML.

In the document below (see Fig. 1.5), we can find several attributes: @`type`, which goes together with the `keyword` element, @`created` with the root element `reference`, and @`href` that goes with the element `fulltext`.

***Note**: This book uses the convention of writing the attribute names preceded by the @ character, to distinguish them from the elements' names. In the real XML documents, the names of the attributes are not preceded by this character.*

In the three cases, the attributes appear in the start tag of the elements, their values are written within quotes and preceded by the equal character.

The list of attributes that can be used with each element must be declared in the DTD or XML schema. The declaration of the attribute must indicate its name, the element that is accompanied by the attribute, whether the attribute is optional or mandatory, and the attribute data type.

There are some restrictions that must be remembered about the attributes:

- a distinction is made between lower and uppercase, although lower case is the recommended way to write the element and attribute names;
- the attribute value must be written within simple or double quotes;
- An element may be accompanied by an unlimited number of attributes (as long as they are declared in the XML schema),

- the same attribute cannot be repeated in the same instance or occurrence of one element; for example, this line would be incorrect: `<keyword type="LCSH" type="DDC">`;
- the order of the attributes is not relevant, and they can be written in any order in the start tag of the element.

A typical decision in XML is deciding when to use elements and when to use attributes. Although there are no specific constraints or rules, usually people opt to use elements and restrict the use of attributes for those cases where some kind of clarification on the element value is needed. For example, one XML document containing one abstract could use an attribute @lang to indicate the language in which the abstract is written; similarly, one document containing keyword elements could include one attribute to indicate the controlled vocabulary the keyword is taken from.

1.4.3 Empty Elements

XML documents can include special types of elements, called *empty elements*. The main characteristic of these elements is that they do not contain any text in between their start and end tags.

Usually, empty elements are used to indicate that a picture, link, or multimedia file must be included in a specific place in the document. Empty elements are also used in HTML. For example, `<img>`, `<hr>`, or `<br>` are some of the empty elements available in HTML to include images, separation lines, and carriage returns within the content of the HTML files.

In XML, there are two ways to write the empty elements in the documents. You can either write a start and end tag with the name of the empty element, with no text in between, or you can use a single tag that will have a slash (/) character just before the > character that indicates the end of the tag. An example is provided below:

```
<graphic />
```

Empty elements must also be declared in the XML schema that establishes the rules for each document type; in the case of the empty elements, usually they will have some attributes that must also be declared in the DTD or schema. In the document shown in Fig. 1.5, it is possible to identify a <`fulltext`> empty element that has an @`href` attribute.

1.4.4 Entities

XML documents can also include *entities*. This is a concept inherited from SGML that is used for different purposes:

- Entities can be used to include special characters in the documents, like accented letters á, è, ü, etc.), characters that have a special function in XML like the *ampersand* (&), greater than (>), smaller than (<), etc. The entities used to represent these characters receive the name of *character type entities*.
- Entities can also be used to add to the document images, video, or any other type of non-XML object. These entities are called *non-processing external entities* (There are additional uses of the XML entities. They can also be used like processing internal entities, to give an alias to complex names or names that are unknown at the time of writing the document, or the processing external entities that refer to external XML documents that can be combined to form a compound XML document.).

In the case of the character type entities, they offer an alternative form to write reserved or special characters in the XML documents. This is necessary to avoid processors understanding a normal character in our text with the beginning of tags and markup (<, > y &). If we write the < character directly in the document, the XML processor could interpret it as the beginning of a tag and this will provoke an error. To avoid these problems, entities provide us with alternative representations for reserved characters:

Reserved character	Alternative representation (Entity)
<	<
>	>
&	&

XML editors are able to manage these entities for the user, doing all the necessary translations between characters. In other words, users do not need to write the entities instead of the reserved characters because the editors will do it for them.

Regarding the non-processing external entities, these were traditionally used in SGML to include images or references to external files within the SGML documents. Currently, this is not the preferred method to incorporate non-XML content within XML documents, and the recommended method is to use empty elements containing an attribute that points to the location of the external file. This is the same method that is used in HTML documents to incorporate images. However, this mechanism can be found in some legacy schemas and it is, therefore, important to know how it works: to include external, non-XML content in the document, an external entity must be declared pointing to the path of the external file; in the XML document, just in the position where the content should be shown, the author will have included a reference to the entity, writing its name in between the & and ; characters. Then, the tool in charge of creating the visualization of the document (this process was called *composition* in SGML) had to resolve the entity and replace that reference with the corresponding image or file, or with a hyperlink pointing to them.

1.4.5 Comments

XML documents can contain comments. Comments are written within the reserved characters <!-- and -->. Comments can extend several lines and include any character; the XML processors won't try to process them. Comments can be written in any place within the XML documents, but not within a tag. Fig. 1.6 shows two comments written within an XML document:

Documents are an interesting way to add clarifications on the purpose of the elements, or any other information that may be useful for the people in charge of processing or reading the document.

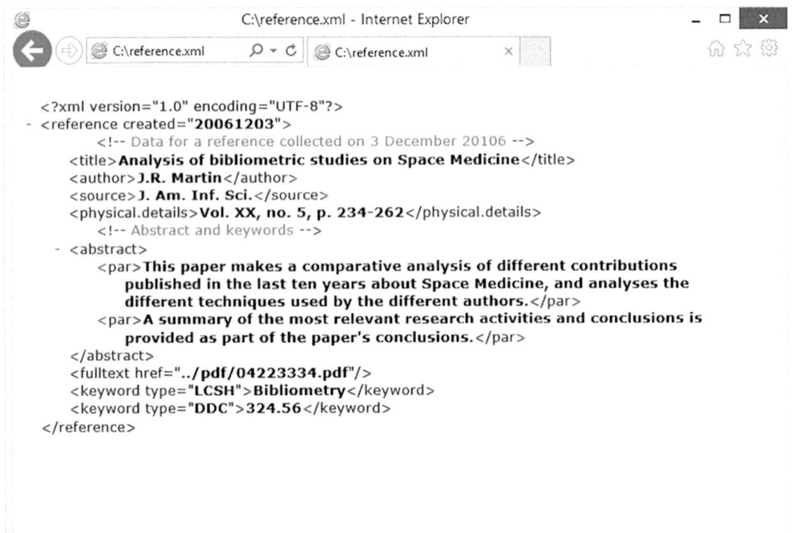

Figure 1.6 Document XML.

1.4.6 Processing Instructions

Another component of XML documents is a special type of line called *processing instructions*. The purpose is to provide XML processing tools with information about how to process the document. Processing instructions offer a way to add to the XML document's commands addressed to the computer programs that will process the XML document. They will be used in different ways depending on the specific implementation or program.

Processing instructions are usually applied to link XML documents with the stylesheets used to indicate how the document must be displayed on screen or printed. They are written at the beginning of the document, just after the XML declaration, between the reserved characters <? and ?>.

1.5 WELL-FORMED DOCUMENTS

XML documents must follow a set of syntactic rules. These rules refer to some basic constraints that documents must fulfill. For example, XML elements must be correctly nested, all the nonempty elements must have start and end tags, and the values of the attributes must be written within quotes. If they do not follow these rules, the software applications will not be able to process them.

When the XML document meets these constraints, we say that the document is *well-formed*. It is important to note that one document may be well-formed but not valid. We say that the document is valid when it meets the constraints imposed in the XML schema or DTD it is related to. Validity depends on the full compliance of the document with the rules in the XML schema or DTD (e.g., use of allowed elements, order of the elements, presence of all the mandatory elements declared in the schema, etc.). One document may be well-formed—in other words, it may be syntactically correct – but not valid, as it may fail to follow the rules in the schema.

Well-formedness is the first requirement that an XML document must fulfill. Then, in addition, the document must be valid according to the rules in its XML schema.

1.6 ANATOMY OF AN XML DOCUMENT

Fig. 1.7 shows a fragment of an XML document open in a web browser. Using this fragment, the main components of an XML document are checked.

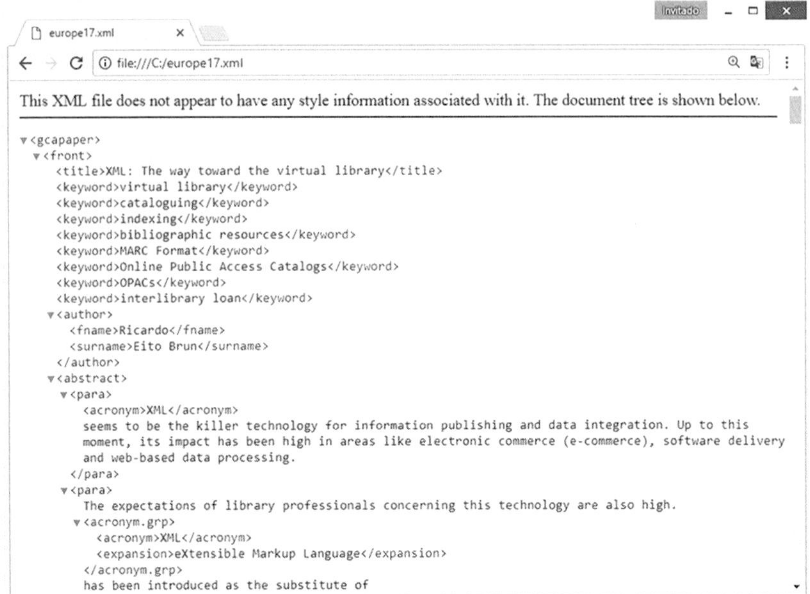

Figure 1.7 XML document.

The root element of this document is <gcapaper>, whose start tag appears at the beginning, just after the XML declaration. In the available fragment, it can be observed that `gcapaper` contains at least one child element called `front`. The picture shows the start and end tags of the front element: <front> and </front>.

Within its tags, there are other elements children of the `front` element: `title`, `keyword`, `author`, and `abstract`. The `title` element appears just one time, but the `keyword` element repeats several times. These elements contain the values corresponding to the title and keywords assigned to the document, and they do not contain any nested child element.

In the case of the `author` element, within its start and end tags, five child elements appear: `fname`, `surname`, `jobtitle`, `address`, and `bio`. The address element is further decomposed into more child elements, and the `bio` element contains two `para` elements that are used to distinguish different paragraphs in the author biography.

The document shows one attribute: `@src` attribute that is used with the `image` element. It can be checked that the attributes are always used in the start tag of the element, and their values are written within quotes. The `image` element is empty, as it does not contain either text or nested elements. The special markup used for empty elements consists of a single, unique tag that ends with the / > characters.

The document is not linked to any stylesheet, so its tags and markup are shown to the user when opening the document with a standard browser. In order to obtain a visual presentation of the document to read online, a stylesheet should be designed. The presence of the tags allows the identification of the data within the document. For example, it would be possible to extract the authors' information, generate a bibliographic citation, etc. Tags also permit the definition of indexing policies, e.g., to build different indexes for authors, affiliations, titles, dates, etc. These strategies are feasible thanks to the use of markup that makes the information within the document explicit and easy to process.

1.7 W3C XML SPECIFICATIONS

W3C has published different specifications for the XML language. The most relevant is the one describing the characteristics of the language and the structure of the XML documents. It was published on February 10th 1998 as XML 1.0. Today, its current version is XML 1.0 5th edition, released as W3C recommendation on November 26th, 2008.

In addition to the specification for the XML language, the W3C has published other related recommendations.

1.7.1 XML Schemas

The schemas are special files that contain the rules that XML documents of a specific type must follow. The schema indicates which elements must be used, whether they are optional or mandatory, how many times one element can appear in the document, the valid attributes that can be used with each element, etc.

There are three W3C recommendations that establish the rules for the design of XML schemas. In the three cases, their second edition was published on October 28, 2004:

- *XML Schema Part 0*: Primer. This is a nonnormative document that describes the purpose and main characteristics of the schemas.
- *XML Schema Part 1*: Structures, which provides the information about the different constructs that can be used when creating a schema for a specific document type.

- *XML Schema Part 2*: Datatypes, where the different data types that can be used in XML documents are described: string, integers, dates, date-time, etc.

On April 5, 2012, two separate recommendations for the XSD language were released: *W3C XML Schema Definition Language (XSD) 1.1 Part 1: Structures* and *W3C XML Schema Definition Language (XSD) 1.1 Part 2: Datatypes*.

1.7.2 Namespaces

Namespaces provide a method to allow the combined use of tags taken from different XML schemas or vocabularies in the same document. The first version of the W3C recommendation for namespaces was released on January 14th, 1999, and the current version is Namespaces in XML 1.1 (Third Edition), available since December 8, 2009.

A namespace corresponds to one vocabulary (a set of XML tags defined with a specific purpose), uniquely identified in the global space of the Web by means of a URI (*Uniform Resource Identifier*). The name of all the tags belonging to that namespace will be preceded by the namespace's URI. In this way, all the tags will have a unique name in the Web, and conflicts are avoided in the case of elements defined in different schemas or vocabularies having the same name.

To avoid writing the full URI of the namespaces, authors of XML documents can use an alias to refer to these URIs. For example, instead of using the full URI for the namespace containing the tags for the elements defined in the Dublin Core vocabulary, `http://purl.org/dc/elements/1.1/`, we can use the `dc` alias. The name of the elements from the Dublin Core namespace can then be written preceded by the `dc` alias; the alias name and the element name will be separated by means of the colon (:) character.

Using the alias in our document, we can resume the elements' names, and use `dc:title` instead of `http://purl.org/dc/elements/1.1/title`, or `dc:creator` instead of `http://purl.org/dc/elements/1.1/creator`. The use of an alias make things easier. In addition, if there is other XML schema or vocabulary defining a title or creator element (with any other purpose), the use of namespaces avoids confusions and misunderstandings. Although the short name of the element may coincide, the full, qualified elements will never by the same, as they are preceded by the identifier of the namespace they belong to. In other words, two title elements from different namespaces will never have the same name:

```
http://purl.org/dc/elements/1.1/title
http://www.uc3m.es/ontweb/patents/title
```

Thanks to the namespaces we can put together, in the same XML document, elements from different vocabularies. The example below (taken from the W3C recommendation) shows an XML document that contains elements from two different namespaces identified by the `bk` and `isbn` aliases). It can be observed that the start and end tags of the elements contain the name of the element preceded by the name of the alias and separated by a colon:

```
<?xml version="1.0"?>
<!—both namespace prefixes are available throughout -->
<bk:book xmlns:bk='urn:loc.gov:books'
      xmlns:isbn='urn:ISBN:0-395-36341-6'>
   <bk:title>Cheaper by the Dozen</bk:title>
   <isbn:number>1568491379</isbn:number>
</bk:book>
```

1.7.3 XLink

The XML Linking Language (XLink) is a W3C recommendation whose version 1.1 was released on May 6, 2010 (version 1.0 was created on June 27, 2001). XLink provides a description of the different types of hyperlinks that can be used in XML documents. It also describes the steps to create links within an XML document. As a general rule, any element can be used as the source of a link, as long as it provides a method—usually an attribute—to encode the target of the link. Links can point to external documents or to specific elements within the same or the target document.

The model proposed by XLink is more complex than the model used in HTML. For example, in XLink it is possible to have links with more than one target. In addition, links in XLink can be defined inline and out-of-line. Inline links are those that are embedded in one of the resources, usually the one acting as the origin of the link. Out-of-line links are an interesting feature that allows the definition of links out of the documents that are being linked. Out-of-line links permit having a set of links defined in a separate document.

XLink defines the `@type` attribute, which can be used with the elements that act as the origin of a link. This attribute can take different values to indicate the type of the link, e.g. a *simple* link that links two resources, or an *extended* link that links one source resource with several target resources. Another value for `@type` is `arc`, used to create two-way links that are not defined inline. In addition to the `@type` attribute, XLink proposes additional attributes that can be used when creating links:

1. `@href`, that will contain the URI of the target resource,
2. `@title`, this is a descriptive title for the link,
3. `@from` and `@to`, that contain the origin and target resources of a link of type "arc". With this type of link it is possible to use the attribute `@role` to indicate the role or function of the resource in the hyperlink,
4. `@show`, that gives the possibility of indicating how the target resource is going to be shown to the user (e.g. embedded within the document, in a different window, or in the same window containing the document with the source link),
5. `@actuate`, that indicates how the user will activate the link. Links may be actuated explicitly by the user (`onRequest`), or automatically when the document is loaded (`onLoad`).

The fragment below shows an example of a simple and an extended link:

```
<author xlink:href="authorData_REito.xml">Ricardo Eito-Brun</
author>
```

Or the equivalent:

```
<author
   xlink:type="simple"
   xlink:href="authorData_REito.xml"
   xlink:show="replace"
   xlink:actuate="user"
   xlink:role="author"
   xlink:title="Author data">
   Ricardo Eito-Brun
</author>
```

In the case of an extended link, its definition would be similar to this:

```
<authors
   xlink:type="extended"
```

```
      xlink:role="author"
      xlink:title="List of authors"
      xlink:show="replace"
      xlink:actuate="user">
      <author xlink:type="locator" xlink:href="REito.xml">Ricardo Eito-
Brun</author>
      <author  xlink:type="locator"  xlink:href="MAMolina.xml">Miguel
Angel Molina</author>
   </authors>
```

1.7.4 XSL (eXtensible Stylesheet Language)

This specification, which is discussed with further detail in the third chapter of the book, defines a language used to design stylesheets that are used to display the documents on screen and to print them on paper. In fact, XSL includes two different languages: XSL FO (*eXtensible Stylesheets Language Formatting Objects*) and XSLT (*eXtensible Stylesheet Language Transformation*). XSL FO is used to create a page-based presentation of the XML content, and it is applied to convert XML content into PDF format.

XSLT stylesheets are used to convert one XML document into another document based on markup. XSLT is applied to convert XML content to HTML, but it can also be used to convert one XML document based on a schema, into another document using a different schema. To manage the transformation process, XSLT stylesheets make use of the XPath (*XML Path Language*) specification. XPath describes how to reach and filter specific nodes (elements, attributes, etc.) within a document.

1.7.5 DOM (Document Object Model)

The purpose of the DOM is to provide an object-oriented interface to process XML documents and to access their nodes using a programming language (like Java, VB.NET, Python, etc.). DOM allows developers to see the XML document like an object that exposes a set of methods and properties. DOM is useful for programmers developing software applications that manage XML content.

1.7.6 CSS (Cascading Stylesheets)

The presentation on screen of XML documents can be managed using the classic CSS stylesheets. CSS is the W3C specification created in the early days of the World Wide Web to improve the mechanisms used for the presentation of HTML documents. With CSS, it is possible to use different fonts, margins, and control the visual appearance of the markup content. Today, although it is feasible to use CSS stylesheets to control the presentation of XML content, the preferred method is XSL stylesheets.

1.7.7 XQuery

This specification defines a query language for XML documents. XQuery is used by developers programming XML-based software solutions. This language is not intended for endusers, as its syntax is complex. It was initially published as a W3C Recommendation on January 23, 2007, and the latest version, XQuery 3.0: An XML Query Language 3.0, was released on April 8, 2014.

1.7.8 SOAP (Simple Object Access Protocol)

This specification is used in the development and integration of software applications that exchange commands and data using XML encoded messages. The SOAP standard is one of the key components of the service-oriented architectures, a technology that proposes the integration of software systems by invoking remote methods using XML to format the calls between the applications.

In service-oriented architectures, an application is made up of one or more web services, defined as application components, which offers data or processing services to other software applications. In a service-oriented architecture, the client applications request the services through the web, by sending messages encoded in XML format via the HTTP protocol. The message will contain the information about the requested service and the parameters needed for its execution. Once the target application receives the message, it will execute the method related to the requested service, and its result will also be encoded in XML and sent back to the application that called the service.

The SOAP standard provides the rules to follow when encoding in XML messages the calls to remove services, and their answers. It was initially defined by Microsoft, Userland Software, and DevelopMentor, and later other players in the software industry joined its development including IBM, HP, and Oracle.

The next XML fragment shows a message encoded in SOAP, which requests the execution of a remote web service called searchByIsbn:

```
<?xml version="1.0" encoding="UTF-8" ?>
<SOAP-ENV:Envelope xmlns:SOAP-ENV="http://schemas.xmlsoap.org/
soap/encoding/">

   <SOAP-ENV:Header>
   </SOAP-ENV:Header>
   <SOAP-ENV:Body>
      <catalog:searchByIsbn xmlns:catalogo="http://catalogo.org/cat">
         <catalog:isbn>
            84-4553-3334-2X
         </catalog:isbn>
      </catalog:searchByIsbn>
   </SOAP-ENV:Body>
</SOAP-ENV:Envelope>
```

The XML message containing the result of the execution of this web service would be similar to the next one:

```
<?xml version="1.0" encoding="UTF-8" ?>
<SOAP-ENV:Envelope xmlns:SOAP-ENV="http://schemas.xmlsoap.org/
soap/encoding/">
   <SOAP-ENV:Header>
   </SOAP-ENV:Header>
   <SOAP-ENV:Body>
      <catalog:searchByIsbnResponse xmlns:catalogo="http://catalogo.
      org/cat">
      <catalog:title>
         Special Cataloguing
      </catalog:title>
      <catalog:author>Marta de Juanes</catalog:author>
      </catalog:searchByIsbnResponse>
   </SOAP-ENV:Body>
</SOAP-ENV:Envelope>
```

When developing software applications based on the service-oriented architecture paradigm, developers must know the web services being provided by the remote servers. To standardize the definition of the set of services provided by the servers, the W3C created a separate specification called WSDL (*Web Service Description Language*).

WSDL establishes the syntax and rules of the XML documents describing the services provided by the target server, as well as the web services' signature (these are the list of parameters or arguments that must be used when calling the remote web services, and the data type it will return). The WSDL document is like a contract between the software application that provides the remote service and its clients.

Today, although the SOAP and WSDL specifications are mature and widely supported by the different programming languages and development environments, an alternative method is widely used in software projects: *RESTfull* web services. This is an implementation of the remote call procedure that is less complex than SOA. The requests are also sent by HTTP, but encoded as part of the URI or within the HTTP request header. The answers to the service calls with the results are nowadays exchanged in the form of XML messages.

1.7.9 XML Signature or XMLDSig

This W3C specification proposes a method to embed digital signatures within XML documents (enveloped signature) or to encode digital signature data for external content (detached signature).

It defines a special namespace, `http://www.w3.org/2000/09/xmldsig#` that contains several elements to encode the information about the signature. This includes, among other data, the algorithm used to generate the signature and the signature's value. The namespace even reserves an element to contain the digital object being signed. This will allow embedding the object within the signature, a process that is called *enveloping signature*.

1.8 CONCLUSIONS

This chapter provides an overview of the main characteristics and the evolution of the XML markup language and the differences between XML content and other markup languages like HTML. The main characteristic of XML is that application designers can create specific tags to distinguish—within the document content—the information that is needed for a particular use of the application.

Designers can create different sets of tags for different document types. The XML specification indicates how these tags must be included in the documents to ensure that they are well-formed and can be further processed and exchanged between applications.

Whenever a set of tags or vocabulary is defined for a specific purpose, it may be formally described in an XML schema or DTD. These are files written in a special syntax that indicates the tags that can be used to codify documents of a specific type, as well as other rules like mandatory and optional elements, valid attributes, the order of the elements, etc. When an XML file follows the rules defined in its XML schema or DTD, the document is said to be valid. A valid document will always be well-formed, but a well-formed document may not always be valid.

Regarding the structure of XML documents, they are made up of a set of nested elements. Elements have a start and end tag, which are written within the < and > characters. Elements can contain text (or any other value) and other child elements nested within their start and ending tags. In this way, the elements of the XML document are hierarchically arranged, and all of them are finally nested within a root element.

In addition to elements, XML documents can contain attributes. Attributes can appear in the start tag of the elements, and they are used to provide some additional information about the value of the element they belong to, e.g., the language in which the value of the element is written, or its provenance.

As markup in XML documents has the purpose of identifying the data and the information, and making the document structure explicit, XML documents do not contain any information explaining how they must be shown, printed, or displayed. The information explaining how to display the content of XML documents must be provided in separate documents called stylesheets. The W3C has published different specifications explaining how to create stylesheets for XML: XSLT and XSL-FO. The advantage of making this distinction between the data and their presentation is that the same content can be repurposed for different devices and displays. XML content does not depend on the presentation of the data or the characteristics of the devices that the users have to access to. This supports optimal strategies like "single sourcing" that are later discussed in this book.

Finally, this chapter has reviewed other W3C specifications that are related to XML, like XML Signature, XQuery, SOAP, WSDL, etc. These specifications provide us with standard methods and tools to handle XML content. The benefit of their definition as W3C standards is that XML remains independent of particular software tools' providers, and the same content can be processed in the same way with tools designed for different companies or by the open source community.

All these features make the XML language a standard, versatile option to ensure the easy management of the data. XML data will always remain easy to process, and the language constitutes a key element in the definition of content management programs, digital preservation strategies, and plans.

CHAPTER 2

Scenarios for Structured Data Management

2.1 XML APPLICATIONS, VOCABULARIES, AND SCHEMAS

XML users can define the tags and markup when encoding the documents. This is a major difference between XML and HTML, as HTML users must use a set of predefined tags.

The definition of the tags and markup to be used in a particular document type must be stated in separate files that receive the name of the XML schemas. The definition of an XML schema requires the analysis of the data to be encoded in a particular document type, the selection of the tags to be used, and a decision on the order, repeatability, and the mandatory or optional character of the elements and attributes. In some cases, it is not necessary to define a new schema, and it is possible to use existing schema previously defined by a third party.

When designing an XML schema for a particular document type, designers must make decisions on the markup granularity. This level of detail is applied when inserting tags in the documents. If we opt for a more detailed markup, we have more opportunities to tag, extract, and process the information and the data in the documents. On the flipside, more granularity involves greater costs when editing the documents. For example, to encode the title of a work, it is possible to use a single tag:

```
<title>An analysis of the productivity of scientific institutions:
data for an efficient management.</title>
```

Or, alternatively, it is possible to use tags with greater granularity:

```
<title><main.title>An analysis of the productivity of scientific
institutions</main.title>
<alternative.title>data for an efficient management.</alternative.
title></title>
```

The identification of the attributes to be used in the documents is another aspect that must be analyzed as part of the definition of schemas for a document type.

XML-based Content Management
DOI: http://dx.doi.org/10.1016/B978-0-08-100204-9.00002-0

The characteristics and rules governing the structure and the valid elements of the document types can be recorded using different files: XML schemas and DTD (Document Type Definitions). Schemas are saved as separate files with the .xsd extension and DTD files with the .dtd extension. DTD were created for SGML documents, and although it is possible to use them to define the structure of XML documents, DTD do not offer the same possibilities as XML schemas. Using XML schemas it is possible to define document types with more detail: for example, you can use different data types for elements and attributes (string, integer, date, datetime, etc.), and you can specify the cardinality of the child elements (for example, to limit the number of child elements that any one element can have). XML tools like Altova® XMLSpy® or Oxygen® offer the capability to design XML schemas visually, without knowing the details of the XML schema's syntax. In the following sections of this chapter the visual icons used by XMLSpy are used to define the main structures that can be used when creating or studying schema.

2.1.1 Understanding XML Schemas

XML schemas are special files that contain the tags and markup that are valid for a particular document type. They are saved with the .xsd extension. These files contain a list of elements and attributes that can be used, in what order they should appear, how they can be nested to build the document hierarchy, and whether they are optional or mandatory. The schema fixes the rules that XML documents of a particular type must fulfill. Each document type is based on a particular XML schema because the tags that are used vary depending on the document type. For example, the information to be marked is different when coding a patent, a medical record, or a technical manual. Every document type has a specific set of tags, defined in a particular XML schema. The document type can be understood as an abstraction of all the documents sharing the same characteristics and purpose: a set of rules for all the documents that have the same purpose and that are processed in the same way.

XML schemas contain the following information:

- Elements that can be used in that document type, along with the attributes they can have.
- The type of information and data that elements and attributes can contain. This is similar to the data types used in relational databases. For example, one element can contain—within their start and end tags—a string, an integer, a date, and other child elements.
- Additional constraints on the content of elements and attributes. These constraints may refer to the maximum or minimum values allowed, ranges of values, etc.

- Flags indicating if elements and attributes are mandatory or optional.
- Flags indicating if the elements can be repeated in a particular context.
- The order of the elements and how they can be nested to create the document hierarchy.

As an example, consider the following XML document:

```
<?xml version="1.0" encoding="UTF-8" ?>

<client xmlns:xsi="http://www.w3.org/2001/XMLSchema-instance" xsi:
noNamespaceSchemaLocation="document.xsd">
     <cif>2345555L</cif>
     <company.name>Gráficas Puerto</company.name>
     <address>Paseo de los Melancólicos, 36</address>
     <contact>
          <first.name>Marta</first.name>
          <last.name>Garrido Suñer</last.name>
     </contact>
     <phone>91-365-43-32</phone>
</client>
```

The rules governing these types of documents must be defined in a schema. The name of the file containing these rules is `document.xsd` as stated in the `xsi:noNamespaceSchemaLocation` attribute of the `<document>` element.

The file `document.xsd` contains several declarations, one separate declaration for each allowed element and attribute. The following picture shows a subset of those declarations:

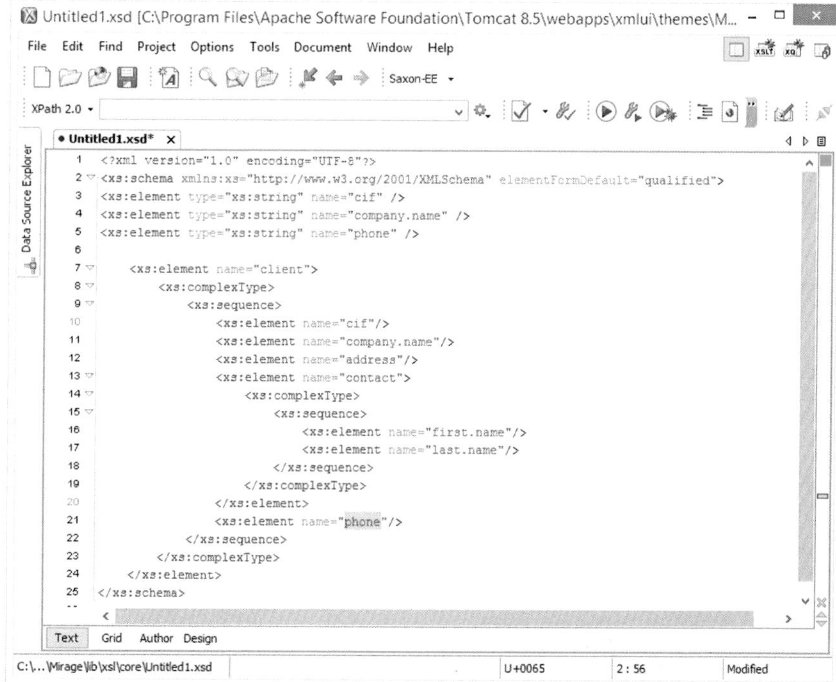

It can be observed that the XSD schema is an XML document (as an example, we can see the first line of the schema is the XML declaration and the schema contains XML documents and tags like `<xs:complexType>`, `<xs:element>`, `<xs:annotation>`, etc.).

In addition, the schema declares the elements that will be used later, when creating the XML documents using the special tag `<xs:element>`. These special elements include an attribute `name`, which contains the name of the element and another attribute that indicates the datatype of each element (e.g. `xs:string`).

The order of the elements in future XML documents is also defined as part of the schema.

All the XML documents that are based on a specific schema must contain a reference to that schema or XSD file. This reference assures the validation of the XML documents by checking whether they follow the rules defined for their document type.

2.1.2 Schema Specifications

XML schemas must be created using the XML syntax and a specific set of tags. The allowed tags are defined as part of one recommendation published by the W3C. The first version of the XSD specification was published in March 2001 and was written by different companies like INSO, Microsoft, ArborText, etc. The current version of the XML Schema Recommendation, published on October 28, 2004, can be downloaded from the W3C web site: http://www.w3.org/XML/Schema#dev

The XML schema specification is made up of three documents:

- *XML Schema Part 0 Primer*—introduces the concept of schema, function, and structure. It can be found at: http://www.w3.org/TR/xmlschema-0/.
- *XML Schema Part 1: Structures*—defines the data structures that can be used when creating XML schemas. It can be found at: http://www.w3.org/TR/xmlschema-1/
- *XML Schema Part 2: Datatypes*—describes the different data types that can be used when declaring elements and attributes. It can be found at: http://www.w3.org/TR/xmlschema-2/

Version 1.1 of the XML schemas was released on April 5, 2012, and includes two separate documents:

- *W3C XML Schema Definition Language (XSD) 1.1 Part 1*: Structures, available at https://www.w3.org/TR/xmlschema11-1/
- *W3C XML Schema Definition Language (XSD) 1.1 Part 2*: Datatypes, available at https://www.w3.org/TR/xmlschema11-2/

In addition to these recommendations, W3C has published some related documents and tools, such as the XSV tool, that can be used to check the correctness of the XML schemas and to check if the XML documents are compliant with the rules defined in a specific schema. It is important to note that standard XML editors, like those described in Chapter 3, XML Authoring and Presentation Tools, provide the capability of checking the correctness and validity of the XML documents by referring to a specific XML schema.

2.2 STRUCTURE OF AN XML SCHEMA

Schemas are XML documents saved with an XSD file extension that use a restricted set of tags defined in a W3C recommendation (a W3C recommendation is a Web standard). As with any other XML document, the schema starts with the XML declaration, which is followed by the root element `<schema>`.

The elements and attributes used in the schemas are usually preceded by the `xs` or `xsd` aliases. These aliases indicate that the tags are taken from a set of reserved names defined in the XML recommendation. According to the recommendation, in the schemas you can find tags including these prefixes: `<xsd:schema>`, `</xsd:schema>`, `<xs:schema>`, and `</xs:schema>`.

The start tag of the `<xs:schema>` element includes a special qualifier: `xmlns:xs="http://www.w3.org/2001/XMLSchema"`. It indicates that when using the xs alias we are pointing to the XML schema namespace where all the reserved tags are defined. As a result, the first tag in an XML schema is similar to the one below:

```
<xs:schema xmlns:xs="http://www.w3.org/2001/XMLSchema">
```

The start and the ending tag of the `<xs:schema>` element contains all the declarations and type definitions in the document type. Declarations indicate the elements and attributes that can be used when creating XML documents of that document type, and the type of data they can contain within their start and ending tags: strings, integer, date, URI, etc. The

XML schema recommendation defines two special XML tags to declare elements and attributes:

`<xs:element>` y `<xs:attribute>`.

In addition to the element and attribute declarations, the XML schema can define data types that can be used in the declaration of elements and attributes. For example, it would be possible to define a datatype `age` that restricts the possible values to an integer between 0 and 100. It is possible to declare both simple and complex data types.

Note: In XML schemas a distinction is made between simple and complex elements.

Simple elements are those whose value is restricted to a specific atomic data type: string, integer, date, etc. Simple elements cannot contain either child elements or attributes.

Complex elements are those that: (1) include at least one attribute or (2) contain at least one child element.

In the next sections the declaration of simple and complex elements in the XML schemas is explained.

2.2.1 Simple Elements

Simple elements contain neither child elements or attributes. These elements only have a name and data type. The data types used in XML schemas are similar to those used in relational databases: integer, string, date, etc.

Within the simple elements a distinction is made between: a) atomic simple elements, which contain an atomic value that cannot be divided, b) simple elements of type list, and c) simple elements of type union.

Note: Using the data types defined in the W3C XML schemas, it is possible to define additional data types applying constraints, e.g. restricting the value to a specific range.

Elements are declared in the XML schema using the `<xs:element>` tag. This element is used to declare both simple and complex elements. In the case of simple elements, the `<xs:element>` element is empty and contain two attributes: `name` and `type`. The first attribute contains the name of the element and the second its data type.

For example, the fragment below contains the declarations of two simple elements called docTitle and issn. Both elements have the `xs:string` data type:

```
<xs:element name="docTitle" type="xs:string"/>
<xs:element name="issn" type="xs:string" minOccurs="0"/>
```

Once we have declared a simple element in the schema it is possible to refer to it when declaring other elements—we can reuse simple elements in different places or contexts.

2.2.2 Complex Elements

Complex elements are those elements that contain at least one attribute or one child element. The term "content model" is used to refer to the child elements that can be contained within the start and ending tags of a specific complex element.

Complex elements can be declared in two different ways: first, as a content model in the declaration of the complex element; and second, in the declaration of the complex element which is a reference to a complex type `<complexType>` previously defined in the schema. Complex types give us the possibility of defining complex content models that can be reused in different places of the schema. For example, a complex type called "publicationData" could be created to incorporate the place of publication, the name of the publisher, and the publication year.

In the case of complex elements that contain child elements, XML schemas support three possible means to combine the child elements: (1) SEQUENCE, (2) ALL, and (3) CHOICE. Two additional methods are available to define the content model: the *mixed content model, ANY,* and empty elements.

The SEQUENCE content model is used to enforce the specific order of the child elements. For example, if we declare an element with name `<book>` whose content model is a sequence of child elements `<title>`, `<subtitle>`, and `<pubYear>`, the XML documents based on this schema are valid only if the three child elements appear in this particular order. If they appear in a different order, the XML document will not be valid. XML schemas include a reserved tag to declare this content model: `<xs:sequence>`.

The CHOICE content model is used to indicate that the element can contain only one of the child elements that are listed in the content model. For example, there may be one element `<publication>` with an identifier that can be the ISBN (`<isbn> element`) or the ISSN (element `<issn>`) depending on its type, but not both at the same time. When creating an XML document based on that schema we should select one of the two elements. XML schemas use the reserved element `<xs:choice>` to create this content model.

The ALL content model is used to indicate that the element can only contain one single occurrence of all of its child elements. The document will not be valid if one child element appears more than one time. In the ALL content model, child elements can appear in any order.

Another content model for complex elements is mixed content. This means that the element can contain both text and child elements.

Note: One example of element with mixed content is the <p> element used in the HTML language. This element can include both textual content and other child elements like <b> to write the text in bold , <i> to write the text in italics, <a> for including a hyperlink, etc. The fragment below shows a <p> element with mixed content:

<p>This paragraph contains data about <b>Cervantes</b>, who wrote <i>Don Quixote</i> and who was born in Alcala de Henares.</p>

In the XML schemas, the mixed content model is specified using the reserved word "mixed=true" in the declaration of the element.

Finally, XML schemas support the ANY content model. ANY is used to indicate that the element can contain any combination of text and child elements, even if they are not declared in the schema. Elements with this content model have no restrictions, and any kind of content can be included within their start and ending tags. When the XML document is validated, the validation tool skips any checks for those elements with the ANY content model.

2.2.3 Global Elements

Sometimes it is necessary to repeat the same element in a different context within the same XML schema. To avoid repeating the declaration of the same element several times, XML schemas allow the declaration of global elements. Global elements may be either simple or complex, using any of the content models described above.

> *Note*: Elements can be declared in a specific context (e.g., within the sequence of the child elements of an existing element), or as global.
>
> In the first case, it is not possible to reuse the element in other declarations of the schema. When the element is declared as global, it is possible to reuse it in different places of the schema. References can be done to global elements in the declaration of the content model of other elements in the schema.

Global elements are declared with `<xs:element>` that are children of the schema root element. The declaration of the element must contain its name and data type. The declaration of global elements does not include any information indicating if the element is mandatory or optional, or the cardinality (minimum or maximum number of times it can appear). These data are indicated in the specific context where the element is reused.

2.2.4 Facets and Constraints

Facets are used in XML schemas to specify constraints on the values of elements and attributes. The assignment of a data type to elements and attributes is a way of adding constraints to potential values, but the facets give the possibility of being more precise. For example, using facets we can limit the values to those in a specific range, or the use of a specific format, mask, or pattern.

Facets can be used with both elements and attributes, and even in the definition of types. XML schemas include several reserved elements to define facets: `<restriction>`, `<length>`, `<minInclusive>`, etc. Some facets are related to a specific data type, e.g., the `TotalDig` facet can only be used with numeric data types.

Some of the facets we can find in XML schemas are the following:

Facet	Description
`Length`	Length or number of characters of the data.
`MinLength`	Minimum number of characters of the data. The value of the element or attribute must have at least the number of characters indicated in this facet.

(*Continued*)

Facet	Description
`MaxLength`	Maximum number of characters of the data. The value of the element or attribute must have, at most, the number of characters indicated in this facet.
`enumeration`	The value of the element or attribute must be one of the values indicated in a closed list.

Patterns are a special type of facet that enforce the format of the data. For example the values of an element or attribute must follow the *AA-nnnn-A* pattern, where *A* refers to uppercase letters and *n* refers to digits. Patterns in XML are similar to the data input masks that are used in some databases to make data entry easier.

2.3 SCENARIOS FOR XML DATA MANAGEMENT

After explaining the concepts of document type and its implementation through XML schemas, this section describes the most relevant schemas and document types in different areas related to information and content management. The origin and the main characteristics of the selected schemas are summarized, as well as examples of their use.

2.4 ARCHIVAL DESCRIPTION: EAD, EAC-CFP, AND EAG

EAD is an XML vocabulary developed by the Society of American Archivists and maintained by the Library of Congress to encode finding aids in electronic format. EAD standardizes the format used to create and exchange descriptions of archival materials (fonds, files, series, and individual documents) and facilitates their publication in the Web and their automated processing by software programs (Szary, 2005; Thurman, 2005).

The Development of EAD started in 1993 with the Berkeley Finding Aid Project, led by Daniel Pitti at the Berkeley University. In March 1995 they developed an SGML DTD with the name *FINDAID DTD*, that was later renamed EAD. In 1998, version 1.0 of EAD was published; this version was later replaced by EAD 2002, and the current version is EAD 3, published in August 2015 and recently adopted by the professional community. EAD is aligned with other archival description standards like ISAD(G), RAD (*Rules for Archival Description*), and APPM (*Archives, Personal Papers and Manuscripts*). It supports multilevel archival description and the traceability between EAD elements and ISAD(G) documentation (Pitti and Duff, 2001).

2.4.1 EAD

Finding aids encoded in EAD are made up of several elements that are hierarchically arranged. Its main structure follows (only the most important structural elements are displayed and intermediate elements are omitted):

```
<ead>
    <control>
    <archdesc level=" ">
        <did>
        <accessrestrict>
        <accruals>
        <acqinfo>
        ............................
        ............................
        <dsc type=" ">
            <c01 level=" ">
                <did>
                <scopecontent>
                ..........................
                ..........................
                <c02 level=" ">
```

The root element is <ead>. It contains an <control> element followed by a mandatory <archdesc> element (see Fig. 2.1).

In the case of multilevel descriptions, the <archdesc> element contains one <dsc> child. And <dsc> contains a nested set of child elements with the description of the nested archival units (e.g. series within a fonds or files within series).

<control> is a mandatory element that contains metadata about the finding aid. These metadata are grouped within several mandatory child elements: <recordid>, <filedesc>, <maintenancestatus>, <maintenanceagency>, and <maintenancehistory>. It <control> can contain other optional child elements, as shown in Fig. 2.2.

<recordid> contains a unique identifier for the finding aid; <filedesc> contains subelements for registering the finding aid title, author, editor, notes, etc.; <maintenancestatus> contains additional metadata like the EAD title, publication status, etc. Finally, <maintenanceagency> and

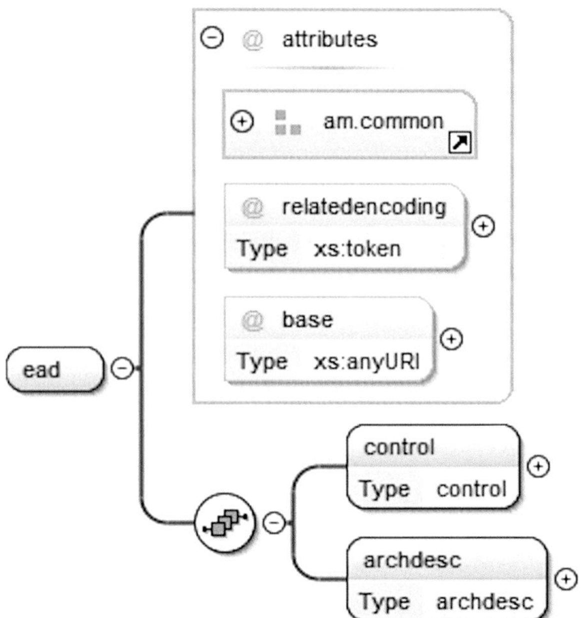

Figure 2.1 EAD schema.

<maintenancehistory> contain the information about the entity creating the EAD document, and the changes done in its different versions.

Besides the <eadheader>, the most important element in the EAD schema is <archdesc>, because it contains the content of the finding aid. It has a mandatory @level attribute, which states the type of archival unit that is being described: fonds, collection, item, subfonds, file, recordgrp, subgrp, class, otherlevel, series, and subseries. This approach gives us the flexibility of using the same schema and elements to describe different archival units. The most important child elements of <archdesc> are shown in Fig. 2.3.

The <archdesc> element includes:

- One `<did>` element, which contains in turn several child elements including the main information of the finding aid.
- Several child elements, described in the table below. The content of these elements consist of a sequence of paragraphs (<p> elements).

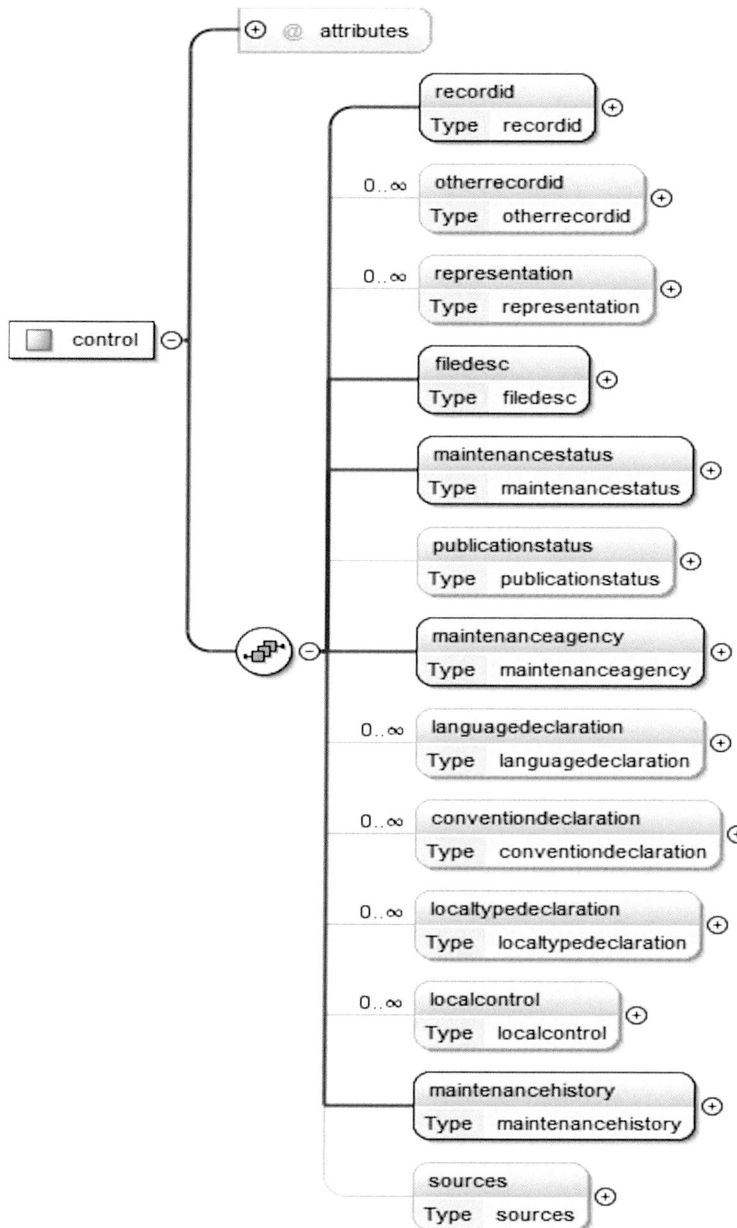

Figure 2.2 XML EAD schema.

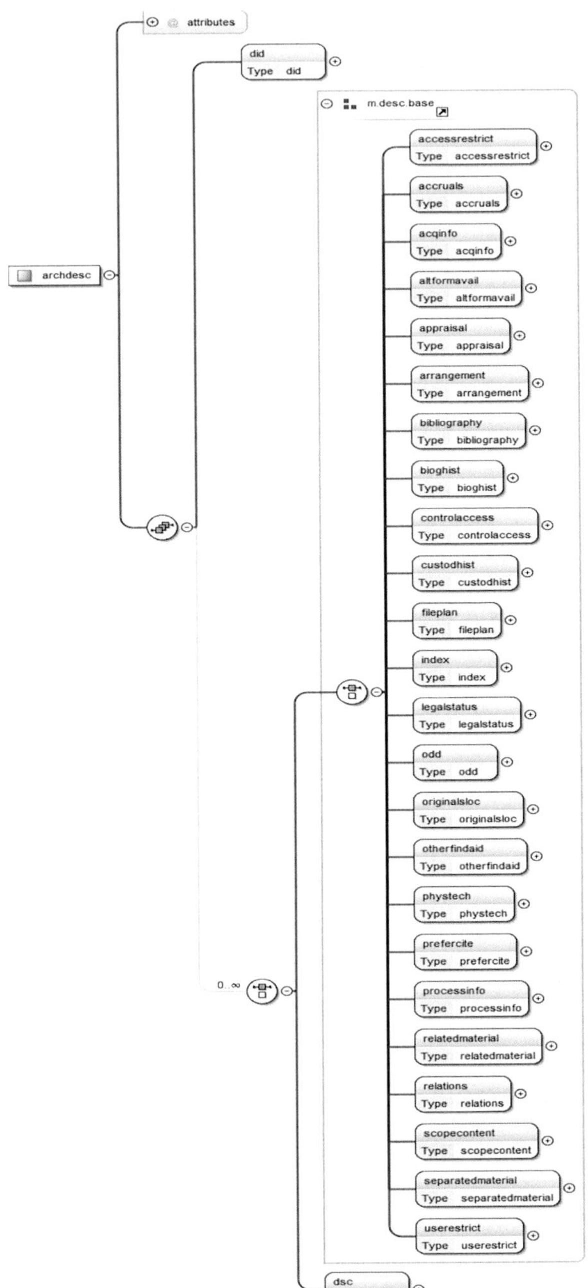

Figure 2.3 EAD XSD document.

Element	Description
<accessrestrict>	Contains information about the availability of the documents and the applicable access restrictions.
<accruals>	Information about the future accruals or transfer of documents.
<acqinfo>	Immediate source of acquisition of the materials being described. Used to identify the source of the materials being described and the circumstances under which they were received, including donations, transfers, purchases, and deposits.
<altformavail>	Indicates the existence of copies of the materials being described, including the type of alternative form, significant control numbers, location, and source for ordering if applicable. The additional formats are typically microforms, photocopies, or digital reproductions.
<appraisal>	A statement of the rationale for decisions related to appraisal and disposition of the materials being described. Such decisions may be based upon the records' current administrative, legal, and fiscal use; their evidential, intrinsic, and informational value; their arrangement and condition; and their relationship to other records. It can include information about destruction actions, sampling, and disposition schedules.
<arrangement>	Logical or physical groupings within a hierarchical structure. This includes how the described materials have been subdivided into smaller units, e.g., record groups into series. It can also indicate the filing sequence of the described materials, for example chronological or alphabetical arrangement.
<bibliography>	Identifies works that are based on, about, or of special value when using the materials being described, or works in which a citation to, or brief description of, the materials occurs. The works may be encoded in <bibref> or as a <table>, <list>, or <chronlist>, or in a series of <p> elements.
<bioghist>	A concise text or chronology that places the archival materials in context by providing information about their creator. Includes significant information about the life of an individual or family, or the administrative history of a corporate body.

(*Continued*)

Element	Description

	It can include a series of <p> elements and/or an element <chronlist>, for example:
	`<bioghist>`
	`    <chronlist>`
	`    <chronitem>`
	`        <date>1903, Dec. 14</date>`
	`        <event>Creation</event>`
	`    </chronitem>`
	`    <chronitem>`
	`        <date>1911, March 14</date>`
	`        <event>Changes its name to SSCCD.</event>`
	`    </chronitem>`
	`    </chronlist>`
	`</bioghist>`

<controlaccess>	Contains access points corresponding to names, topics, places, functions, occupations, titles, and genre terms that represent the contexts and content of the materials being described. <controlaccess> is used to support authority-controlled searching across finding aids. It can include different child elements, depending on the type of access point: • <persname> • <corpname> • <famname> • <geogname> • <subject> • <occupation> • <function> • <genreform> used for access points that refer to the access form, techniques, or physical characteristics of the document. • <name> a generic element that is used only if the type of the name used as the access point is unknown (that is to say, if it is not clear whether the name corresponds to a person, entity, etc.) • <title> used for access points that correspond to titles of works. • <head> used to group together the different access points by type, using a header or title before all the access points of the same type. For all each child element listed in this box, it is possible to use one attribute @source to indicate, in the controlled

(Continued)

Element	Description

	vocabulary, where the access point is taken from: aat (Art & Architecture Thesaurus), lctgm (Thesaurus for Graphic Materials), gmgpc (Thesaurus for Graphic Materials), lcnaf (Library of Congress Name Authority File), ulan (Union List of Artists Names), etc.
	It is also possible to include a formal identifier for the value used as an access point by means of the @identifier attribute.
	Example:
	`<controlaccess>`
	`<head>Subject headings</head>`
	`<subject source="lcsh">Bibliographies</subject>`
	`<subject>History of books</subject>`
	`<head>People</head>`
	`<persname>Mateo Flandro</persname>`
	`<head>Geog Location</head>`
	`<geogname>Zaragoza</geogname>`
	`</controlaccess>`
	EAD allows for the tagging of the names of persons, families, entities, titles, etc., in other parts of the finding aid (not only in the access points), using the same elements: <persname>, <famname>, <subject>, etc. Once the information is tagged at any place within the finding aid, it can be indexed and processed for different purposes.

<custodhist>	Describes both physical possession and intellectual ownership by providing details of changes of ownership and/or custody that may be significant in terms of authority, integrity, and interpretation.
<fileplan>	A filing plan is usually identified by the type of system used, e.g., alphabetical, numerical, alpha-numerical, decimal, color-coded, etc. It is often hierarchical and may include the filing guidelines of the originating entity.
<index>	Provides an alphabetical overview of subjects, people, entities, etc, represented in the collection, with references to the containers where the materials can be located. Includes child elements <indexentry>. Each <indexentry> element includes a name or access point encoded using the <persname>, <corpname>,

(*Continued*)

Element	Description
	etc., elements, and references or links to the appropriate sections or containers, for example: <index> <indexentry> <corpname>A.P. Watt & Son</corpname> <ref>47.5</ref> </indexentry> <indexentry> <persname>Watt, Janet</corpname> <ref>48.5</ref> </indexentry> </index>
<legalstatus>	Used to record the status of the material being described as defined by the law.
<odd>	Reserved to encode the information that cannot be recorded in any other EAD field (Other Descriptive Data). It is defined as an element *"for recording additional information about the described materials that is not easily incorporated into one of the other named elements within <archdesc> and <c>....."*
<originalsloc>	Contains information about the existence, location, or destruction of the original documents described in the finding aid. It is used when the description unit is made up of copies. This element must not be confused with <altformavail>, which contains information about the existing copies of the documentation that it is being described.
<otherfindaid>	Contains references to related guides or finding aids that provide information about the same description unit.
<phystech>	Physical conditions of the documentation that have an impact on its storage, use, and preservation. This element is also used to indicate when it is necessary to use specific hardware, software, or a dedicated device to read the documents.
<prefercite>	Preferred method that is used when referring to the documents being described. This is the citation to use when writing about the archival unit.
<processinfo>	Information about the processing activities, both manual and automated, that are executed on the documentation, with "*basic information about*

(*Continued*)

Element	Description
	accessioning, arranging, describing, preserving, storing, conserving, or otherwise preparing the described materials for research use."
<relatedmaterial>	Information about documents external to the documents being described, not related by provenance, which may be of interest to the researchers. The related documents may be held in the same, or different, archive/institution. <relatedmaterial> includes one or several <archref>, elements (each related documentation set is encoded in an independent <archref> element).
<relations>	Contains information entities (archival, bibliographic, persons, families, locations, etc.) that are related to the materials being described. Contains <relationentry> elements that specify each relation. It can also embed other XML data with information about the related entity within an <objectxmlwrap> element. The content model for <relations> defines the elements <date>, <daterange>, and <dateset> for specifying the time when the relation went into effect.
<scopecontent>	Provides a description of the scope and content of the documents being described. It should refer to the main persons, entities, places, topics, and events covered or related to the generation of the documents.
<separatedmaterial>	Used to refer to other archival materials that are related to the documents being described by provenance, and that are held separately from it (e.g., in a different archive).
<userestrict>	Applicable restrictions to cite, publish, or reproduce the contents of the documentation. This element contains constraints related to access of the documentation (EAD includes a separate element to encode access constraints, <accessrestrict>). It can be filled to indicate that there are no restrictions.
<dsc>	In the case of multilevel descriptions, the <dsc> element shall be used to group together all the components included in the description unit. For example, if one finding aid is used to describe a fond, the finding aid can contain descriptions for its series, all nested together within an element <dsc>.

The elements described in the previous table can be written in any order (the XML schema for EAD does not enforce the use of a specific order). All these elements are optional and can be repeated within <archdesc>. The only constraint is that they must be written after the <did> element.

The element <did> *(Descriptive Information)* is the main data block in each level that can be included in the finding aid. Fig. 2.4 shows the content model of this element.

Its child elements are described in the next table (the description of the elements that have already been described in the table with the child elements of <archdesc> is omitted):

Element	Description
<abstract>	Brief descriptive summary for the documentation.
<container>	Used in the <did> elements with the nested components (these nested components are encoded with <c> elements within the <dsc> element) to specify the container where the documents being described are stored.
<dao>	The Digital Archival Object's purpose is to link the finding aids to digital representations of the materials. The link can be established with the @href attribute of this element. Another mandatory attribute of the <dao> element is the @daotype, which takes one of these values: borndigital, derived, unknown, or otherdaotype. The @coverage optional element can be used to indicate if the digital representation corresponds with the complete documentation or only to one of its parts (by taking the values whole or in-part, respectively).
<daoset>	Used to group together several <dao> elements containing digital representations of the documents.
<didnote>	Used to include any additional, explanatory information that is hard to accommodate in the other elements.
<langmaterial>	Language of the documents described. Each language is encoded in a separate <language> element nested within <langmaterial>.

(*Continued*)

Element	Description
	These languages should not be confused with the language in which the finding aid (EAD document) is written. The language used to write the EAD document is indicated in the <languagedeclaration> element that is nested within <control>.
<materialspec>	Includes data that depends on the type of material being described, e.g. the scale in maps and plans.
<origination>	Name of the entity, person or family that has generated the archival materials. This element may contain other child elements like <persname>, <corpname>, or <famname>. For example, its value can be directly written in the <originator> element: <originator>Ramiro Brun</originator> Or detailed with subelements: <originator> <persame normal="Brun, Ramiro">Ramiro Brun</persname> </originator> In the second example the use of a normalized form for the name of the person is written within the @normal attribute.
<physdescset>	Used to group together several <physdesc> elements.
<physdesc>	Physical description, extension and format of the archival material. The content must be written directly within its start and ending tags, in a simple, unstructured statement, for example: <physdesc>149 fotografías</physdesc>
<physdescstructured>	Similar to <physdesc>, this element is used to provide the physical description of the materials in a structured form, using its child elements <descriptivenote>, <dimensions>, <physfacet>, <quantity> and <unittype>, for example: <physdescstructured coverage="whole" physdescstructuredtype="spaceoccupied"> <quantity>12</quantity> <unittype>linear feet</unittype> </physdescstructured>

(*Continued*)

Element	Description
`<physloc>`	Physical location of the description unit (call number or any other method used to indicate where the materials are located).
`<repository>`	Name of the archive or entity that holds the archival materials and gives access to the materials. It is possible to write the name of the archive using its child elements <address>, <corpname>, <famname>, <name>, or <persname>.
`<unitdate>`	Inclusive dates of the records / archival materials, expressed in a single, unstructured statement. `<unitdate>1931-1999</unitdate>`

`<unitdatestructured>`	Inclusive dates of the records / archival materials, expressed in a structured statement using its child elements <daterange>, <dateset> and <datesingle>, for example:
	`<unitdatestructured unitdatetype="inclusive">`
	`<daterange>`
	`<fromdate notafter="1962">1962</fromdate>`
	`<todate notafter="1968">1968</todate>`
	`</daterange>`
	`</unitdatestructured>`

`<unitid>`	Unique identifier of the materials; two optional attributes, @`countrycode` and @`repositorycode` contain the code of the country (according to *ISO 3166* codes) and the code that identifies the archive holding the materials. `<unitid>` is not intended to contain the call number or physical location of the materials (this information should be written in the `<physloc>` element).
`<unittitle>`	Title given to the materials.

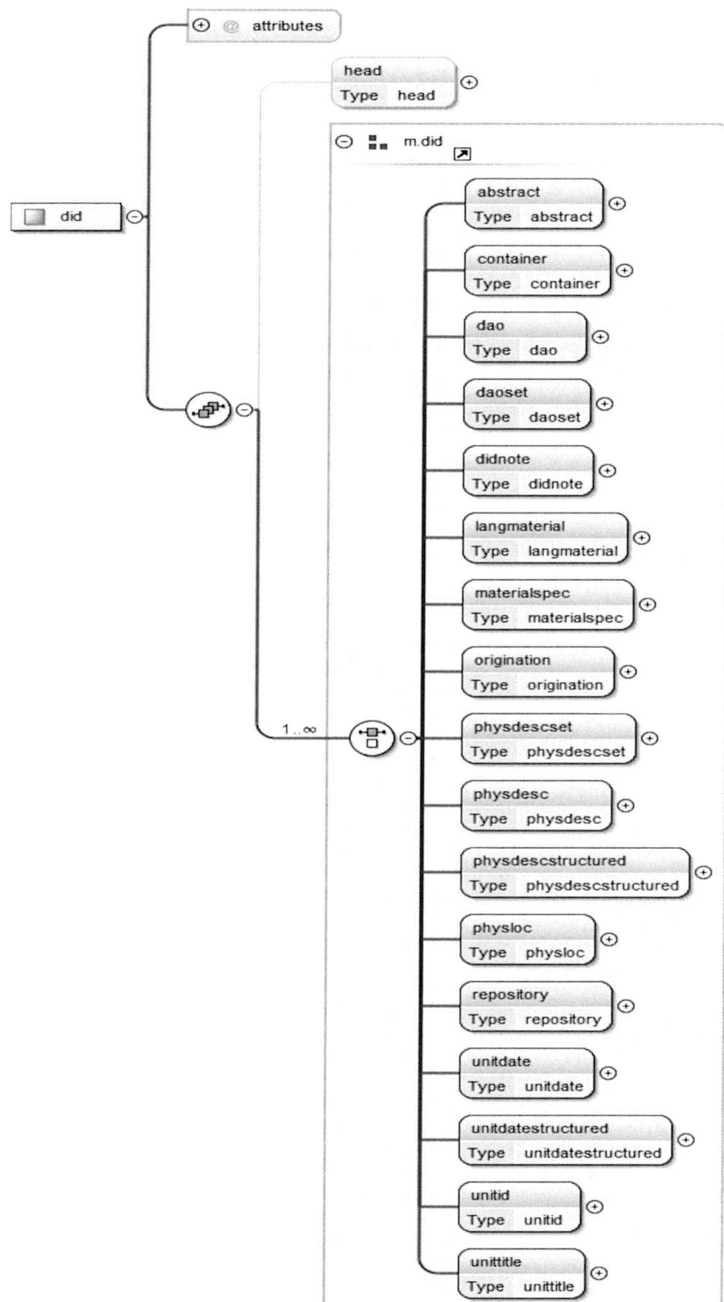

Figure 2.4 EAD XSD schema.

The example below, taken from the official EAD3 documentation, shows the structure and the elements of the <did> element:

```
<archdesc localtype="inventory" level="subgrp">
    <did>
      <repository>
            <corpname>
                  <part>Minnesota Historical Society</part>
            </corpname>
      </repository>
      <origination>
            <corpname>
                  <part>Minnesota.</part>
                  <part>Game and Fish Department</part>
            </corpname>
      </origination>
      <unittitle>Game laws violation records</unittitle>
      <unitdate>1908-1928</unitdate>
      <abstract>Records of prosecutions for and seizures
of property resulting from violation of the state's hunting and
fishing laws.</abstract>
      <physdesc>2.25 cu. ft. (7 v. and 1 folder in 3
boxes)</physdesc>
    </did>
[...]
</archdesc>
```

2.4.2 EAC-CPF

Archivists have, at their disposal, another XML schema that can be used to describe authority records (Pitti, 2004a). In addition, because of the relationship between EAD and ISAD(G), it is possible to establish an equivalence between EAC-CPF and the ISAAR(CPF) standard proposed by the ICA *(International Council of Archives).*

EAC documents have a root element with a name `<eac>`, which contains two mandatory child elements:

1. `<eacheader>, with data` related to the authority record, its author, creation date, update dates, etc.
2. `<condesc>`, with the information about the person, family, or institution described in the authority record. This element contains the description of the entity, the preferred and alternative names, as well

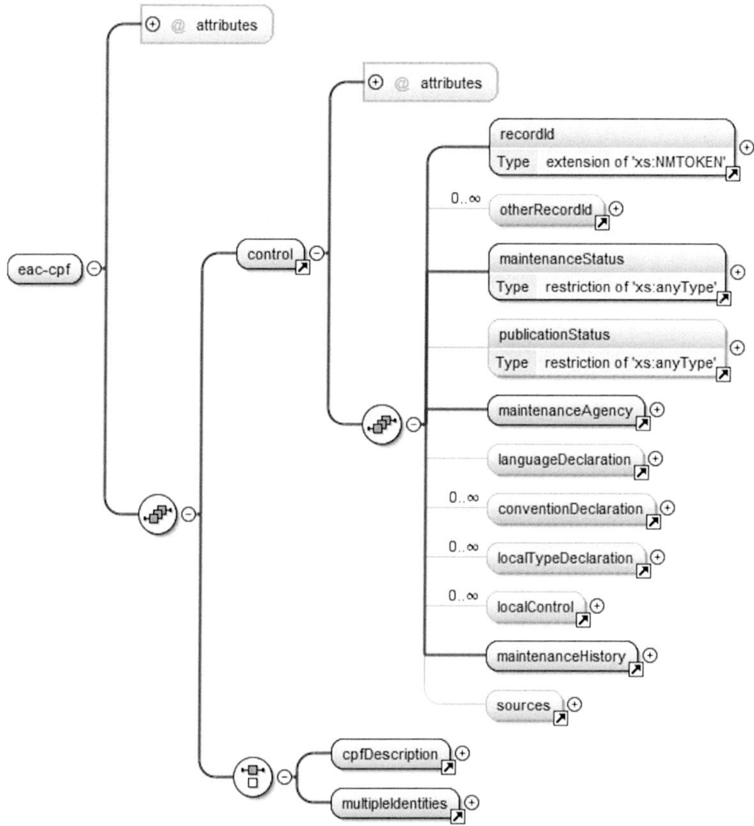

Figure 2.5 EAC-CPF XSD document.

as relationships with other EAC authority records and information resources.

Fig. 2.5 shows the basic structure of the EAC documents.

The root element `<eac-cpf>` includes the child elements <control>, <cpfDescription>, and <multipleIdentifiers>.

<control> contains the metadata for the authority record. Similar to the <control> element used in EAD3, it contains at least these mandatory child elements:

Element	Description
`<recordid>`	Unique identifier for the EAC authority record.
`<maintenanceStatus>`	This field indicates the status of the record, which can be one of the following: "cancelled", "deleted", "deletedReplaced", "deletedSplit", "derived", "new", or "revised".

(Continued)

Element	Description
<maintenanceHistory>	It contains all the changes done in the EAC authority record. Each change is recorded in a separate <maintenanceEvent> child element. <maintenanceEvent> contains separate child elements for encoding the type of event <eventType>, the time of the event <eventDateTime>, its agent <agentType> and <agentName>, and one optional description of the maintenance tasks in <eventDescription>. The values for the <eventType> element are one of the following: *"cancelled, "created", "deleted", "derived", "revised", or "updated".*
<languageDeclaration>	This optional element is used to encode the language in which the authority record is written. Each language is indicated in a separate <language> element.
<maintenanceAgency>	Agency maintaining the EAC authority record.

2.4.2.1 Element <cpfDescription>

This element conforms the basis for the authority record. It has the following child elements:

Element	Description
<identity>	Mandatory element that contains the names used to refer to the entity, both the preferred and the nonpreferred. <identity> includes the child elements <entityId>, <entityType>, <nameEntry>, and <descriptiveNote>. <entityType> Indicate the type of the entity the authority record refers to, using one of these values: "person", "corporateBody", or "family". <nameEntry> can include one or several child elements such as <parts>, <useDates>, <authorizedform>, and <alternativeForm>.
<description>	Optional element containing the descriptive data for the person, family, or institution, its history or bibliography, functions, context in which it developed its activity, etc. This element includes several child elements, for example: <existDates>, <place>, <legalStatus>, <function>, <occupation>, <generalContext>, <structureOrGenealogy>, and <biogHist>. The content of this elements consists of textual descriptions encoded using paragraphs (elements <p>), lists (<list>), or terms in the case of functions.

(*Continued*)

Element	Description
<relations>	This optional element contains references to other EAC-CPF authority records that are related to the entity, person, or family being described. Relations to functions and other resources can also be encoded as child elements of <relations> using different child elements: <cpfRelations>, <resourceRelations>, and <functionRelations>. Relationships can be given a title, a description, and a date range. It is also possible to embed XML data with additional information about the related entity.
<alternativeSet>	This is an optional document used to incorporate alternative authority records that refer to the same entity. This element contains one or more <setComponent> child elements, each one containing a different authority record. This element is useful to aggregate data that refers to the same person, institution, or family. <setComponent> points to the alternative records: <alternativeSet> <setComponent xlink:href="http://nla.gov.au/anbd.aut-an35335937" xlink:type="simple"> <componentEntry>NLA record.</componentEntry> </setComponent> </alternativeSet>

Fig. 2.6 shows the structure of the <cpfDescription> element in EAC.

2.4.2.2 Element <multipleIdentifies>

This optional element is used to group together several <cpfDescription> in the same authority record. This function may be useful in the case of entities that are the result of several entities collaborating together, each having an independent description.

2.4.3 EAG (Encoded Archival Guide)

EAG was published as a preliminary schema in 2002 by the *Subdirección General de los Archivos Estatales de España*, with the aim of providing a DTD to encode guides or archives in electronic format (Desantes, 2005). The document type was intended to solve some of the constraints observed in EAD. EAD focuses on the description of the

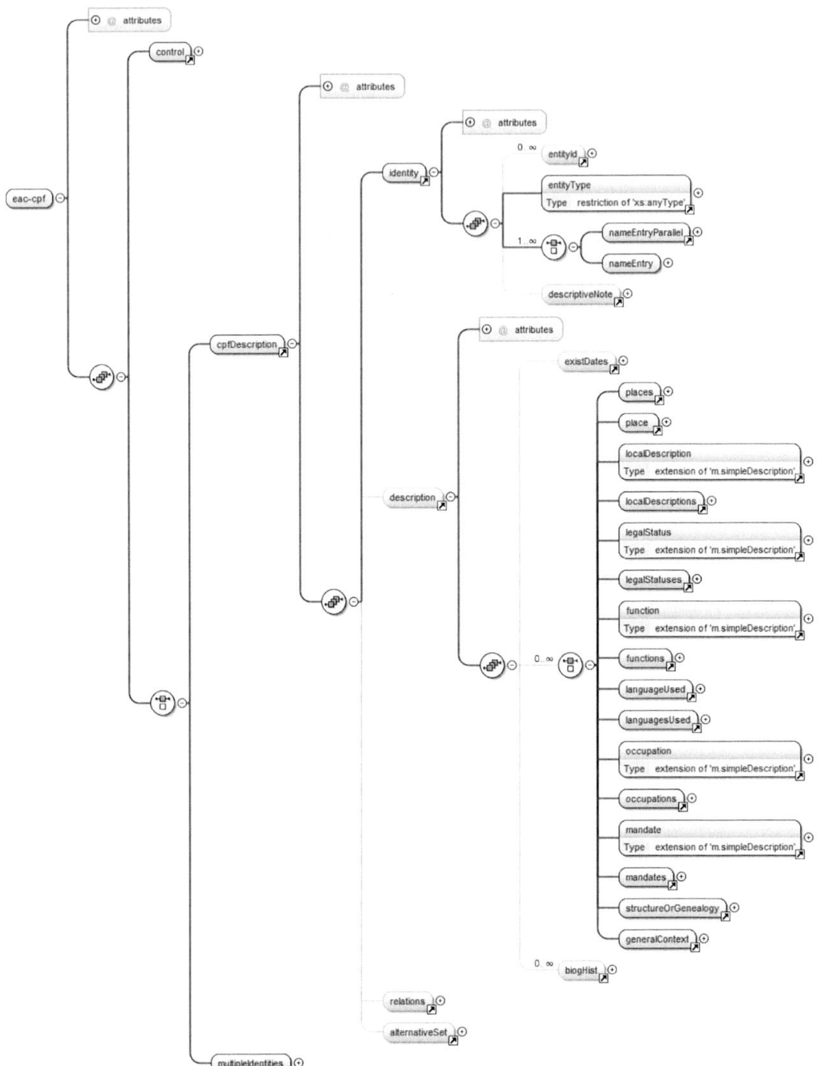

Figure 2.6 EAC-CPF XSD schema.

archival materials and documents, but additional, different elements were needed to encode information about the archive: its internal organization, location, contact details, opening hours, services, managers, etc. As an example, EAG incorporates elements like `<telephone>`, `<fax>`,

`<webpage>`, `<timetable>`, or `<repositoryHist>`, `<services>`, etc., among others.

The root element in the EAG schema is `<eag>`, which contains three child elements:

- `<control>`—with the same structure as the <control> element in EAD, and used to encode data about the XML document itself, identifier, language, maintenance agency, evolution, etc.
- `<archguide>`—has the main content of the guide. It is possible to encode, within the same XML document, the guides for more than one archive.
- <relation>—optional element that can be used to create relations with other EAG records or with records that describe holdings.

The structure of the EAG records is aligned with the one used in EAD and EAC-CPF, which makes it easer to learn and use these XML schemas. Archivists who used to work with EAD found it easier to create and maintain EAC-CPF and EAG records. In addition, the three types of records can be linked together, thereby establishing a complex information system containing the data about the archives (EAG), their holdings (EAD), and the authority records used as access points to index the data.

2.5 METS (METADATA ENCODING & TRANSMISSION STANDARD)

METS offers an XML schema for the exchange of complex, digital documents (Cundiff, 2004). One electronic document can be made up of several files. For example, one digital book can be composed by several, digitized image files in TIFF format, text files generated by an optical character recognition (OCR) process, and audio files that relate to the content of the pages of the book. In these cases, the document contains several image, audio, and text files that must be displayed and shown to the user in a coordinated way. In other words, special metadata must be added to understand the structure and the relationships between the different files.

METS offers the metadata needed to encode and represent the structure of complex, digital documents. It is a schema that allows for management of the structural metadata of the digital objects. Besides that, METS also gives the choice of attaching descriptive metadata to the digital object using popular schemas like MARC, Dublin Core, and MODS (McCallum, 2004; Seadle, 2002).

The origin of METS goes back to the design of one schema of structural metadata as part of the MOA2 (*Making of America II*) Project. *Making of America II* was led by the US DFL (*Digital Library Federation*). They created an XML DTD with the name MOA2 and software tools to encode and exchange digitized information resources with their descriptive, administrative, and structural metadata. When the MOA2 project finished, DLF continued evolving the format, and this evolution resulted in the first version of METS.

METS provides us with an XML schema. Today, the Network Development and MARC Standards Office of the Library of Congress is in charge of its maintenance and evolution, and the latest version available is 1.11, published in May 2015.

A METS document is an XML document that can encode the following data (Nicholson, 2006):

1. The list of all the files that are part of the digital object. These files may be images, audio, text, or any other media.
2. The structure and logical organization of these files. Logical organization refers to the sequence in which the files must be shown, their organization into chapters and sections, or any other group, as well as the parallelism between them (for example, the parallelism between a digitized image and the text file with its content obtained by OCR).
3. The descriptive metadata of the digital object as a whole, or any of its parts. Descriptive metadata is encoded using an existing schema such as Dublin Core, MODS, or MARC.
4. Administrative metadata for the digital object as a whole, or for any of its parts. These metadata cover information related to rights management, provenance, and origin of the digital representations, data about the digitized document, etc.
5. Hyperlinks between the different parts of the digital object (section, subsections, etc.). These links are called structural hyperlinks.
6. The behavior attached to the different parts of the digital object. This is one of the most complex parts, because they link the sections of the digital object with external applications that are used to make a process.

The METS document also includes some metadata related to itself: author, creation date, last update date, etc.

2.5.1 Structure of METS documents

To encode the data mentioned above, the METS schema provides the document structure shown in Fig. 2.7.

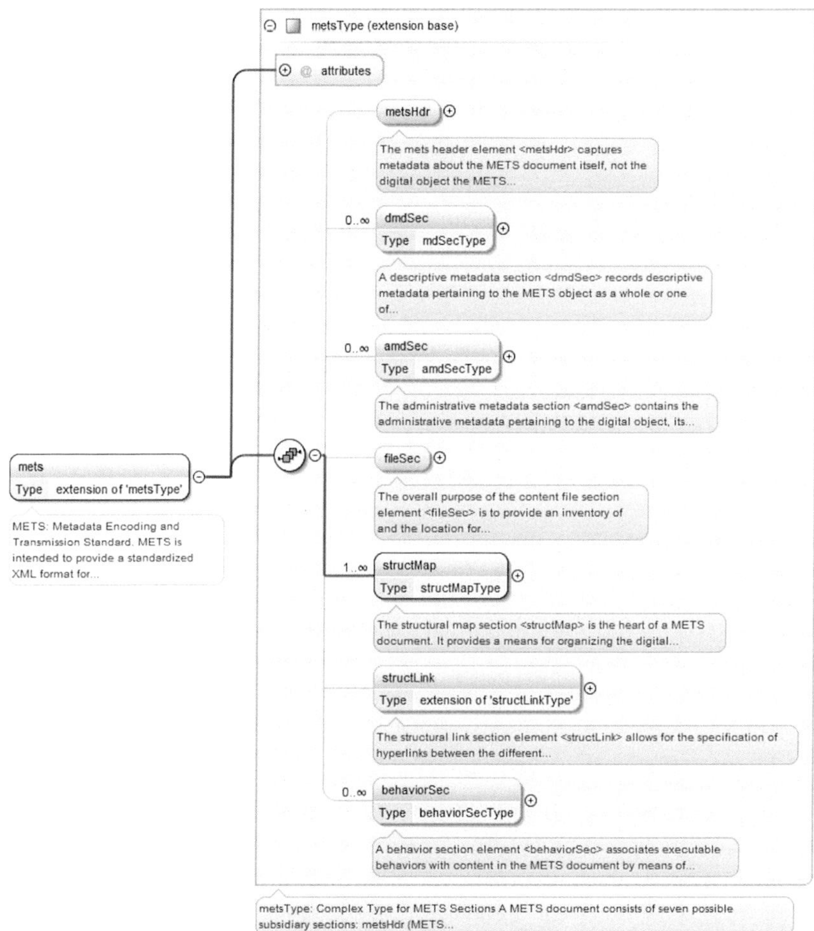

Figure 2.7 METS XSD document.

The `<mets>` element is the root element. It contains these child elements:

- `<metsHdr>`—header that contains the metadata about the METS document: creator, creation date, last update date, etc. It is optional and nonrepeatable.

- `<dmdSec>`—descriptive metadata of the digital object or any of its sections. This element is optional and repeatable.
- `<amdSec>`—administrative metadata of the digital object or its sections. It is optional and repeatable too.
- `<fileSect>`—list of all the files that compose the digital object. In most of the cases, this list is made up of digitized image files. The element is optional and repeatable.
- `<structMap>`—also known as the structural map of the document, it describes the logical organization of the files listed in the `<fileSect>` element. The structural map must indicate at least the sequence in which the digitized images must be displayed, as well as their organization in chapters, sections, subsections, etc.

  `<structMap>` is the only element declared as mandatory. It can also be repeated.
- `<structLink>`—contains the links between the different parts of the digital object: chapters, sections, etc. It is optional and nonrepeatable.
- `<behaviorSec>`—contains the behaviors attached to the digital object. It is optional and repeatable.

2.5.1.1 Element <dmdSec>

The `<dmdSec>` element, which contains the descriptive metadata of the digital object, provides the basic data about the document, and is used to index and retrieve the digital object or its constituent parts. One of the features of the METS schema is that it does not define descriptive metadata. Instead, use existing metadata schemas like Dublin Core, MODS, and MARCXML. The child elements of `<dmdSec>` can be a `<mdRef>` element or a `<mdWrap>` element, depending on the method we want to use to link the descriptive metadata:
- `<mdRef>` used when the descriptive metadata is stored in an external file; the URL of this external file—or an alternative identifier—is encoded in the METS element.
- `<mdWrap>` used when embedding the metadata inside the METS document, within this element.

2.5.1.2 Element `<amdSec>`

This element contains the administrative metadata of the digital object or its parts. These metadata help manage the information about rights and intellectual property and the source document is used to obtain the digitized version of the document, preservation activities completed on the files, etc.

<admSec> has four child elements, as shown in Fig. 2.8.

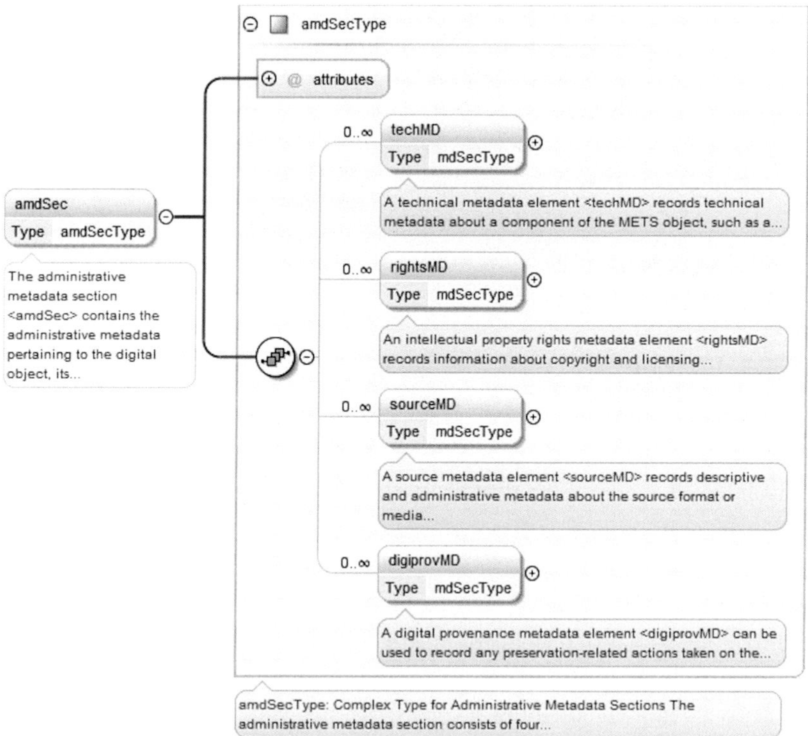

Figure 2.8 METS XSD schema.

- <techMD>—this element contains the technical metadata, that is to say, the format of the files, their technical characteristics, compression method, etc.
- <rightsMD>—metadata about rights management and intellectual property rights.
- <sourceMD>—information about the source document on which the digital object is based.
- <digiprovMD>—data about the provenance of the digitized copies that made up the digital object.

  The content of these four elements (<techMD>, <rightsMD>, <sourceMD>, and <digiprovMD>) is not declared in the METS schema.

As with `<dmdSec>`, it is possible to refer to metadata encoded in an external file (using the `<mdRef>` element) or embed the metadata within the child elements of `<mdWrap>`. Using this approach the <amdSec> child elements share the same attributes and children as <dmdSec>.

Regarding the existing XML metadata schemas that can be used to complete these elements, METS proposes the following alternatives for the administrative metadata:

- *Schema for Technical Metadata for Text*, `textmd.xsd`, created by Jerome McDonough from the New York University.
- *MIX—Metadata for Digital Images Standards*
- *Schema for Rights Declaration Schema*
- *PREMIS*

2.5.1.3 Element `<fileSec>`

This element contains the list of all the files that are part of the digital object. It can include a reference to external files (pointing to their URL, DOI, etc.), or embed the content of the files within the METS document (embedded files can be XML or binary files).

2.5.1.4 Element `<structMap>`

The structural map describes the relationship between the files in the digital object, grouping them in parts, chapters, sections, etc. The `<structMap>` element includes several divisions, each division encoded in a separate `<div>` element. The `<div>` elements can be nested to create complex hierarchical arrangements of the sections.

2.6 TEI (TEXT ENCODING INITIATIVE)

TEI is one of the early initiatives in structural data management. It was created in 1987—before the creation of XML—with the purpose of encoding the full text of documents and textual corpus. TEI was the result of an initiative of the ACL (Association for Computational Linguistics), ALLC (Association for Literary and Linguistic Computing), and ACH (Association for Computing and the Humanities). The Project was funded by the US National Endowment for the Humanities, Mellon Foundation, Canadian Social

Sciences and Humanities Research Council, and the 3rd Framework Programme for Linguistic Research and Engineering of the European Union.

The objective of TEI was to create a markup language based on SGML to encode and exchange texts. Using SGML as a basis, the tagged documents are independent of any specific technical solution or provider. In addition, using a standard like SGML supports the conversion of the content to electronic format for its preservation and access. The TEI document type includes tags to encode the content of different types of documents, and includes the metadata needed for cataloging and searching in large text databases (McCarthy et al., 2012; Di Monte and Serafin, 2017).

The latest version available of TEI is P5 version 3.1.0, fully aligned with XML (Erjavec, 2010; Halsell, 2013). To make the adoption of TEI easier for organisations, the TEI Consortium published a reduced version called *TEI Lite* (Burnard and Sperberg-McQueen, 2012). It is a simplified version of the schema that includes only the most popular elements. As TEI is designed to accommodate different types of texts, its complete definition includes a big number of tags (version P5 has around 495 elements). These elements are grouped in several *TagSets,* each TagSet having the elements needed to encode different characteristics of the documents. TagSets are defined in separate XML schemas.

TEI documents have, as their root, the `<TEI>` element. This element refers to the namespace http://www.tei-c.org/ns/1.0.

TEI documents have a header with metadata about the document, and the full text of the encoded document. The header—*TEI Header*—is encoded in the `<teiHeader>` element, and the full text of the document is encoded in one `<text>` element.

Fig. 2.9 shows the basic components of a *TEI Lite* document.

The <text> element is the most important part of the document. Its content is organized into three child elements:

- `<front>`—optional element that contains the transcription of the initial pages of the document, preliminary pages, dedication, etc.
- `<body>`—mandatory element for the main text of the document.
- `<back>`—optional element containing the annexes, bibliography, or any other section appearing at the end of the work. TEI documents can contain several works or contributions; to handle these cases the

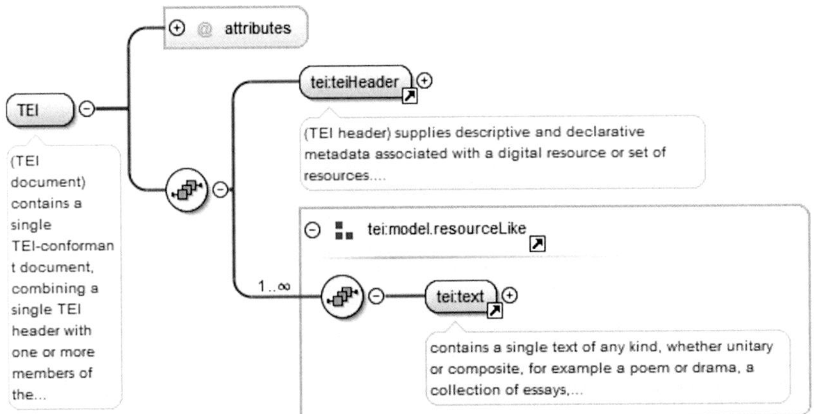

Figure 2.9 TEI XSD schema.

schema includes the <group> element, which can be used to nest different works, as shown in this example:

```
<TEI.2>
     <teiHeader>...</teiHeader>
     <text>
        <front>...</front>
        <group>
           <text> <front>...<back>...</text>
           <text> <front>...<back>...</text>
           <text> <front>...<back>...</text>
        </group>
        <back>...</back>
     </text>
</TEI.2>
```

The content of the `<body>`, `<front>`, and `<back>` elements are grouped into sections and subsections that correspond to the different parts and chapters of the work. TEI uses the generic <div> element to differentiate each part. The `<div>` element can have other <div> child elements which can be accompanied by the @`type` attribute to indicate chapter, section, etc. The values for this attribute are not defined in the TEI schema.

`<div>` elements can also have a header encoded in a `<head>` element and a `<trailer>` element that acts as colophon. Between the header and the trailer it is possible to include all the necessary elements to identify the paragraphs, sections, images, tables, lists, hypertext links, etc. The table below describes the most frequent elements in *TEI.*

Element	Description
<p>	Paragraphs. Each paragraph is encoded in a separate <p> element.
<s>	Used to encode sentences delimited by punctuation marks.
<q>	Used to encode citations and text fragments that correspond to the literal transcription of sentences said by an individual. This element can be accompanied by the @who attribute, which provides attribution to the speaker.
<emph>	Used to emphasize several words.
<rs>	Used to tag text that refers to one person, place, etc. It has one @type attribute indicating the type of entity the text refers to. <rs> is similar to another TEI element, <name>, which is also used to tag the name of people, entities, places, etc. The main difference between <rs> and <name> is that the use of the second one is restricted to proper names. For example, a reference to the *president of the US* should be encoded with <rs>, but a reference to *Obama* should be encoded with <name>. It is also possible to include the <name> element within the <rs>. <rs> can have one @key attribute that contains the normalized name of the person, entity, place, etc., the text fragment refers to.
<foreign>	Used to encode one or more words written in a language other than the main language of the work. The attribute @xml:lang is used to indicate in which language the word(s) is written.
<title>	Used to tag the title of one work (book, article, journal, etc.) cited in the text. The type of the work is indicated with the @level attribute. Its values are declared in the schema as follows: *a* (title of an analytic work), *j* (periodic publication), *m* (monograph), *s* (serial), and *u* (for unpublished material such as dissertations).
<pb>	This empty element is used to indicate a page break. It is useful when retaining the information about a printed material. <pb> is particular to the <milestone> element, used to keep data about any break in the printed work that is being encoded in electronic format.
<lb>	Empty element used to indicate the presence of line breaks. It is useful when retaining the information about the printed version of the work that has been encoded electronically. <lb> is particular to the <milestone> element.

(*Continued*)

Element	Description
<name>	Used to tag the proper name of a person, place, organization, etc. It has these attributes: 1. type, which contains the type of entity (its values are not declared in the schema), 2. reg, which contains the authorized or preferred name for the person, entity, or place. 3. key, which can contain one code for the authorized form of the name.
<date>	Used to encode dates. It can be accompanied by the @value attribute, which contains the date in normalized form (year-month-day, e.g. 1973-07-22). This element has an optional attribute, @calendar, to indicate the type of calendar used.
<time>	Used to encode time. It can have the attributes: @value, which contains the time in a normalized form, @type, which accepts the *am*, *pm*, *24h* and *descriptive* values, and @zone, which indicates the time zone.
<list>, <item>, and <label>	Used to encode lists. Each list is encoded with a <list> element. This <list> element has one separate <item> element for each entry in the list. <list> can have one @type attribute with the values: *ordered*, *bulleted*, *simple*, and *gloss* (the last one is used to encode a list of definitions). Before the <ítem> elements the list can have one title encoded in the <head> element. The <item> element has an optional @n attribute to encode the number of the alphanumeric code that precedes the entry. In addition, each <item> element can be preceded by the <label> element which contains the code or term that is shown before the entry text. This element is useful for lists that contain definitions—to tag the term being defined. Lists can be embedded within other lists in TEI documents by nesting <list> elements within the <item> elements.
<table>, <row>, and <cell>	Used to create tables. <table> is used to create one table and has the attributes @rows and @cols, which indicate the number of rows and columns. When using <table>, each row has a separate <row> element. <row> elements have one child element <cell> for each cell in the row.

(*Continued*)

Element	Description
	The <cell> elements contain the content of the cell. If the width or height of the cell must be expanded the @rows and @cols attributes can be used to indicate the number of cells that must be expanded.
<figure> and <graphic>	<figure> is used to add images to the document. It has one @entity attribute that contains the reference to an external entity that points to the file with the image. <figure> can have child elements such as <figDesc> with a description of the image and <head> for the image's title. As an example, this fragment shows the use of the <figure> element. First, the <!ENTITY... line is used to declare the image (one tif file). Then the @entity attribute points to this image.

```
<!ENTITY sevillaTO SYSTEM "sevilla1.tif" NDATA tiff>
<figure entity="sevillaTO">
  <head>Torre del Oro, Sevilla</head>
  <figDesc>Foto tomada en 1924 por Carlos Montero
  </figDesc>
</figure>
```

Element	Description
	TEI also uses another element—<graphic>—to include images in GIF, JPEG, PNG, TIFF, and CGM format pointing to the image file URL.
<bibl> and <listBibl>	Used to encode bibliographic references. <bibl> has child elements to distinguish the different bibliographic data: <author>, <date>, <editor>, <biblScope>, <imprint>, <pubPlace>, <publisher>, and <title>. When encoding a bibliographic reference with <bibl>, its child elements can be used in any order. It is also possible to write the reference as a single text line within the <bibl> element, without using its child elements. <listBibl> is used to group together several bibliographic references.

In addition to the elements listed above, TEI documents can contain internal links that point to other sections of the same document, and external links pointing to other documents. Internal links are encoded with the <ptr> and <ref> elements. The first one is an empty element and the second one is not empty and can contain the text that acts as the source of the link.

The links to external documents are encoded with the <xptr> and <xref> elements. Similar to the previous ones, the first one is empty and the second one can contain the text used as the source of the link.

2.7 DITA (DARWIN INFORMATION TYPING ARCHITECTURE)

Another well known and frequently used XML document type is DITA. DITA is not used in the area of digital humanities—unlike the previous schemas—but in the preparation of technical documents (user manuals, operation guides, etc.), and it has become the most relevant XML schema in the elaboration of technical documentation for software products.

DITA offers a flexible schema that can be used in other, alternative scenarios that require the elaboration of XML documents in a format easy to process and reuse (Kelley, 2017; Evia et al., 2016).

The origin of DITA goes back to 1999, when IBM designed the schema. In 2004, the maintenance of the DITA specification was transferred to OASIS, a nonprofit consortium that managed the development and adoption of open standards for the global information society. The latest version of DITA is 1.2, published on December 2010.

Content in DITA is organized into topics, defined as basic units of content and reuse. The DITA specification provides this definition: "*DITA topic is a titled unit of information that can be understood in isolation and used in multiple contexts. It should be short enough to address a single subject or answer a single question but long enough to make sense on its own and be authored as a self-contained unit.*" Topics can be generic or specialized into one of these types: concept, tasks, reference, or learning content. The origin of this classification of topics is necessary for encoding user guides and manuals. A best practice for these documents is to make a distinction between the pages that provide the conceptual information needed to understand the product features and the procedural information needed to accomplish the tasks using the software application. Each topic can be stored in a separate file with the .xml or .dita extension.

In addition to topics, DITA also defines the concept of a map. One map is defined as, "...documents that organize topics and other resources into structured collections of information." The maps are special files containing a hierarchical arrangement of the content topics, which are stored externally to the map file. The DITA map contains references to content topics nested in a way that is useful to navigate the publication and find information. Maps are saved in files with the .ditamap extension and act as the navigational tools to access the different topics that compose the publication.

Another relevant feature of DITA is that new types of topics can be created by specializing the generic topic or any of its types (concept, tasks, etc.). By using the extension mechanisms provided by DITA the schema can be extended to accommodate additional tags to support new information and data encoding needs.

One DITA publication is made up of several files. Each topic is kept in a different XML file; at least one DITA map with the organization and arrangement of the topics should be included. The different files that compose a DITA publication have a different structure. In the next sections the structure of DITA topics, their specialization, and DITA maps are explained.

Generic DITA topics have the <topic> element as their root. This element must have a mandatory @id attribute, which is used as a unique identifier for the topic.

The first element in the document, within the root element, is the <title> element that contains the title of the topic. In addition to the main title, DITA offers the possibility to define alternative titles that can be used when browsing or searching the publication. These two alternative titles can be optionally encoded within the <titlealts> elements. <titlealts> have, as children, the <navtitle> and the <searchtitle> element. The tool used to manage the DITA publication uses these titles when building the navigation tools or when displaying the item in a list of search results.

After the title add an optional <shortdesc> or <abstract> element. The first one contains a brief summary of the topic content (no longer than a paragraph); the second one contains a more detailed overview of its content and has at least one <shortdesc> child element.

Metadata about the topic itself can be encoded using the <prolog> element. Data in this element should not be shown when displaying the topic information, although it is useful for managing the topic. The DITA schema defines different metadata to be used in the <prolog>, like <author>, <Publisher>, <critdates>, <created>, <revised>, <copyright> – divided into <copyryear> and <copyrholder> – or <metadata> that contains <keywords>, <audience>, <prodinfo>, etc.

After these elements, the schema requires the presence of a <body> element. The <body> element contains the text of the topic, encoded using different block and inline elements. DITA uses the same elements as HTML to encode the content, so readers who are used to working with HTML will find no major issues when working with DITA.

The table below shows the main elements used in DITA to tag the text and include multimedia elements in the body of the topic:

Element	Description
<p>	Paragraphs. Each paragraph is encoded in a separate <p> element.
<i>	Inline element used to display text in italics.
<b>	Used to emphasize several words.
<section>	Content in the topic may be divided into different sections. Each <section> element is used to distinguish between the sections. In DITA, sections may have a title that is tagged with the <title> element, just after the start tag of the <section> element. One interesting feature in DITA is that <section> elements cannot be nested within other <section> elements. DITA also includes a <div> element that can be used to separate the content into different divisions.
<ul>, <ol> and <li>	These elements are used to encode lists. Each list is encoded with a <ul> or <ol> element, depending on the use of unordered or ordered list. Every entry in the list has a separate <li> element.
<dl>, <dlentry>, <dt> and <dd>.	Used to encode lists of definitions. The list is included within the <dl> element. Each entry has a separate <dlentry> element, which contains a <dt> element for the term and a <dd> element for the definition.
<simpletable>, <sthead>, <strow> and <stentry>	Used to create tables. <simpletable> is used to create one table, which can have an optional header row, <sthead>, and one or more rows (each row encoded with the <strow> element). In addition, each <strow> (as well as <sthead>) has one separate <stentry> for each cell in the table.
<fig>, <title> and <image>	<fig> is used to add images to the document. It has as child elements <title> and <image>. <title> contains the title of the image and <image> the URL of the image file. This URL is indicated in the @href attribute of <image>. Another attribute that can be used with <image> is @align. The <image> file can be directly used without embedding it in a <fig> element.
<pre>	This element is used to tag a block as pre-formatted text. This text is displayed in monospaced characters.

(*Continued*)

Element	Description
`<tt>`	This inline element is used to tag a text fragment as monospaced or teletype.
`<sup>` and `<sub>`	This inline element is used to indicate that the tagged text must be displayed as superscript or subscript.
`<xref>`	This element is used to create hyperlinks. `<xref>` has a @href attribute where we can type the target of the link. The text that is used as the origin of the link is written between the <xref> element start and ending tags.

Other elements defined in DITA – that are related to the encoding of technical documentation – are used to distinguish the use of commands (<cmdnames>, window titles (<wintitle>), blocks of code (<codeblock>), filenames (<filepath>), application messages (<msgblock>), etc.

After the <body> it is possible to use the <related-links> element. This element provides a functionality similar to "See also" or "See related topics", which are statements routinely used in online help systems and documentation. <related-links> contain one or more <link> elements pointing to other topics where it is possible to find related information. The text used as origin of the link is indicated in the <linktext> element, which is a child of <link>. If this <linktext> element is not provided, the application used to handle the DITA content will try to generate source text from the DITA topic that is identified as the target of the link.

Generic DITA topics are specialized into other type of topics depending on the information they provide. The specification makes a distinction between concept, task, and reference topics. The main structure of these topics is similar to the one used for the generic topics, with a few differences.

First, the root and the <body> elements are renamed depending on the topic type. For example, for concept topics the root <concept> or <conbody> is used instead of <body>. For tasks, <task> is the root element and <taskbody> is used. In this case there are more options because tasks include different elements to distinguish between the context of the tasks and its steps, with specific elements like <context> and <steps>. <context> is contains a textual description encoded with the elements described in the previous section (<p>, <table>, <ul>, etc.). In the case of <steps>, this element contains a sequence of <step> elements. Each <step> contains a command <cmd> and the results of its execution in an <stepresult> element. <stepresult> can include typical elements like paragraphs, tables, lists, etc. Finally, reference topics have <reference> as a root element and <body> is renamed as <refbody>. They can contain different sections with the typical elements used in the generic topics.

Another type of topic widely used in DITA documents is a glossary of terms (<glossentry>). This topic has two elements, <glossterm> and <glossdef>, and each contains the term and its definition. DITA also includes the <glossgroup> element which can be used to group several entries of the glossary together in a single document. Each entry in the glossary has a unique identifier to support hyperlinks from other topics.

Maps are used in DITA to organize content and topics. The map can be a table of contents or a navigational aid that gives access to the collection of topics that make up the publication. The root element of the DITA map is the <map> element. Within this element this a <title> element followed by the list of topics.

Each topic that is referenced in the DITA map has a separate <topicref> element and the @href attribute points to the identifier of the target topic.

Another element that can be used when creating the map is <topichead>. With this element it is possible to add an entry to the map that does not point to a topic, but instead simply provides text used to group other entries. The text shown is written in its @navtitle attribute.

```
<map>
  <topichead navtitle="Books">
    <topicref href="hardback.dita"/>
    <topicref href="paperback.dita"/>
  </topichead>
</map>
```

2.8 CONCLUSIONS

This chapter provided information about typical structured data management requirements in different scenarios: archival science, digital humanities, exchange of digital objects and technical communication.

A preliminary step when working with XML and structured data management is to gain an understanding of the most popular schemas and document types in order to get familiar with the structure and markup used in these schemas. Depending on the specific needs and application requirements, information specialists can focus on different schemas or DTD. Once the selection has been made, authors and editors must gain knowledge on the schema structure, its elements and attributes, etc. This provided the information needed to start working with some of the most popular schemas: EAD, TEI, DITA, and METS. To make the understanding of these schemas easier, an introduction to the schema constructs, features, and possibilities was provided in the preliminary section of this chapter.

CHAPTER 3

XML Authoring and Presentation Tools

3.1 XML AUTHORING TOOLS

The creation of XML documents can be done with any text editor, but authors can benefit from dedicated tools to ensure that documents are well-formed and valid. XML authoring tools guide the user in inserting tags and markups, and they enforce the application of constraints as defined in the XML schema or DTD.

The main advantages of using XML authoring tools are the following:

1. Assistance for the user in the selection and insertion of the tags that are valid in a specific context. This ensures that the finished documents are valid—XML authoring tools do not allow authors to include elements or attributes not permitted in the schema.
2. Automatic checks ensure the documents are well-formed and valid, according to the schema selected.
3. Organization of the documents in projects. Documents that are part of the same project or collection may be grouped together under the same folder.
4. Conversion and publication of XML documents by applying XSLT transformations.

XML authoring tools also incorporate the typical features of word processing tools, like spell checking or WYSIWYG modes. Typically, the XML authoring tools offer different views of the documents being edited:

1. WYSIWYG view, where document content is edited. This view shows the document content using an authoring template that applies different styles to the document elements. For example, titles and headings are shown with a bigger font size, in different colors, etc. XML elements that correspond to tables, lists, and images are also shown as such. XML authoring tools support the creation of these WYSIWYG templates for the different document types.
2. For the end users, using the WYSIWYG view is like working with a standard word processing tool. The only difference is that they can

XML-based Content Management
DOI: http://dx.doi.org/10.1016/B978-0-08-100204-9.00003-2

display or hide the information about the tags surrounding each element.

3. Raw XML content. This view displays the resulting XML content, with all the start and end tags, attributes, etc. Some XML authoring tools avoid making changes in this view, to avoid the accidental removal of tags.
4. Grid view. This view displays the XML document using a grid, similar to a table where the elements are nested according to the rules defined in the schema. This view can be useful for document types that do not impose a complex hierarchy of elements with several nesting levels.

Using an XML authoring tool, the writer does not need to manually add the start and end tags of the documents. Tags are added by choosing the element or attribute from a list. The content of this list comes from the XML schema on which the document is based. When the author selects the element from this list, the tool will automatically add its start and end tags, and the author can write the content inside these tags. The tools avoid the accidental removal of the start and end tags, that is to say, we can remove the full element, but we cannot remove one of its tags. With this functionality, the tools ensure that the documents are always well-formed.

Attributes can be added to our documents in a similar way. The tool provides a list of attributes that are allowed for the element in which they are positioned. We just need to type the attribute value, and the tool will add the corresponding markup in the correct place of the document (in the case of the attributes, they are added to the start tag of the element, preceded by the equal sign, and their values are written within double quotation marks).

XML authoring tools guide the user in the application of the rules defined in the XML schema or DTD. When creating a new document, the author must first select the XML schema or DTD on which the document is based. Then, depending on the part of the document where the author is positioned (this is called the "context"), the XML authoring tool will permit only the insertion of the elements and attributes that are allowed in the XML schema in that specific context. It will not be possible to add tags for elements or attributes that have not declared in the schema or written in the elements, in an order different than the sequence defined in the schema. If the schema declares mandatory elements or attributes, the document will not be validated until we add all the required elements or attributes.

Fig. 3.1 shows an XML authoring tool. The window is divided into two main areas: one area at the left, where the author can type the content of the document, and one area at the right that contains two panels. In the left-hand side panel, we are positioned at the <para> element (this element is the current context). The panel in the upper part shows the attributes that can be used in the element where we are situated. The panel in the lower part displays the list of all the elements that are allowed in that context: these are the elements that can be added as children of the <para> element. Any of these elements can be added to the current position just by clicking on them.

This feature, common in all the XML authoring tools, ensure that documents are well-formed and valid.

One characteristic of the XML authoring tools is that they are not limited to a specific DTD or schema. The tools can interpret any XML schema or DTD. The tools also support the inclusion of entities—like special characters that must be avoided when writing XML content, like &, < or >. Fig. 3.2 shows a panel where the user can directly select the special characters and add them to the document.

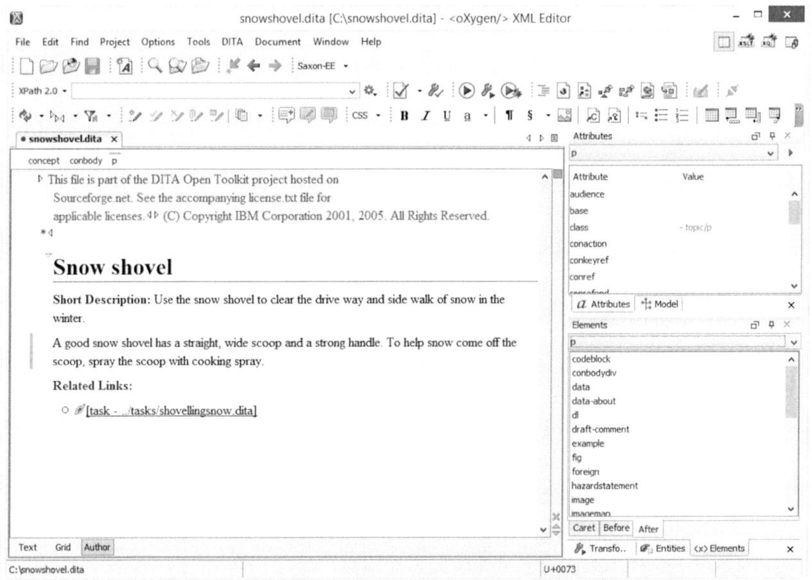

Figure 3.1 XML editor.

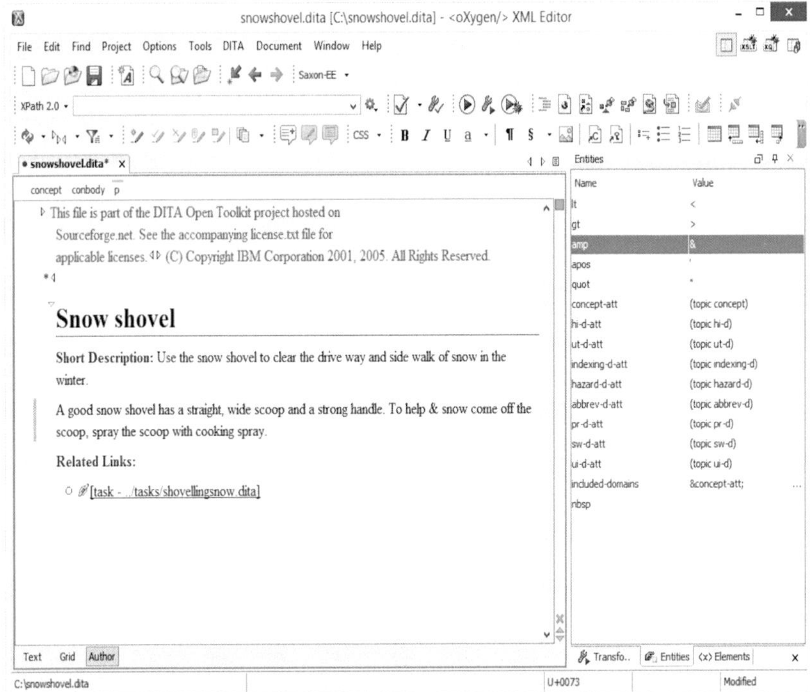

Figure 3.2 XML editor.

The creation of stylesheets is not part of the function provided by XML authoring tools, and we should use other dedicated tools to design the stylesheets. But with the XML authoring tools we can link stylesheets to the XML document, and apply and check how the document will be displayed to the end user with a standard browser (see Fig. 3.3).

Another feature supported by some XML authoring tools is the use of templates based on forms to create and update XML documents. When using form-based interfaces the tags are hidden from the user, therefore, the user simply needs to complete the content of the available fields. These fields are mapped to XML elements and attributes declared in the XML schema or DTD. Using templates based on forms is a useful approach in reducing the perception of complexity that is associated to XML. But when working with complex schemas that support different levels of nested elements, and elements with mixed content models combining both text and child elements, it may be difficult to map the document structure and hierarchy to a set of fields in a form. This means that

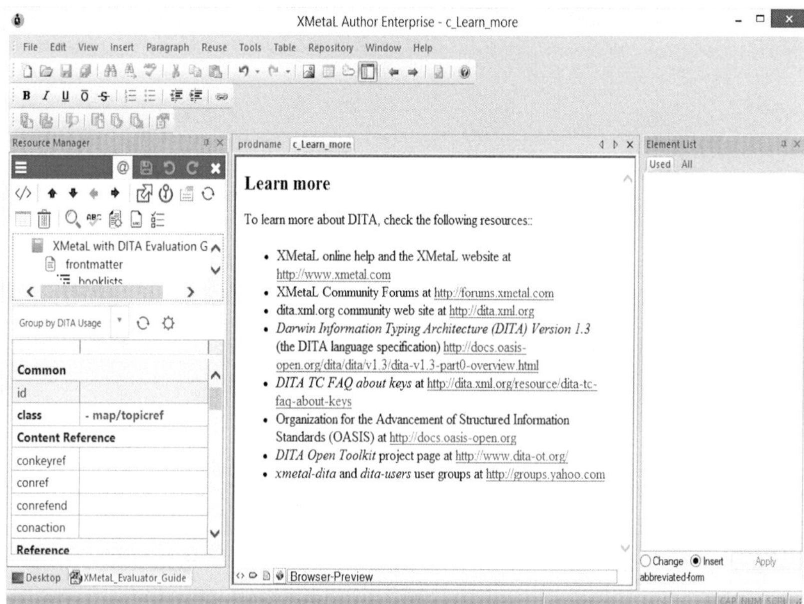

Figure 3.3 XML editor.

the possibility of working with forms may be limited to noncomplex DTD or schemas. Fig. 3.4 shows one form used to create documents with the Altove *Authentic*® tool.

3.2 PRESENTATION OF XML DOCUMENTS

XML differentiates between the structure and content of the documents, and the way they are displayed or presented. XML markup does not indicate how documents must be shown. The presentation of the XML documents must be specified in a separate file called a stylesheet. The structure of the stylesheets is defined as per W3C recommendations.

The use of stylesheets ensures the consistent presentation of all the documents in the same collection. In addition, it is possible to change the presentation of all the documents by linking them to a different stylesheet. One of the benefits of the stylesheets is that the presentation of the documents can be updated without changing the XML documents: we just need to update the stylesheet, and the change will be applied automatically to the presentation of all the XML documents that are linked to that stylesheet.

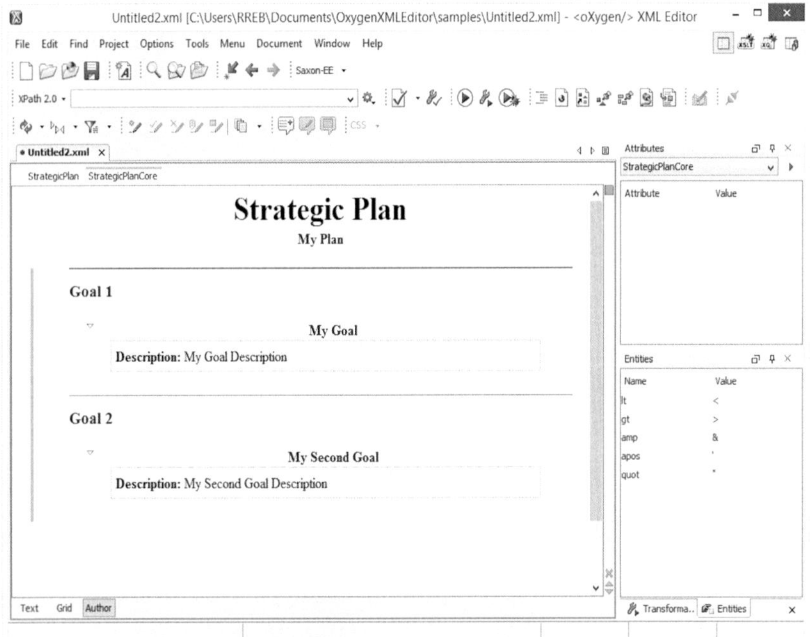

Figure 3.4 XML editor—form view.

3.2.1 Types of Stylesheets

There are different types of stylesheets for XML documents, all of them published as W3C recommendations:

- CSS (*Cascading Style Sheets*), which are inherited from HTML.
- XSLT (*XML Stylesheet Language Transformation*), which are used to convert XML documents to HTML, so their content can be opened with a standard Internet browser. XSLT stylesheets are also used to convert an XML document into another XML document based on a different XML schema.
- XSL FO (*XML Stylesheet Language Formatting Objects*), which are used to convert XML documents into a page-oriented format suitable for printing, typically PDF (*Portable Document Format*).

Regardless the type of the stylesheet used, XML documents must contain a reference to the external file that defines the stylesheet. When an Internet browser downloads one XML document that is linked to a stylesheet, the browser will download the stylesheet and will apply its rules and instructions on the XML document. As a result, the XML document shall be displayed according to the rules in the stylesheet. Fig. 3.5 shows the different types of stylesheets and their purpose.

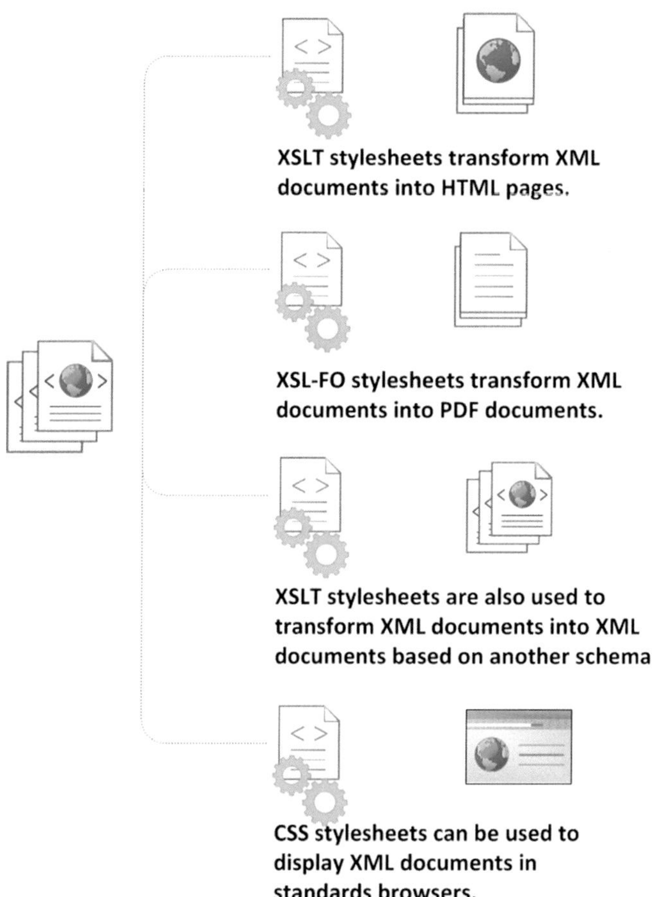

Figure 3.5 Purpose of the different stylesheets.

Designers of stylesheets can use dedicated tools like Altova StyleVision or Altova MapForce. These tools support the visual creation of stylesheets, by mapping the elements and attributes defined in an XML schema to the HTML elements or to elements in another target XML schema. Using these tools, designers do not need to know the specific syntax of the XSL language, and can check the result obtained with their stylesheets in an iterative way.

3.2.1.1 CSS Stylesheets

CSS or *Cascading Style Sheets* is a W3C recommendation initially created for the presentation of HTML documents. These stylesheets can also be applied to XML content. Where we are using XSLT stylesheets to convert XML to HTML, CSS is still a key component and their properties must be known.

CSS was created because of the limited capabilities of the HTML language to present information in an attractive way. HTML language includes some elements for using bold and italic fonts, but it does not support the possibility of combining different font-types, line-heights, margins, etc. CSS offers these additional capabilities.

CSS stylesheets are made up of rules. Each rule includes instructions on how to present the different instances or occurrences of a specific HTML element. Instructions in CSS rules are called declarations. Each declaration gives a value to a CSS property. The W3C recommendation defines the properties that can be used and the allowed values. For example, *fontfamily, fontsize, margin-left*, etc., are some of the properties defined in the W3C recommendation. In declarations, the name of the property is followed by a colon (:) and its value. CSS rules can contain several declarations. Declarations in the same rule are separated by the ; character.

The next line shows a CSS rule:

title {font-family : Arial ; color : blue ; font-size : 12pt }

The rule is applied for all the instances of the `<title>` element, which is the *selector* of the rule. The rule includes three declarations, written between { and }. The first declaration assigns the Arial value to the *font-family* property; the second assigns the *blue* value to the *color* property; the third assigns the 12pt value to the *font-size* property. The names of the properties are separated by their values with a colon (:), and the declarations are separated with the ; character.

CSS stylesheets are stored as separate, independent files with the .css extension. Saving the CSS stylesheet as a separate file gives the possibility of linking and applying the same stylesheet within multiple documents. We just need to add the link to the CSS stylesheet to the XML documents. This is done with a `<?xml-stylesheet...?>` processing instruction that is written after the XML declaration, similar to this:

```
<?xml-stylesheet type="text/css" href="cssfilepath.css">
```

In this declaration, `type` indicates the type of the stylesheet, and `href` the full path to the CSS file containing the instructions for the presentation of the document.

For example, the following XML document contains a link to a CSS stylesheet that is stored in the `registry.css` file. The link between the

XML document and the stylesheet is created with the `<?xml-stylesheet...?>` processing instruction:

```
<?xml version="1.0"?>
<?xml-stylesheet type="text/css" href="registry.css"?>
<record>
      <title>Styles and formatting</title>
   <abstract>This document contains some examples about...</abstract>
   .......................................
</record>
```

CSS offers different possibilities for managing the presentation of XML documents, however, this type of stylesheets is more limited than XSLT. Some of the constraints of CSS are:

- The order in which the elements of the XML document are shown cannot be changed. With CSS stylesheets we can hide or show specific elements of the XML document, but we cannot change the order, and they will be shown in the same order they appear in the XML document.
- It is difficult to add new content to the content already in the XML document. With CSS there are constraints to add information like field names, images, etc., if they are not part of the XML document on which the stylesheet is applied.
- There are constraints to display the contents of the XML document as tables or lists.

We can conclude that the direct use of CSS stylesheets to present XML documents is not the best choice, although this approach can be used to render XML documents that do not require a complex visualization. To get better results and to have more control on the way documents are presented, use XSLT and XSL-FO stylesheets.

3.2.1.2 XSLT Stylesheets

XSLT (*eXtensible Stylesheet Language Transformations*) is a language based on XML for transforming XML documents into other markup-based languages. XSLT stylesheets are typically used to transform or convert XML documents to HTML. The resulting HTML content can be easily interpreted and displayed by standard Internet browsers (in this case, the browser interprets the XSLT stylesheet linked to the XML document and generates its presentation). XSLT can also be used to make batch conversions of XML documents to HTML persistent files that will be later published on a web site (in this case, the

Internet browser will download the HTML file that is the result of the transformation).

XSLT is also relevant when dealing with software applications that exchange data in the XML format. If the XML data has to be converted in different schemas, XSLT can be used to define the rules that will guide this conversion. The XSLT stylesheet will include rules that establish the equivalence between the elements and attributes of the source and the target schemas, as well as the operations that must be done when the data require some kind of processing and a straight equivalence cannot be defined.

XSL Transformations (XSLT) was published as a W3C recommendation in 1999. Version 2.0 was published in January 2007 (Available at: http://www.w3.org/TR/xslt). XSLT is closely related to another W3C specification: *XPath*. XPath defines how to refer to specific locations of an XML document (XPath versions 1.0 and 2.0 were published as recommendations at the same time as the corresponding XSLT versions.). XSLT stylesheets are also XMLS documents, but they use the reserved elements and attributes that are defined in the W3C recommendations for the design of presentation rules. XSLT stylesheets are saved in separate files with the `.xsl` extension.

Regarding the syntax of the XSLT stylesheets, they must start with the XML declaration:

```
<?xml version="1.0" encoding="UTF-8"?>
```

After the XML declaration, we will find the `<stylesheet>` root element. This element will contain the XSLT transformation rules. Each rule is written in a `<template>` element. The rules specify which are the nodes (elements or attributes), where the rule is to be applied, and the transformation that must be done with them. The next lines show a simple rule:

```
<template match="//author">

    <h2>
        <value-of select="." />
    </h2>

</template>
```

This rule is applied to all the instances of the `<author>` element. This is indicated with the `@match` attribute of the `<template>` element, regardless of its position in the document hierarchy (this is indicated with the // characters before the element name).

The start and end tags of the `<template>` element contain the transformation for each `<author>` element. Whenever the processor (or the browser) finds an `<author>` element, it does that transformation. In the example, the transformation will do the following: first, it writes the `<h2>` tag in the output document. After the tag, the `<value-of select="." />` element indicates that the value of the element being processed (that is to say, the `<author>` element) must be added to the output document. After that, the processor must write into the output document the `</h2>` tag. The rule ends here. In this example, each `<author>` element is transformed or converted to an `<h2>` element. XSLT stylesheets will consist of a set of rules similar to the previous one. These rules indicate how to transform an XML document into a target HTML or XML document.

XSLT possibilities go beyond the transformation of conversion between tags. With XSLT we can also add to the output document text and images that are not part of the source XML documents. XSLT also allows reordering or changing the order of the elements of the source document when doing their presentation. For example, the bibliographic references in one XML document that contain a bibliography could be presented—using XSLT stylesheets—in an order that is different from the order in the source document. The important point is that this can be directly managed in the XSLT file, without modifying the source XML document (XSLT defines a special element, <sort> to order sequences of elements and to display them in an order different to the order they have in the document. This element has two attributes: (1) select, which takes as a value the name of the element to be used as sort criteria, and (2) order, which indicates the use of an ascendent or descendent order.).

XSLT also gives control on the order in which the rules are executed. They also support mathematical operations on the data available in the source XML documents (sum, average, etc.).

XSLT stylesheets are linked to XML documents by means of a processing instruction similar to that described for the CSS stylesheets:

```
<?xml-stylesheet type="text/xsl" href="hojaEstilo.xsl"?>
```

The `@type` attribute gets the *text/xsl* value (In some cases it is possible to use the text/xml value instead of text/xsl.), and `@href` must include the path to the XSLT file we want to apply.

3.2.1.3 XSL-FO Stylesheet

XSL-FO (*eXtensible StyleSheets Language—Formatting Objects*) is the third type of stylesheet that can be used to display XML documents. XSL-FO is oriented toward the presentation of documents in a page-based format suitable for printing. For example, with XSL-FO we can create a presentation for XML documents containing a page header and footer, landscape or portrait page displays, etc. XSL-FO is a W3C recommendation too, whose version 1.1 was published in December 2006 (Available at: http://www.w3.org/TR/xsl/).

When applying XSL-FO stylesheets to XML documents, the XML document is first transformed to another XML document that contain XSL-FO specific tags. Then, this intermediate document is converted to PDF format. The intermediate XML document contains the textual content of the source XML files with special XSL-FO elements and attributes. In the process of applying XSL-FO, there are two steps: (1) the transformation of the source XML document into another XML file that contains XSL-FO markup, and (2) the conversion of the intermediate XML document to PDF, or other format, that retains the information about how to print the document. Designers working with specialized XML tools do not need to manage these steps, because the tool will complete the transformations as a single step.

The next XML fragment shows a sample intermediate XML document that contains XSL-FO markup (An XSL-FO tutorial is available at: http://www.xml.com/lpt/a/2002/03/20/xsl-fo.html.). In this example we can see the tags used to define the page format, margins, page sequences, etc.

```
<?xml version="1.0" encoding="UTF-8"?>
<root xmlns="http://www.w3.org/1999/XSL/Format" font-size="16pt">
   <layout-master-set>
      <simple-page-master
         margin-right="15mm" margin-left="15mm"
         margin-bottom="15mm" margin-top="15mm"
         page-width="210mm" page-height="297mm"
         master-name="bookpage">
         <region-body region-name="bookpage-body"
         margin-bottom="5mm" margin-top="5mm" />
      </simple-page-master>
   </layout-master-set>
   <page-sequence master-reference="bookpage">
```

```
        <title>Hello world example</title>
        <flow flow-name="bookpage-body">
            <block>Hello XSLFO!</block>
        </flow>
    </page-sequence>
</root>
```

Although the development of the XSL-FO specification was not as fast as XSLT, today there are alternate tools that implement the XSL-FO specification and that can be used to generate PDF files from XML documents. The tools that support XSL-FO include, among others: Altova Stylevision, RenderX XEP Engine, Ecrion XF Designer, and the Oxygen suite.

3.2.2 Recommendations on Stylesheets

Before moving forward with a more detailed description of the possibilities of the XSLT stylesheets, the characteristics of the different types of stylesheets are summarized:

1. CSS—are inherited from HTML and can be used to get a presentation of the XML documents suitable for reading the documents that hides the markup. However, they offer limited capabilities to change the order of the elements and to add text or images that are not part of the source XML documents.
2. XSLT—are used to convert or transform one XML document into another XML document or HTML page. XSLT is in-between stylesheets and programming languages, and it supports features like iterating through the elements of the document, applying conditions on elements or attribute values, and/or doing mathematical operations on the element or attribute values. With XSLT we can change the order used to display the elements without changing the source XML files. We can also display or hide elements depending on specific characteristics (values of the element or its attributes, presence of attributes, etc.).
3. XSL-FO—are used to generate a presentation suitable for printing, typically to generate a PDF document from the source XML file. The resultant presentation will consist of a sequence of pages.

The creation of stylesheets for XML documents is a process that requires different iterations and trials until the desired presentation is obtained. Stylesheet designers must be familiar with the XML schema of the documents, as the creation of the stylesheet must define rules for the different elements and attributes in the schema. Once the stylesheet is ready, it can be linked to the documents to ensure their consistent display and presentation. It is even possible to link the same document to different stylesheets (in a dynamic way), to generate different outputs or presentation of the same content depending on business specific requirements. If the presentation of the documents must be changed in the future, we just need to update the stylesheet, but the content of the XML documents do not need to be modified.

3.3 CONTENT TRANSFORMATION WITH XSLT

XSLT is the preferred method to manage the presentation of XML documents, typically by converting the XML document to an HTML page (on the fly or by means of a batch process). This section provides additional details on XSLT, in particular:

- the structure of XSLT stylesheets.
- the method to apply XSLT stylesheets to XML documents.
- the XPath language.
- the main elements of the XSLT specification.

3.3.1 The Structure of XSLT Stylesheets

XSLT stylesheets are XML documents. They must be well-formed documents stored in files with the `.xsl` extension. These XML documents use a set of reserved elements and attributes, which have a specific purpose. The reserved element and attribute names are preceded by the URI or alias of the namespace defined by the W3C for stylesheets:

```
http://www.w3.org/1999/XSL/Transform
```

The start and end tags of the root element of XSLT stylesheets are similar to this one:

```
<xsl:stylesheet version="1.0" xmlns:xsl="http://www.w3.org/1999/
XSL/Transform">
………
</xsl:stylesheet>
```

Between the start and the end tags of the root element <xsl:stylesheet>, we can create the specific rules for the transformation of the document element and attributes.

The main element of XSLT stylesheets is <xsl:template>, which defines transformation rules to be applied on XML elements or attributes. For example, we have the following XML document:

```
<?xml version="1.0" encoding="UTF-8"?>
<cities>

     <city>
          <name>Madrid</name>
          <inhabitants>3500000</inhabitants>
     </city>
     <city>
          <name>Málaga</name>
          <inhabitants>800000</inhabitants>
     </city>
     <city>
          <name>Toledo</name>
          <inhabitants>50000</inhabitants >
     </city>

</cities>
```

The document contains three <name> elements. This is the sample rule to apply:

```
<template match="//author">

   <h2>
        <value-of select="." />
   </h2>

</template>
```

The XSLT rule executes three times (one per each <name> element in the source XML document). In all the cases, the transformation is done, and the final document looks similar to this:

```
<?xml version="1.0" encoding="UTF-8"?>
<h2>Madrid</h2>3500000
<h2>Málaga</h2>800000
<h2>Toledo</h2>50000
```

The resulting document is not a well-formed document. To ensure that the output document, obtained after applying the stylesheet, is a well-formed XML document, we need to implement some changes in the XSLT, by adding the next lines:

```
<?xml version="1.0" encoding="UTF-8"?>
<xsl:stylesheet version="1.0" xmlns:xsl="http://www.w3.org/1999/
XSL/Transform">

  <xsl:template match="/">
    <html>
        <head>
        <title>XSLT transformation</title>
        </head>
        <body>
              <xsl:apply-templates select=”name” />
        </body>
    </html>
  </xsl:template>
  <xsl:template match=”//name”>
    <h2>
        <xsl:value-of select=”.” />
    </h2>
  </xsl:template>

</xsl:stylesheet>
```

There are several changes in the stylesheet. First, a new rule has been added:

```
  <xsl:template match="/">
    <html>
        <head>
        <title>Sample XSLT</title>
        </head>
        <body>
            <xsl:apply-templates select=”name” />
        </body>
    </html>
  </xsl:template>
```

This rule is triggered for the document's root node (this is the meaning given to the `@match` attribute of the `<xsl:template>` element the / value). Because the document has a single root node, this rule will be executed only once. Its execution adds the following content and tags to the document:

```
<html>
    <head>
    <title>Sample XSLT</title>
    </head>
    <body>
```

Going back to the XSLT stylesheet, after writing the `<body>` tag in the output, we find these XSLT reserved elements:

```
<xsl:apply-templates select="name" />
```

`<xsl:apply-templates>` is a reserved XLST element that tells the processor that it has to execute a specific rule. When the processor completes the execution of the rule being called by `<xsl:apply-templates>`, it continues executing the XSLT steps after this call.

`<xsl:apply-templates>` includes a `@select` attribute that indicates the rule that must be run. In the example, this attribute contains the *name* value. This means that—at that specific point—the next rule must be executed:

```
<xsl:template match="//name">

    <h2>
        <xsl:value-of select="." />
    </h2>

</xsl:template>
```

The rule is triggered for all the instances of the `<name>` element. Its execution writes in the output document the `<h2>` tag, followed by the value of the element being processed and by the `</h2>` tag. After running this rule, the execution flow goes back to the rule that called the rule of the <name> element. After processing all the rules for the `<name>` element, the processor will add these tags to the output document:

```
    </body>

</html>
```

The result of applying the sample stylesheet on the document used as an example is an HTML document like to the next one:

```
<html>

  <head>
      <title>Sample XSLT</title>
  </head>
```

```
    <body>
        <h2>Madrid</h2>
        <h2>Málaga</h2>
        <h2>Toledo</h2>
    </body>
</html>
```

After linking the XML document to the stylesheet, the XML document can be open with a standard browser. It will show the content that corresponds to the target HTML file generated by the transformation.

We can see a different XLST example executed on the same document. In this case, the XSLT must display the content of the document in tabular format. The table shall have a separate row for each city. Each row will have two cells: one for the name of city and another for the number of inhabitants.

To create the HTML table in the output document, we will use the HTML elements: <table>, <tr>, <th>, and <td>. The stylesheet will include a specific rule for the <city> element. These rules shall be called by the <xsl:apply-templates> elements when processing the document's root node.

The final XSLT stylesheet is shown below:

```
<?xml version="1.0" encoding="UTF-8"?>
<xsl:stylesheet version="1.0" xmlns:xsl="http://www.w3.org/TR/WD-xsl">
    <xsl:template match="/">
        <html>
            <head>
            <title>Sample XSLT</title>
            </head>
            <body>
            <table width="90%" border="1">
                <xsl:apply-templates select="//city" />
            </table>
            </body>
        </html>
    </xsl:template>
    <xsl:template match="city">
        <tr>
        <td><xsl:value-of select="./name" /></td>
```

```
        <td><xsl:value-of select="./inhabitants" /></td>
        </tr>
    </xsl:template>
  </xsl:stylesheet>
```

The stylesheet works as follows: when starting the processing of the source XML document, the following tags are added to the output document:

```
<html>
    <head>
    <title>Sample XSLT</title>
    </head>
    <body>
    <table width="90%" border="1">
```

The last tag starts a new table with a width of 90% of the window space. Then, the execution of the rule for the <city> element is requested with this line:

```
<xsl:apply-templates select="//city" />
```

This call will process the rule defined for the <city> element, for all the instances. The rule to process the <city> element is shown below:

```
<xsl:template match="city">
    <tr>
    <td>Name: <xsl:value-of select="./name" /></td>
    <td>Number of inhabitants: <xsl:value-of
    select="./inhabitants" /></td>
    </tr>
</xsl:template>
```

For each <city> element a <tr> tag is added to the document (this element in HTML corresponds to the start of a new table row). Then the <td> tag is added, which means the creation of a table cell. After <td> the XSLT reserved element <xsl:value-of> is used to indicate that the value of the <name> element that is a child of <city> must be added to the output. The @select attribute of the <xsl:value-of> indicates that, by taking the value: "./name". After writing this value in the output document, the rule writes the </td> tag to close the cell.

Something similar is done in the XSLT rule to add a second cell that will contain the value of the <inhabitants> element. The </tr> tag is added after adding this second cell. Finally, the stylesheet adds to the output document these tags:

```
            </table>
        </body>
    </html>
```

The document generated by the stylesheet is the next one:

```
<html>

   <head>
        <title>Sample XSLT</title>
   </head>
   <body>
        <table width="90%" border="1">
          <tr>
               <td>Madrid</td>
               <td>3500000</td>
          </tr>
          <tr>
               <td>Malaga</td>
               <td>800000</td>
          </tr>
          <tr>
               <td>Toledo</td>
               <td>50000</td>
          </tr>
        </table>
   </body>

</html>
```

If this document is opened from a standard browser, the result is an HTML table with the contents of the XML document.

3.3.2 Reserved Elements in XSLT

XSLT stylesheets can include:

- Text that is written directly in the output document generated by the transformation.
- HTML or XML tags that are written to the output document generated by the transformation.

- XSLT reserved elements that make actions (like getting the value of elements from the source document), sort elements, and call other rules in the stylesheet, etc.

For example, the next XSLT rule includes:

- Text to be added to the output document: the strings "Name:" and "Number of inhabitants:"
- HTML tags used to format the document as an HTML table: `<tr>`, `<td>`, `</td>` and `</tr>`.
- XSLT reserved elements like `<xsl:value-of select="./name" />` and `<xsl:value-of select="./inhabitants" />`). These elements are used in XSLT to get the value of elements in the source XML document.

```
<xsl:template match="city">
   <tr>
        <td>Name:
             <xsl:value-of select="./name" />
        </td>
        <td>Number of inhabitants:
             <xsl:value-of select="./inhabitants" />
        </td>
   </tr>
</xsl:template>
```

3.3.3 Sorting Elements

By default, XSLT rules are triggered as elements and attributes are found in the XML source document. This means the execution of the XSLT rules depends on the order of the elements of the source document. This behavior can be changed, and as part of the XSLT stylesheet we can alter the order in which the elements are processed. This can be done with the `<xsl:sort>` element. This element gives the choice of sorting the elements in the XML source document to process them in an order that is different than the order they currently have.

The `<xsl:sort>` element can be included within the `<xsl:apply-templates>` or the `<xsl:for-each>` elements. `<xsl:sort>` can have two attributes:

- `@select`—it takes as a value the name of the element used sort criteria.
- `@order`—it indicates if an ascendant or descendent order must be applied.

Going back to the previous example, the XSLT stylesheet could be updated to sort the cities by name, in descending order. The final XSLT is the next one (changes appear in bold):

```
<?xml version="1.0" encoding="UTF-8"?>
<xsl:stylesheet version="1.0" xmlns:xsl="http://www.w3.org/1999/
XSL/Transform">

  <xsl:template match="/">
    <html>
        <head>
        <title>Sample XSLT</title>
        </head>
        <body>
        <table width="90%" border="1">
            <xsl:apply-templates select="//city">
            <xsl:sort select="./name" order="descending" />
            </xsl:apply-templates>
        </table>
        </body>
    </html>
  </xsl:template>
  <xsl:template match="city">
    <tr>
    <td><xsl:value-of select="./name" /></td>
    <td><xsl:value-of select="./inhabitants" /></td>
    </tr>
  </xsl:template>

</xsl:stylesheet>
```

To use a different element as sort criteria, it would be enough to change the name of the `@select` attribute of the `<xsl:sort>` element.

3.3.4 Linking XSLT Stylesheets to XML Documents

To link and apply one stylesheet to one XML document, one processing instruction must be added to the XML document, for example:

```
<?xml-stylesheet type="text/xsl" href="pathstylesheet.xsl"?>
```

This processing instruction links the XML document to an XSLT stylesheet available at the URL: http://www.myserver.com/docs/xml/stylesheet.xsl.

```
<?xml version="1.0"?>
<?xml-stylesheet type="text/xsl" href=" http://www.myserver.com/
docs/xml/stylesheet.xsl"?>
<document>
    <title>JAVA programming</title>
    <pages>456</pages>
    <pubYear>2017</pubYear>
</document>
```

Instead of using absolute URLs, it is possible to use relative URLs (relative with respect to the folder where the XML documents are located). For example, if the XML documents are in the same folder as the XSLT file, the link could be:

```
<?xml version="1.0"?>
<?xml-stylesheet type="text/xsl" href="stylesheet.xsl"?>
<document>
    <title>Java programming</title>
    <pages>456</pages>
    <pubYear>2017</pubYear>
</document>
```

If the stylesheet file is located in the parent folder of the folder containing the XML documents, the relative link would look like:

```
<?xml version="1.0"?>
<?xml-stylesheet type="text/xsl" href="../stylesheet.xsl"?>
<document>
    <title>Java programming</title>
    <pages>456</pages>
    <pubYear>2017</pubYear>
</document>
```

3.3.5 XPath Expressions

The XSLT element `<xsl:template>` includes a `@match` attribute that is used to select the elements and attributes to be transformed by the rule. The value of this attribute must be a valid XPath expression.

XPath is another XML specification that defines the syntax to get the nodes (elements and attributes) of XML documents. XPath expressions are used not only in the `@match` attribute of the `<xsl:template>` element.

It is also used with the @select attribute with <xsl:value-of> and <xsl:apply-templates>. The result of an XPath expression is a node or a set of nodes from the XML document. When defining XPath expressions, we must consider:

- The content where the expression will be evaluated.
- The direction of the expression.
- The conditions that the XML nodes must meet to be selected.

Regarding the context, XPath expressions are evaluated from a specific node that acts as reference or context. The node that is being processed is the context for the XPath expression. For example, in the next rule:

```
<xsl:template match="city">
    <tr>
    <td><xsl:value-of select="./name" /></td>
    <td><xsl:value-of select="./inhabitants" /></td>
    </tr>
</xsl:template>
```

The context is the XML node that corresponds to each occurrence of the <city> element. The expressions in the rule, e.g. the <xsl:vale-of...> elements, will be evaluated using the <city> elements as reference.

Once the context is fixed, XPath expressions can indicate the direction of the search. The direction can focus on:

- The child nodes of the node used as context.
- The descendant nodes of the node used as context.
- The parent node of the node used as context.
- The ancestors of the node used as context.
- Any combination of the previous.

XPath defines some reserved words to cover the previous cases:

self	The expression is evaluated for the node that is being processed (the context node).
child	The expression is evaluated for all the nodes that are children of the context node. That is to say, all the nodes that depend on it.
parent	The expression is evaluated for the parent node of the context node.
descendant	The expression is evaluated for all the nodes that depend on the context node, at any level in the hierarchy.
descendant-or-self	The expression will be evaluated for the context node and for all its descendants.

ancestor	The expression will be evaluated for all the ancestors of the context node.
ancestor-or-self	The expression will be evaluated for the context node and all its ancestors.
following-sibling	The expression will be evaluated for all the nodes that appear just after the context node, in the same hierarchical level.
preceding-sibling	The expression will be evaluated for all the nodes that appear just before the context node, in the same hierarchical level.
attribute	The expression will be evaluated for the attributes of the context node.

Finally, XPath expressions can also indicate that nodes must meet to be selected and processed. Conditions may be one of the following:

- The node must have a specific name.
- The node must have a specific attribute.
- The node must have one attribute with a specific value.
- The node must have one child element.

Conditions are also known as predicates. They are written within square brackets and can make use of the reserved words child, descendants, etc. Predicates can compare the value of an element or attribute with another value using the following criteria: = , ¡= , > , < , >= , <= . Several conditions can be combined with the and/or operators, and special functions can be used:

- position()—to get those nodes in a specific position (first, second, etc.)
- last()—to get the last node.
- count()—to count the number of nodes.
- starts-with()—to get the nodes whose value starts with a specific string.
- name()—to check the name of the node.

Next we can see different XPath expressions that can be used in the definition of XSLT stylesheets. In these expressions, the direction is indicated and then, after the double colon (::), a condition or predicate can be stated.

`child::*`

This expression gets all the children of the context node. The asterisk indicates that we must select all the nodes in the target direction.

`descendant::*`

This expression gets all the descendants of the context node, regardless of their name and type.

child::book

This expression gets all the child nodes of the context node, which corresponds to <book> elements. Other children that are not <book> will not be retrieved.

parent::*

This expression gets the parent node of the context node.

child::book[position()=3]

This expression gets the third <book> element that is a child of the context node. The position()=3 tells the processor to get only the <book> element situated in the third position of the list of child elements.

child::book[last()]

This expression gets the last <book> element that is a child of the context node.

child::*[last()]

This expression gets the last child of the context node.

descendant::*[attribute::price]

This expression gets all the descendants of the context node that have a @price attribute.

descendant::libro[attribute::price]

This expression will get all the <book> elements that are descendants of the context node if they have a @price attribute.

descendant::*[attribute::price>'35']

This expression gets all the descendants of the context node that have a @price attribute with a value higher than 35.

child::book[child::subtitle]

This expression gets all the <book> elements that are children of the context node, if they contain a <subtitle> child element.

child::book[attribute::price>'35' and attribute::price<'50']

This expression gets all the <book> elements that are children of the context node that have a @price attribute with a value in between 35 and 50.

child::book[starts-with(child::title, "User manual")]

This expression gets all the <book> elements that are children of the context node whose <title> element starts with "User manual...".

child::book[count(child::author)>1]

This expression gets all the <book> elements that are children of the context node and have more than one <author> child element.

XPath expressions can be written using an abbreviated syntax, as described in the table below:

Expression	Abbreviated form	Description
child		This is the direction used by default, so there is no need to use any alternative representation.
self	.	Instead of self, we can use one point (.)
parent	..	Instead of parents, we can use two points (..)
descendant	//	Instead of descendant, the characters // can be used.
Attribute	@	Instead of the work attribute, the @ character can be used.

The next table shows the equivalence between the complete and the abbreviated syntax for some XPath expressions:

Full syntax	Abbreviated syntax
child::*	*
descendant::*	//*
child::book	Book
parent::*	..*
child::book[position()=3]	book[position()=3] book[2]
child::book[last()]	book[last()] book[end()]
child::*[last()]	*[last()]
descendant::*[attribute::price]	//*[@price]
child::book[child::subtitle]	book[subtitle]
child::book[attribute::price>'3500' and attribute::price<'5000']	book[@price>'3500' and @price<'5000']
descendant::*[attribute::price>'3500']	//*[@price>'3500']
child::book[attribute::price>'3500'] [attribute::price<'5000']	book[@price>'h3500'] [@price<'5000']
child::book[starts-with(child::title, "Don Quijote")]	book[starts-with(title, "Don Quijote")]
child::book[count(child::author)>1]	book[count(author)>1]

3.3.6 Reference of the Most Important XSLT Elements

The aim of this section is to provide a quick description to the most important elements we can use when creating XSLT stylesheets: `<xsl:stylesheet>`, `<xsl:value-of>`, `<xsl:apply-templates>`, `<xsl:template>`, etc. Some of them have already been introduced in the previous examples in this chapter. All these XSLT elements are preceded by the xsl alias, which is an abbreviation for the full XSLT namespace URI.

In the next stylesheet, the markup that corresponds to the start and end tags of the reserved XSLT elements is shown in bold:

```
<?xml version="1.0" encoding="UTF-8"?>
<xsl:stylesheet version="1.0" xmlns:xsl="http://www.w3.org/TR/WD-xsl">

  <xsl:template match="/">
    <html>
        <head>
        <title>Sample XSLT</title>
        </head>
        <body>
        <table width="90%" border="1">
            <xsl:apply-templates select="//city" />
        </table>
        </body>
    </html>
  </xsl:template>
  <xsl:template match="city">
      <tr>
      <td><xsl:value-of select="./name" /></td>
      <td><xsl:value-of select="./inhabitants" /></td>
      </tr>
  </xsl:template>

</xsl:stylesheet>
```

3.3.6.1 Element <xsl:stylesheet>

This element is the root element of the XSLT stylesheet. All the other elements must be included within its start and end tags.

3.3.6.2 Element <xsl:template>

This element is used to create transformation rules. XSLT stylesheets must have at least one <xsl:template> element. <xsl:template> elements must be children of <xsl:stylesheet>. Within the start and end tag of <xsl:template> we will write the transformation to be done with the nodes the rule is applied to.

<xsl:template> has two attributes:

- @match, which contains an XPath expression used to indicate the nodes in which the rule will be applied. If this attribute takes as a value the / character, the rule will be applied on the document root (it will be the first rule applied in the transformation).

- `@name`, which can be optionally used to give a name to the rule. Rules with a name can be called later from other rules in the stylesheet, by means of the `<xsl:call-template>` element.

3.3.6.3 Element <xsl:apply-templates>

This element is used inside other rules, to request the execution of the rest of the rules in the stylesheet.

3.3.6.4 Element <xsl:call-template>

This element can be used to request the execution of a specific rule. The target rule will be called using its name (the names of the rules are indicated in the @`name` attribute of the `<xsl:template>` element. <xsl:call-template> must have a @name attribute that will take as a value the name of the rule to be executed.

This element is similar to `<xsl:apply-template>`. The difference between these elements is that, when a rule is called with `<xsl:call-template>`, the context used to assess the XPath expressions remains the same. In `<xsl:apply-template>`, the context will change as we move from one rule to another.

3.3.6.5 Element <xsl:value-of>

This element writes the value of the node that is being processed—or the value of any of its related nodes – in the output document. `<xsl:value-of>` must have a `@select` attribute containing an XPath expression that will select the nodes whose values must be written to the output file.

For example, the next rule will be applied to all the occurrences of the `<book>` element. The rule uses two `<xsl:value-of>` elements. In both cases, there is a `@select` attribute with an XPath expression. The expressions just contain the name of one element. This is telling the XSLT processor that it must write—in the output document—the values of the `<title>` and `<pubYear>` elements that are children of the `<book>` elements.

```
<xsl:template match="book">
<h3><xsl:value-of select="title" /></h3>
<p><xsl:value-of select="pubYear" />, ISBN:
<xsl:value-of select="isbn" /></p>
</xsl:template>
```

3.3.6.6 Element <xsl:for-each>

This element can be used to iterate through a collection of nodes. `<xsl:for-each>` has a `@select` attribute that will take as a value an XPath expression. This expression selects the nodes that are going to be processed. The context used to assess the rule changes as we iterate through the nodes.

For example, the next stylesheet shows how to iterate through a collection of `<flight>` elements:

```
<?xml version="1.0" encoding="UTF-8"?>
<xsl:stylesheet version="1.0" xmlns:xsl="http://www.w3.org/1999/
XSL/Transform">

   <xsl:template match="/">
     <html>
          <head>
               <title>Schedule of flights</title>
          </head>
          <body>
          <h3>Schedule. Flights from London </h3>
          <table border="1" width="85%">
          <xsl:for-each select="//flight">
          <tr>
               <td><xsl:value-of select="@number" /></td>
               <td><xsl:value-of select="@destination" /></td>
               <td><xsl:value-of select="@company" /></td>
               <td><xsl:value-of select="@time" /></td>
          </tr>
          </xsl:for-each>
          </table>
          </body>
     </html>
   </xsl:template>

</xsl:stylesheet>
```

3.3.6.7 Element <xsl:if>

This element can be used for the conditional execution of tasks. If the node meets a specified condition, the transformation will be executed. Otherwise, it will not be done. The `<xsl:if>` element has a `@test` attribute containing an XPath expression. This expression will be evaluated.

If the evaluation returns true, the code within the <xsl:if> element will be executed. <xsl:if> must appear within a <xsl:template> or <xsl:for-each> element. The XPath expression in @test will be evaluated in the active context.

For example, this stylesheet includes a condition to show in the output document only the flights with the destination JFK. To do that, we have added the <xsl:if> element with the test condition: @destination='JFK'.

```
<?xml version="1.0" encoding="UTF-8"?>
<xsl:stylesheet version="1.0" xmlns:xsl="http://www.w3.org/1999/
XSL/Transform">

   <xsl:template match="/">
     <html>
     <head>
          <title>Flight schedule</title>
     </head>
     <body>
     <h3>Schedule. Flights from London</h3>
     <table border="1" width="85%">
       <xsl:for-each select="//flight">
              <xsl:if test="@destino='JFK'">
              <tr>
              <td><xsl:value-of select="@number" /></td>
              <td><xsl:value-of select="@destination" /></td>
              <td><xsl:value-of select="@company" /></td>
              <td><xsl:value-of select="@time" /></td>
              </tr>
              </xsl:if>
       </xsl:for-each>
     </table>
     </body>
     </html>
   </xsl:template>

</xsl:stylesheet>
```

3.3.6.8 Elements <xsl:choose>, <xsl:when>, and <xsl:otherwise>

This element also supports the conditional execution of the XSLT code (similar to <xsl:if>). But <xsl:if> just allows the execution of XSLT code if the condition is met, and it is not possible to define conditional executions of XSLT if the condition is not met, or if there are different alternatives.

<xsl:choose>, <xsl:when> and <xsl:otherwise> can be used together to indicate which transformations must be done in case the conditions are met, and what to do in any other cases.

- <xsl:choose> will have one or more <xsl:when> children, and a single <xsl:otherwise> child.
- <xsl:when> has a @test attribute containing the XPath expression to be evaluated. If the condition is met, the XSLT code within the <xsl:when> element will be executed.
- <xsl:otherwise> will include the XSLT code that will be executed if the conditions indicated in the previous <xsl:when> elements are not met.

The structure of these elements is shown below:

```
<xsl:choose>
   <xsl:when test="expression">
      .....
      .....
      .....
   </xsl:when>
   <xsl:when test="expression2">
      .....
      .....
      .....
   </xsl:when>
   <xsl:otherwise>
      .....
      .....
   </xsl:otherwise>
</xsl:choose>
```

<xsl:choose> can be written inside the <xsl:template> and <xsl:for-each> elements.

3.3.6.9 Element <xsl:sort>

This element can be used to sort the elements being processed in the output document. By default, the processed nodes are copied to the output document in the same order they have in the source XML document.

With <xsl:sort> we can change that order. <xsl:sort> can appear within the <xsl:apply-templates> and <xsl:for-each> elements. It is an empty element that can have these attributes:

- @select: it contains an XPath expression that selects the element or attribute to be used as sort criteria.
- @order: it indicates if an ascending or descending order must be applied, with the values ascending or descending.
- @data-type: it contains the data type of the element or attribute used as sort criteria. It is possible to distinguish between text and number.
- @case-order: it is used to indicate if upper or lower cases must be sorted first. It can take the values upper-first or lower-first.
- @lang: it indicates the language of the values of the element or attribute used as search criteria.

The next stylesheet shows the information about the flights, ordered by the flight number:

```
<?xml version="1.0" encoding="UTF-8"?>
<xsl:stylesheet version="1.0" xmlns:xsl="http://www.w3.org/1999/
XSL/Transform">

   <xsl:template match="/">
        <html>
        <head><title>Flight schedule</title></head>
        <body>
        <h3>Schedule. Flights from London</h3>
        <table border="1" width="85%">
        <xsl:for-each select="//flight">
             <xsl:sort select="@number" order="ascending" />
             <tr>
                  <td><xsl:value-of select="@number" /></td>
                  <td><xsl:value-of select="@destination" /></td>
                  <td><xsl:value-of select="@company" /></td>
                  <td><xsl:value-of select="@time" /></td>
             </tr>
        </xsl:for-each>
        </table>
        </body>
        </html>
   </xsl:template>
</xsl:stylesheet>
```

3.3.6.10 Elements <xsl:import> and <xsl:include>

XSLT stylesheets can be modular and kept in separate files. XSLT stylesheets can include references to other XSLT files containing additional rules. The inclusion of these references can be done using the `<xsl:import>` and `<xsl:include>` elements. They will have a `@href` attribute that takes as a value the absolute or relative URL of the stylesheet we want to use. Both elements are empty elements.

3.3.6.11 Element <xsl:output>

This element can be used to indicate the type of transformation made by the stylesheet. This element is typically written after the start tag of the `<xsl:stylesheet>` element. It is empty and it can have these attributes:

- `@method`: it says if the transformation will result in an HTML, XML, or plain text (text) document.
- `@encoding`: character set used in the output document.
- `@indent`: it indicates if the processor must add the indentation to the output document. It can be yes or no values.
- `@omit-xml-declaration`: it indicates if the XML declaration must be omitted in the output document. It can be yes or no values.

3.3.6.12 Element <xsl:copy-of>

This element is used to copy to the output file a set of nodes (elements or attributes) of the source XML document. When copying one element with this element, all their child elements and attributes will also be copied. The element is useful when we want to convert an XML document to another XML document.

3.3.7 Example of an XSLT Transformation

This section contains an example where the source XML document is transformed to HTML using XSLT. The source document contains a table that uses the CALS markup:

```
<?xml version="1.0"?>
<table>

    <title>Sample table</title>
    <tgroup cols="3" align="left">
        <thead>
            <row>
                <entry>Name</entry>
```

```
                <entry>LastName</entry>
                <entry>BirthDate</entry>
            </row>
        </thead>
        <tbody>
            <row>
                <entry>Ricardo</entry>
                <entry>Barrueco</entry>
                <entry>22-Jan-1967</entry>
            </row>
            <row>
                <entry>Luisa</entry>
                <entry>Campillo</entry>
                <entry>2-Feb-1971</entry>
            </row>
            <row>
                <entry>Juan Carlos</entry>
                <entry>Galeano</entry>
                <entry>12-Jan-1968</entry>
            </row>
            <row>
                <entry>Marta</entry>
                <entry>Pareja</entry>
                <entry>6-Jul-1967</entry>
            </row>
            <row>
                <entry>Aida</entry>
                <entry>Montaner</entry>
                <entry>15-Sep-1972</entry>
            </row>
        </tbody>
    </tgroup>
</table>
```

We want to transform this document into an HTML document with a table. To transform the document, we have to apply these rules:

- The `<table>` element in the source document shall be transformed to the HTML `<table>` element.

- The <row> element in the source document shall be transformed to the HTML <tr> element, with the exception of the <row> elements that are children of <thead>. These elements shall be converted to the HTML <th> element.
- The <entry> elements shall be converted to HTML <td> elements.
- The <title> element shall be converted to the HTML <caption> element.

This is the stylesheet where the rules above are defined:

```
<?xml version="1.0" encoding="UTF-8"?>
<xsl:stylesheet version="1.0" xmlns:xsl="http://www.w3.org/1999/
XSL/Transform">

    <xsl:output method="html" version="4.0" encoding="UTF-8"
    indent="yes"/>
    <xsl:template match="/">
        <html>
        <head><title>Output document with table</title></head>
        <body>
            <xsl:apply-templates />
        </body>
        </html>
    </xsl:template>
    <xsl:template match="table">
        <table width="90%" border="1">
        <caption><xsl:value-of select="title" /></caption>
        <xsl:for-each select="//row">
            <tr>
            <xsl:for-each select="*">
                <xsl:choose>
                <xsl:when test="name(../..)='thead'">
                    <th><xsl:value-of select="." /></th>
                </xsl:when>
                <xsl:otherwise>
                    <td><xsl:value-of select="." /></td>
                </xsl:otherwise>
                </xsl:choose>
            </xsl:for-each>
            </tr>
```

```
        </xsl:for-each>
      </table>
    </xsl:template>

</xsl:stylesheet>
```

The stylesheet uses the <xsl:for-each> XSLT elements to iterate through the <row> and <entry> elements of the source XML document. <xsl:choose>, <xsl:when> and <xsl:otherwise> are used to check if the parent of the <row> element is <thead>. If the parent is <thead>, the row belongs to the table header, its cells are converted to <th> elements. If the row does not belong to the table header, its cells are converted to <td> elements.

The same result could be achieved with a different approach, e.g., using the <xsl:element> and <xsl:attribute> elements, for example:

```
<?xml version="1.0" encoding="UTF-8"?>
<xsl:stylesheet version="1.0" xmlns:xsl="http://www.w3.org/1999/XSL/
Transform">
<xsl:output method="xml" version="1.0" encoding="UTF-8" indent="yes"/>

   <xsl:template match="/">
        <xsl:element    name="html"    namespace="http://www.w3.org/
        Profiles/XHTML-transitional">
          <xsl:element name="head">
            <xsl:element name="title">
              <xsl:text>Sample HTML table </xsl:text>
            </xsl:element>
          </xsl:element>
          <xsl:element name="body">
              <xsl:apply-templates select="table" />
          </xsl:element>
        </xsl:element>
     </xsl:template>
   <xsl:template match="table">
        <xsl:element name="table">
            <xsl:attribute name="border">
                <xsl:text>1</xsl:text>
            </xsl:attribute>
            <xsl:attribute name="width">
                <xsl:text>90%</xsl:text>
            </xsl:attribute>
```

```
        </xsl:element>
      <xsl:element name="caption">
            <xsl:value-of select="title" />
      </xsl:element>
      <xsl:for-each select="//row">
      <xsl:element name="tr">
            <xsl:for-each select="*">
            <xsl:choose>
                <xsl:when test="name(../..)='thead'">
                    <xsl:element name="th">
                        <xsl:value-of select="." />
                    </xsl:element>
              </xsl:when>
              <xsl:otherwise>
                    <xsl:element name="td">
                        <xsl:value-of select="." />
                    </xsl:element>
              </xsl:otherwise>
          </xsl:choose>
          </xsl:for-each>
      </xsl:element>
      </xsl:for-each>
    </xsl:template>
  </xsl:stylesheet>
```

3.4 CONCLUSIONS

This chapter has discussed the functionalities of XML authoring tools, and how they assist users in writing well-formed, valid documents, and the possibilities that the XSLT and XSL-FO standards offer to create readable displays of the XML content.

Both XSLT and XSL-FO are key components in an XML-based content management strategy. XSLT not only provides a language to publish the XML documents in a readable way by converting the XML content into HTML. XSLT can also be used to transform a set of input XML files into another set of XML files based on a different schema. This functionality of XSLT is especially relevant when defining data exchange processes between software applications and information systems. On the other hand, XSL-FO stylesheets are aimed to create a presentation of the XML documents that are suitable for printing (usually, by converting the XML documents to PDF).

The definition of the output format, templates, and visual characteristics is then one of the most important steps in the strategic deployment of an XML-based solution. If the definition of document types and the adoption of XML schemas was the first decision, the strategy also requires the preparation of the different stylesheets needed to publish the content. Different tools, like those mentioned in this chapter, are available to create the stylesheets. The main advantage of these specialized tools is that they reduce the complexity of the XSLT and XSL-FO languages, as transformations can be visually created, using drag and drop features or mapping the elements in the source XML schema, to the equivalent elements in the target schema. In any case, the stylesheets can also be directly created like any other XML document, using the elements reserved for this purpose in the W3C XSLT recommendation.

CHAPTER 4

Databases for XML Data

4.1 INDEXING XML CONTENT: SOLR

Solr is a popular indexing tool developed as part of the the Apache open source project. It was built on top of a previous indexing engine that was also developed as open source, Lucene, in 2004 by Yonik Seely. The latest available version is 6.5, released in 2016.

Solr's main functionality is full text indexing and searching. It can index the full text of files in different formats (PDF, XML, word processing, CSV files, etc.), extracting the words and text strings that appear in the documents and tokenizing the words to support different queries: keywords, phrases, wildcards, boolean operators, etc.

Although Solr can be directly deployed in web sites (public or private) to give access to documents and text-based assets, the tool is also intended to be integrated with other software solutions written in Java or in any other language (Solr provides an interface based on RESTful web services that can be invoked from scripts and programming code). The result of invoking Solr web services will be an answer encoded in XML or JSON format that can be further processed.

Note: JSON (JavaScript Object Notation) is a lightweight text format used for data exchange in the development of software applications. JSON can be considered as an alternative to XML because both languages are used for interchanging data between software applications in an easy to process format. JSON does not offer the capabilities of XML for encoding complex, persistent documents.

Solr architecture includes different components: request handlers that are in charge of processing the incoming requests; the search components that run the queries against the index and that handle facets, spelling or highlighting; the parser that analyzes the queries sent by the user; the tokenizer, which analyzes the input texts and extracts keywords and tokens; and the response writer that generates the results to the queries in XML, CSV, or JSON formats.

XML-based Content Management
DOI: http://dx.doi.org/10.1016/B978-0-08-100204-9.00004-4

4.1.1 Installing and Running Solr

The installation of Solr is straightforward. From the Solr website it is possible to download a compressed file that must be uncompressed in any folder in a server running the Java Runtime Edition (JRE) (The file can be downloaded from: http://lucene.apache.org/solr/mirrors-solr-latest-redir.html.). The indexer can be initiated by going (using the command line) to the folder where SOLR is uncompressed, and executing the following command:

```
> solr start –p 8983
```

Solr runs by default in port 8983 of the server. Additional commands are available to stop the tool—`solr stop –p 8983`, restart it—`solr restart`, get its status—`solr status`, or help on the commands: `solr –help`.

Once the server is up and running, the administration interface can be accessed using a standard browser. With this tool the administrators can create indexes, define fields and documents metadata, run queries, etc. It can be opened at the URL:

```
http://localhost:8983
```

The administrator interface (Fig. 4.1) displays the main components within Solr: instances and cores. The instance corresponds to the application server, which can handle multiple cores or indexes. When deploying Solr in distributed environments, data in the index can be partitioned into *shards* managed by different instances. Each shard corresponds to a part of the index. In distributed deployments there will be a master instance of Solr that replicates the content of the index to one or more slave instances.

4.1.2 Creating Indexes with SOLR

New indexes or cores can be created from the administration tool and the command line (Fig. 4.2). A new core can be created by running this command:

```
> solr create –c CoreName
```

Cores can be created from the **Core Admin** tab, clicking on the **Add Core** button from the administration interface. Cores are empty and must be fed with the documents to be indexed.

Deletion of cores can also be done at any time (Fig. 4.3) from the command line with the command:

```
> solr delete –c CoreName
```

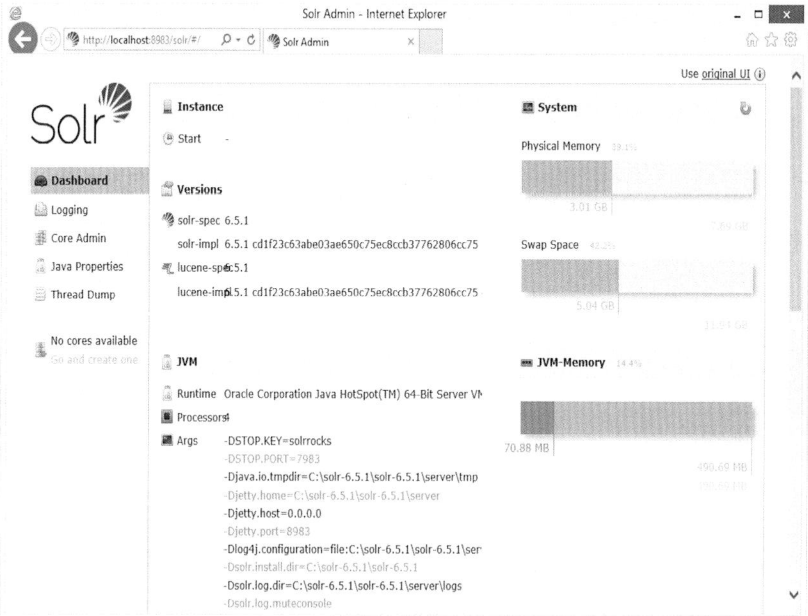

Figure 4.1 Solr administration interface.

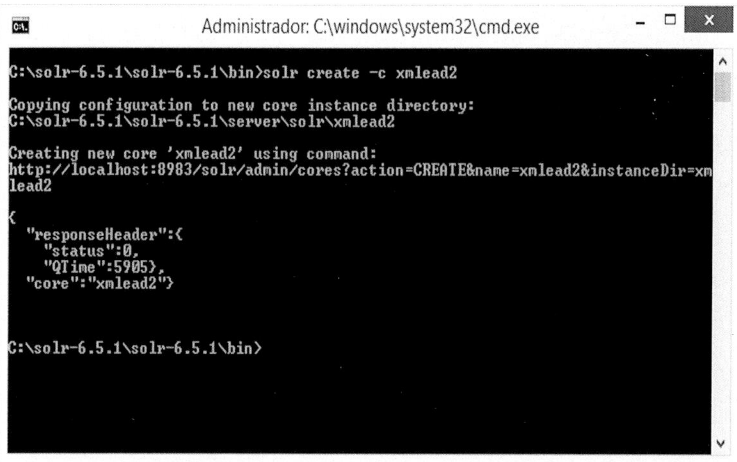

Figure 4.2 Solr—core creation.

4.1.3 Indexing XML Content

Solr has the capability of indexing content in different formats: PDF, Word, HTML, XML, etc. In the case of XML there are two possibilities: (1) indexing XML data written in *Solr XML* format, and (2) indexing of arbitrary XML files based on any other schema.

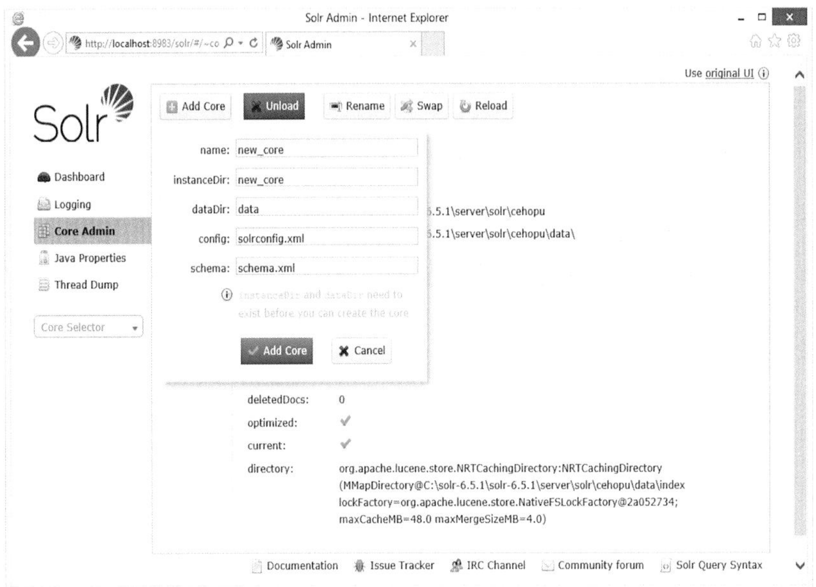

Figure 4.3 Solr—core creation.

Solr XML format refers to one XML schema used to pass structured data or documents' metadata to the indexer. Solr XML files have different <doc> elements for each document or item to be indexed. Each <doc> element includes one or more child elements <field> with the document's metadata. The example below shows the content of one Solr XML file that could be used as an input for Solr:

```
<add>
<doc>

   <field name="id">F8V7067-APL-KIT</field>
   <field name="name">Belkin Mobile Power Cord for iPod w/ Dock</field>
   <field name="manu">Belkin</field>
   <field name="cat">connector</field>
   <field name="features">car power adapter, white</field>
   <field name="weight">4.0</field>
   <field name="price">19.95</field>
   <field name="popularity">1</field>
   <field name="inStock">false</field>

</doc>
```

```
<doc>
    <field name="id">IW-02</field>
    <field name="name">iPod &amp; iPod Mini USB 2.0 Cable</field>
    <field name="manu">Belkin</field>
    <field name="cat">connector</field>
    <field name="features">car power adapter for iPod, white</field>
    <field name="weight">2.0</field>
    <field name="price">11.50</field>
    <field name="popularity">1</field>
    <field name="inStock">false</field>
</doc>
</add>
```

Sending *Solr XML* files to the indexer can be done in three different ways: a) from the web administration tool, b) using the post command, or c) programmatically with the specific command provided by the API.

Using the web administration tool, the administrator must select the core where the Solr XML document has to be indexed by selecting it from the drop down list available at the left hand side of the page (Fig. 4.4); then, we can click on the **Documents** menu.

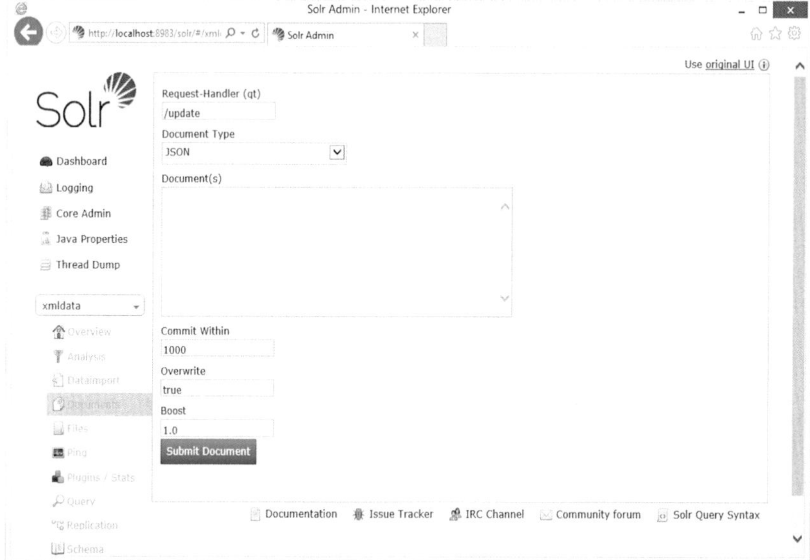

Figure 4.4 Solr—document submission.

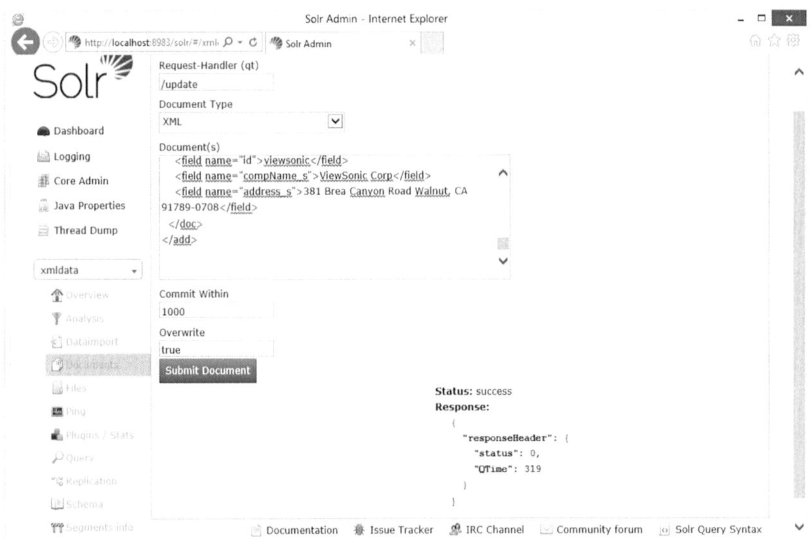

Figure 4.5 Solr—document submission.

In the **Document type** drop down list, the format of the input document will be selected (XML in this case), and the metadata in Solr XML is typed in the **Document(s)** text box (Fig. 4.5). The process is completed by clicking on **Submit document**. A message about the status of the operation will be shown at the bottom of the page.

The `post` command is another alternative for loading several Solr XML documents at one time. This command can be executed from the command line. We must go to the bin subfolder situated in the folder where Solr is uncompressed and run this command (it will work only on Linux computers):

```
./post –c corename *.xml
```

The post command can also be used for crawling external web sites, for example:

```
./post –c gettingstarted http://www.uc3m.com –recursive 3 –delay 1
```

If Solr is installed in a computer running the Microsoft Windows operating system, the post command is available, but its execution is slightly different:

```
java –Dc=corename –jar example/exampledocs/post.jar path/*.xml
```

In the previous command, the path/*.xml should be changed to point to the path where the XML documents to be indexed are saved. Documents' metadata are indexed as the Solr XML documents are

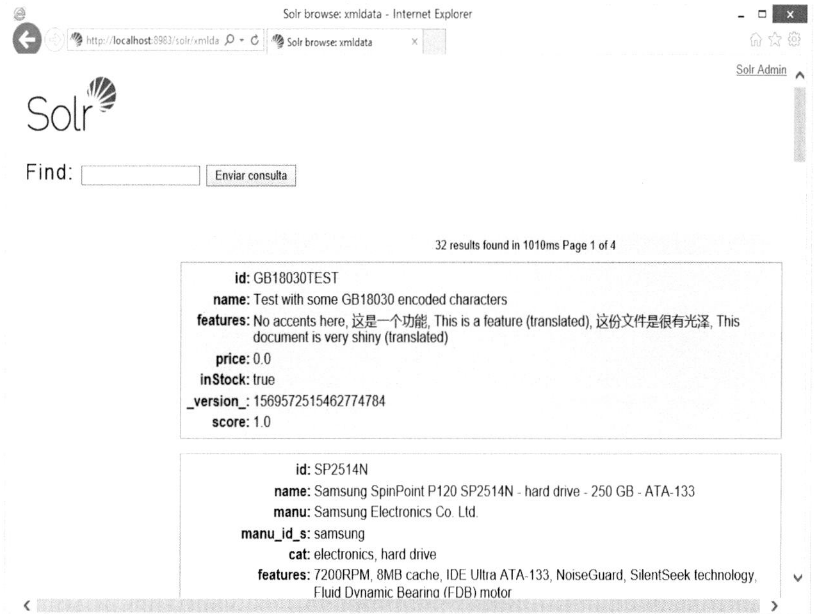

Figure 4.6 Solr—search documents.

processed. It is possible to check their inclusion in the index from the web administration tool (by running specific queries) (Fig. 4.6), or using the URL below from a standard web browser (this URL is used to get a list of all the indexed documents).

```
http://localhost:8983/solr/xmldata/browse
```

Data indexed by Solr can also be queried using URLs, as shown in the next example:

```
http://localhost:8983/solr/xmldata/select?indent=on&q=samsung
&wt=xml
```

The first part of the URL, `http://localhost:8983/solr/xmldata/select?`, must include the name of the core to be searched (xmldata is shown in this example). After `select?`, the following parameters can be added:

- `q`—this is the query containing the keywords or phrases or field combinations to be matched.
- `wt`—the format in which the results of the query must be returned. It can be XML or JSON.
- `indent`—if set to `on` the results in XML format will be automatically indented.

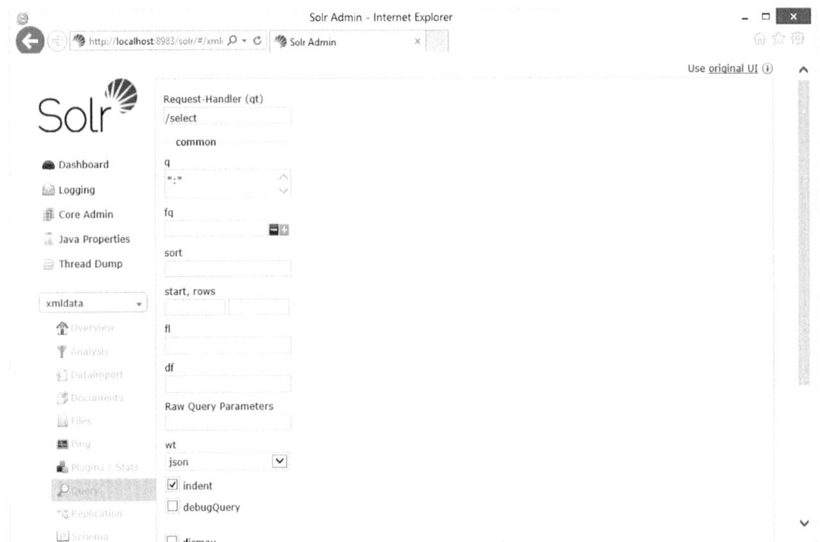

Figure 4.7 Solr—query page.

- `rows`—number of items per page, used to paginate the search results.
- `fl`—this parameter indicates which fields or metadata must be shown in the list of results. Fields will be separated by commas.

Queries can also be tested from the web administration tool as seen in Fig. 4.7.

4.1.4 Updating and Removing Items From the Index

Solr provides a way to update metadata and delete items from the indexes. These tasks can be done by telling the Solr XML file which data have to be updated or removed. The next XML fragment shows the Solr XML file used to update the content of the weight and price fields in an existing document: The special field id is used to uniquely identify the document or item to be updated. The `<field>` elements containing the `@update` attribute contain the metadata to be updated and their new values.

```
<add>
<doc>

    <field name="id">F8V7067-APL-KIT</field>
    <field name="weight" update=”set”>5.0</field>
```

```
        <field name="price" update="set">39.95</field>
        <field name="distributor" update="add">CENALSA</field>
    </doc>
    </add>
```

Removal of documents from the index can also be done by passing a Solr XML file similar to the next one:

```
    <delete>
        <id>1342</id>
        <id>4316</id>
    </delete>
```

The file above will remove the files from the index with the identifiers 1342 and 4316. Besides deleting documents by their identifiers, it is possible to remove the items that match a specific search criteria. The next Solr XML file would remove all the items containing words starting with *photogra*:

```
    <delete>
        <query>photogra*</query>
    </delete>
```

4.1.5 Indexing Arbitrary XML Files

Solr uses the Solr XML format to pass to the indexer the documents' metadata in a structured format. We can transform the source XML data into Solr XML format to index XML documents in any other schema. To ensure that the XML file can be retrieved, a special field storing the document URL, or a file naming convention, could be used so the file path can be sent as part of the search results containing the indexed metadata. The creation of the Solr XML file to be used as input from the source XML documents could be done with an XSLT transformation.

Besides this approach, Solr supports the indexing of arbitrary XML files without transforming the data to Solr XML format.

The first step to complete is the definition of the fields or metadata to keep in the index (Fig. 4.8). This can be done from the web administration tool in the **Schema** tab (the core where the documents are going to be indexed must be selected first). In the **Schema** page is possible to add new fields to the index, indicating its name and data type.

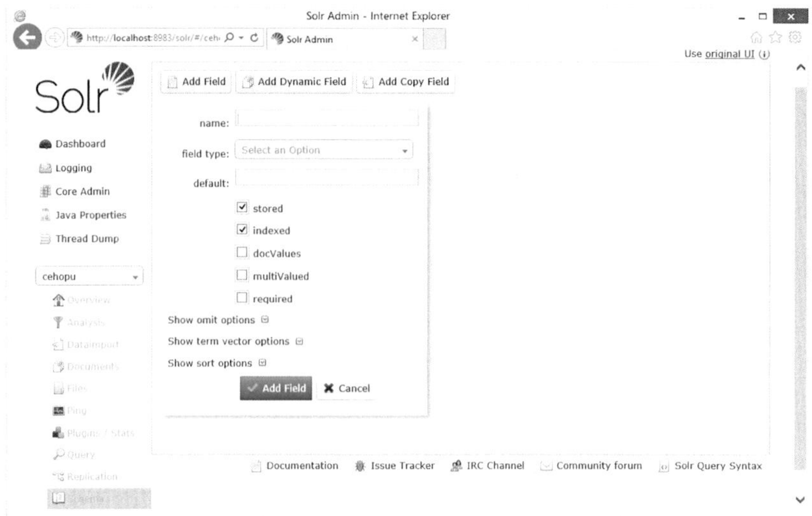

Figure 4.8 Solr—fields definition.

When defining the fields in the index it is possible to mark several checks:

- Stored—to allow retrieving the values of field in the queries.
- Indexed—to allow querying the new field.
- docValues—in this case the value of the field will be put in a column-oriented DocValues structure
- Multivalued—this means that a single document can contain multiple values for this field.
- Required—makes the field mandatory, and documents that do not contain this field will not be processed.

An analysis must be done to identify and define the fields that we want to have in the Solr index for the elements and attributes used in the XML schemas on which the documents to be indexed are based.

Next, some configuration changes have to be completed:

1. Firstly, a *data import handle* must be registered. This is done by editing the `solrconfig.xml` file that is available in the `conf` subfolder situated under the folder for the core we want to use.

   In this file, these lines have to be manually added:

```
<requestHandler name="/dataimport" class="org.apache.solr.handler.
dataimport.DataImportHandler">
    <lst name="defaults">
```

```
    <str name="config">xmleadconfig.xml</str>
    </lst>
</requestHandler>
<updateRequestsProcessorChain>
<processor class="solr.UUIDUpdateProcessorFactory">
<str name="fieldName">id</str>
</processor>
<processor class="solr.LogUpdateProcessorFactory" />
<processor class="solr.RunUpdateProcessorFactory" />
</updateRequestsProcessorChain>
```

The line `<str name="config">xmleadconfig.xml</str>` tells Solr that there is one file with the name `xmleadconfig.xml` that contains the rules to extract and map the content from the XML documents.

2. Next, an XML configuration file with the same name as the one used in the previous step—`xmleadconfig.xml`—must be created. This file will contain the equivalence between the SOLR fields created in the index and the XML elements and attributes whose values must be used as inputs for those fields. The example below shows the content of one of these configuration files:

```
<?xml version="1.0" encoding="UTF-8" ?>
<dataConfig>
<dataSource type="FileDataSource" />
<document>
<entity name="f" processor="FileListEntityProcessor"
fileName=".*.xml$" recursive="true" rootEntity="false"
dataSource="null" baseDir="../inputDocs">
<entity name="eaddoc" processor="XPathEntityProcessor"
forEach="/ead" url="${f.fileAbsolutePath}">
<field column="id" xpath="/ead/archdesc/did/unitid" />
<field column="title" xpath="/ead/archdesc/did/unittitle" />
<field column="otherData" xpath="/ead/archdesc/odd/p" />
<field column="creator" xpath="/ead/archdesc/did/origination" />
<field column="pubDate" xpath="/ead/archdesc/did/unitdate" />
<field column="fulltext" xpath="/ead/eadheader" flatten="true" />
</entity>
</entity>
</document>
</dataConfig>
```

The first `<entity>` element contains several attributes. `@BaseDir` points to the folder containing the XML files to be indexed.

The second `<entity>` element contains one `@forEach` attribute. Its value must be the XML element in the file that is used to separate the different records we want to index. If the XML file corresponds to a single document, this attribute will take as a value the name of the root element of the XML file.

Finally, the configuration file includes several `<field>` elements. Each `<field>` element will have a `@column` attribute with the name of the SOLR field to be populated, and one `@xpath` attribute with the path of the XML node whose value will be used to populate the field. Solr supports a partial implementation of XPath to locate nodes in the source XML documents.

Once this configuration files are created, it is possible to index the files using the web administration tool (Fig. 4.9). After selecting the target core, the **DataImport** tab is accessible.

Indexing can be run by clicking on **Execute**. After indexing the XML files, we can see the content added to the index from the browser, by requesting this URL:

```
http://localhost:8983/solr/xmldata/browse
```

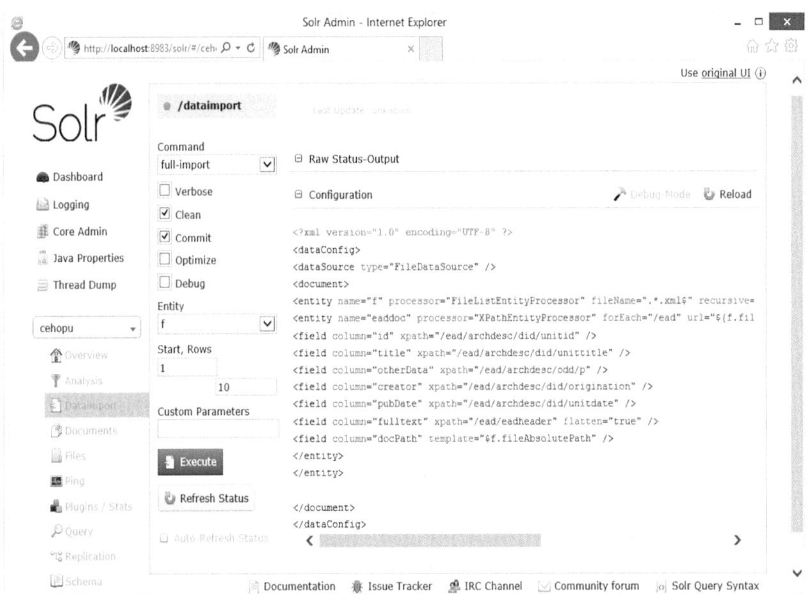

Figure 4.9 Solr—indexing.

Once the index is created and populated, it can be integrated with other tools by using the Restfull web services or the Java integration capabilities of Solr.

Solr is an interesting solution to index XML content and gives access to the repository of XML data, but it is important to remark that XML content is not kept in a dedicated database: Solr simply indexes the files and keeps the documents' metadata, but it does not store the files and it does not support typical database operations like content edition and updates.

The next section of this chapter describes other alternatives that can be used to manage XML data: native XML databases.

4.2 NATIVE XML DATABASES

In addition to document indexing tools like Solr, there are other tools for managing XML data. One of the most popular types of applications is the native XML database (Cornish, 2004; Lu et al., 2006). These databases are designed to cope with XML documents stored in XML format in a secure, central repository. They implement search and retrieval capabilities based on the W3C XQuery and XPath recommendations.

Native XML databases differ from relational databases because they do not organize the data into tables, rows, and columns. Instead of that, they keep the XML documents stored as a unit, and index their content to support different types of queries:

1. Structured queries, e.g., getting those XML documents that contain a specific element or attribute.
2. Value-based queries, like getting the documents with elements or attributes that contain a specific value.

If relational databases support SQL (structure query language), XML databases support the XQuery language. This language not only provides search capabilities, but it can also be used to add, update, and delete content from the XML database.

XML databases offer other functions common to other database tools:

1. Support for large amounts of data (for example, the BDB XML database can handle up to 256 terabytes).
2. Multiuser support and concurrent access.
3. Management of transactions to avoid overwriting of the same data by different users and ensure data integrity.
4. Replication methods to distribute data between different databases.

5. Availability of APIs (application programming interfaces) that allow the integration of the XML database functionality in external applications written in different programming languages.

There are different tools that can be included in the category of native XML databases. The next sections discuss some of them to provide working examples of these types of solutions.

4.2.1 Oracle Berkeley DB XML

Oracle Berkeley DB XML (referred to here as BDB XML) is the evolution of one open source project based on the Berkeley DB database. This project was acquired by Oracle—one of the most important players in the database market—which is now distributing the tool. BDB XML is an embeddable XML database. This means that it does not follow a client–server architecture. Instead, the database can be directly linked into the software applications that make use of the XML data. This approach simplifies the development of XML-based software solutions and the architecture of the final applications.

The next sections describe the BDB XML installation process, the main concepts behind this database, and the most relevant commands that can be used to create databases or containers, adding documents, and querying data. A separate section provides an example on how to work with BDB XML from an external application written in the PHP programming language.

4.2.1.1 Installing and Running BDB XML

BDB XML can be downloaded from the Oracle web site (Available from: http://www.oracle.com/technetwork/database/database-technologies/berkeleydb/downloads/index.html.). The latest version available is 6.1.4, and there are installers for Windows. Installing the tool only requires running the executable installer. The installation of the tool in computers running Windows will add a new folder at `C:\Program Files\Oracle\Berkeley DB XML 6.1.4`. The installer also adds a menu entry for the tool in the Start menu, giving access to the command line shell, examples and documentation (Fig. 4.10).

Management of databases and documents can be done through the command line shell.

It is possible to create different databases—called *containers*. They will store the XML documents, the indexes, and additional metadata that can be attached to the XML documents. A difference between the native

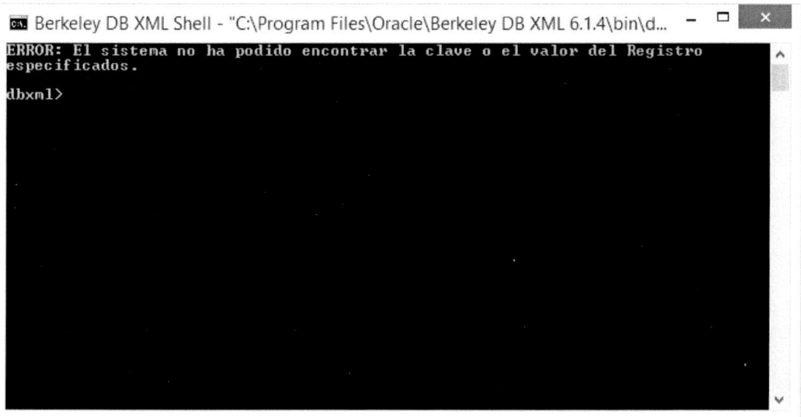

Figure 4.10 BDB XML console.

XML databases and the indexing tools like Solr is that the databases store the XML documents, not only the indexes. Regarding the metadata, they are kept in the database but they are not part of the XML documents. This means that if the XML documents are extracted from the BDB XML database, their attached metadata will not be available outside of the database.

The same container can include XML documents based on different schemas. When creating containers it is possible to indicate whether the documents must be validated, or not, against the schema they point to. The schema files must be available in a reachable URL to run the document validation.

The most common operations with BDB XML are:

1. Creating a container.
2. Adding documents to the container.
3. Adding metadata to the documents.
4. Querying documents.

4.2.1.2 Creating Containers

The creation of containers can be done with the `createContainer` command. This command will be followed by the name of the container (containers are stored in separate files with the `.dbxml` extension). The following command creates a container with the name `eadfiles`:

```
dbxml > createContainer eadfiles.dbxml
```

Containers can be of two types, depending on the method they use to store the documents: *document containers* or *node containers*. Document containers store the XML documents as they are with no changes. Node containers stores the nodes (elements and attributes) of the documents as separate units, in an optimized format. XML documents are always displayed with their original aspect with no specific implications for the end user. The use of document containers is only recommended if there is a need to keep the blank space of the source XML documents. By default, new containers are created as node containers.

To ensure that the XML documents are validated against their schemas before they are stored in the container, the creation of the container must include the `d validate` parameter, as follows:

```
dbxml > createContainer eadfiles.dbxml d validate
```

If the documents are not valid, they will not be stored in the database.

4.2.1.3 Adding Documents to the Containers

Once the container is created, it is possible to add XML documents to it. This can be done from the command line using the `putDocument` command. The following commands will be used with XML documents stored as separate files:

```
dbxml > openContainer eadfiles.dbxml
dbxml > putDocument "docID" xmlfilename.xml f
```

The first command opens the container where the document will be added. In the second command—`putDocument`—the first parameter is the identifier given to the document and the second one is the path and the filename of the XML file to be added to the container. The f letter is used to indicate that we are adding a file. `putDocument` can also be run using, as an example, the XML data itself (instead of the name of the file); in this case, the s letter will be used instead of f.

Note: When writing the document path as part of the dbxml commands in Windows, it is necessary to use the/character instead of \. If the path contains blank spaces, it must be written within quotes.

Documents in the container can be retrieved by their name, using the `getDocuments` command. This command takes, as an argument, the name of the document. The successful execution of this command will return one message that says the document has been found. To display the content of the XML document, we have to run the `print` command (Fig. 4.11).

Administrador: Berkeley DB XML Shell - DBXML

```
      <corpname role="propietario">Almendralejo, Ayuntamiento</corpname>
      <subject>Saneamiento urbano</subject>
    </controlaccess>
    <odd>
      <p>Construcci├│n de una red de alcantarillado de diez kil├│metros en Almed
ralejo (Badajoz) con pozos de registro en todos los cambios de alineaci├│n y poz
os de descarga en las extremidades de la tuber├¡a. Todo apunta a que Eduardo Tor
roja llevara la direcci├│n de las obras aunque no consta en ning├║n documento</p
>
    </odd>
    <relatedmaterial>
      <archref xlink:href="../expt/ETM-004-001.xml">
        <unittitle>Proyecto de replanteo de alcantarillado de Almedralejo [Exp.
004]</unittitle>
        <unitdate>1926-1928 (Proyecto)</unitdate>
      </archref>
    </relatedmaterial>
  </archdesc>
</ead>

dbxml> getDocuments "ETM-04"
1 documents found

dbxml> print_
```

Figure 4.11 BDBXML—access document.

BDB XML offers one utility for the bulk load of XML documents into containers: `dbxml_load_container`. This executable file is available in the `bin` subfolder of the BDB XML installation folder. It will take these arguments:

- −c, with the name of the container.
- −f, that points to one file containing the list of files to be uploaded.
- −p that contains the path where the files to be uploaded are available.
- −s that indicates the storage method to be used: `node` or `wholedoc`.

4.2.1.4 Adding Metadata to XML Documents

XML documents can be assigned metadata, which will be stored in the container, but external to the XML documents. The `setMetaData command` is used to attach metadata to the documents. It receives as arguments the name of the document, the namespace (by default an empty string), the metadata name, and its data type and value. For example, the next command assigns the metadata `creator` with the value `Ricardo Eito` to the EAD010 document:

```
dbxml > setMetaData EAD010 '' creator string 'Ricardo Eito'
```

4.2.1.5 Querying Documents

Documents added to the container can be searched using XQuery. Queries can be run from the command line using the syntax below:

```
dbxml > query 'collection("eadbx.dbxml")//unittitle'
```

After the reserved word `query` we have to write, within quotes, the context of the query—that is to say, the container we want to search— followed by one XPath expression. In the example above, we are searching in the `eadbx.dbxml` container, for all the instances of the `<unittitle>` element located in any place of the document hierarchy. Other possibilities available when defining queries are:

1. Getting the text of one element, removing its tags, e.g:

```
dbxml > query 'collection("eadbx.dbxml")//unittitle/string()'
```

2. Getting the text of one attribute, without tags:

```
dbxml > query 'collection("eadbx.dbxml")//archdesc/@level'
```

3. Getting the text of one element at a specific location of the document hierarchy:

```
dbxml > query 'collection("eadbx.dbxml")/ead/archdesc/did/
unitdate/string()'
```

4. Getting the elements if some conditions are met, e.g., they have a child element or an attribute. In this cases, the conditions to be fulfilled must be written between square brackets:

```
dbxml>query'collection("eadbx.dbxml")/ead/archdesc[@level]/
string()'
dbxml>query'collection("eadbx.dbxml")//archdesc[@level="funds"]/
did/unittitle'
```

5. Getting nodes that contain a specific word:

```
dbxml > query 'collection("eadbx.dbxml")//archdesc[contains(./did/
unittitle,"hotel")]'
```

When running queries in BDB XML the tool will return the number of nodes retrieved. The `print` command must be run to display the results.

Metadata attached to the documents can also be searched, for example, to get the documents whose creator metadata is "John Smith", we should run this query:

```
dbxml> query 'collection("ead.dbxml")/ead[dbxml:metadata("creator")
="John Smith"]'
```

4.2.1.6 Indexes

BDB XML creates and maintains indexes for the different nodes found in the documents. Automatic index maintenance can be activated or deactivated with the `setAutoIndexing` command, which will be followed by the arguments `on` or `off`.

If autoindexing is deactivated, the database administrator can create and add indexes to the container using the `addIndex` command. This command will take these arguments:

1. The namespace, by default it is an empty string.
2. The node (element or attribute) to be indexed.
3. The type of the index.

The type of the index can be indicated using four keywords separated by dashes that refer to the type of path, the type of the node to be indexed, the type of key, and the type of comparison to do with the values. As an example, the next command will create an index optimized to check the presence of the `<unittitle>` element in the documents:

```
dbxml > addIndex "" unittitle node-element-presence-none
```

A different command can be used to create an index on the `<unitid>` element to check equality conditions:

```
dbxml > addIndex "" unitid node-element-string-equality
```

4.2.1.7 Programming BDB XML

BDB XML is an embeddable database. This means that it is expected to be used from other software applications that will interact with the database tool via BDB XML API. Software developers building XML data management solutions can implement calls to this API from code written in different programming languages: Java, C, C++, PHP, etc.

This section includes some sample code fragments written in the PHP language to illustrate the use of the BDB XML API,. The first example shows how to load documents into one container:

```
<?php
function fnLoadFile($sFileID, $sFilePath)
{

        print "This function process the files";
        $mgr = new XmlManager();
        $container = $mgr->openContainer("C:\AUTHFILE.dbxml");
        print "Processing the file $sFileID\n";
```

```
        $xmlInput = $mgr->createLocalFileInputStream($sFilePath);
        $container->putDocument($sFileID, $xmlInput);
        }
?>
<html>
    <body>
        <?php
        if ($handle = opendir('C:\eac-cpf'))
        {
            while (false !== ($file = readdir($handle)))
            {
                $filepath = "c:";
                $filepath .= "\\";
                $filepath .= "eac-cpf\\";
                $filepath .= $file;
                if ($pos = strpos($file, ".xml"))
                    fnLoadFile($file, $filepath);
            }
            closedir($handle);
        }
        ?>
    </body>
</html>
```

The next example shows how to run a query and display the names of the retrieved documents:

```
<html>
        <body>
        <?php
        $mgr = new XmlManager();
        $container = $mgr->openContainer("c:\ead.dbxml");
        $query = "collection()//unititle[contains(., 'Barcelona'])";
        $results = $mgr->query($query);
           echo $results->size();
           while($results->hasNext())
           {
                $val = $results->next();
```

```
                $doc = $val->asDocument();
                echo $doc->getName();
        }
        ?>
</body>
</html>
```

As indicated in previous sections of this chapter, all the native XML databases offer integration and programming capabilities similar to those available in BDB XML. By using their APIs, it is possible to build different applications to store and search XML data repositories.

4.3 IXIASOFT TEXTML

TEXTML is a native, embeddable XML database developed by the Canadian company IxiaSoft. This was one of the first software applications developed to cover the needs of managing unstructured XML data. IxiaSoft has also developed the DITA CMS solution based on TEXTML and it has been adapted by companies working with the DITA standard in the technical communication domain.

The fault-tolerance architecture of TEXML is an excellent representative of native XML data management solutions. The server can handle collections of documents based on different schemas, and through the Administration Console the administrators can manage servers, collections, documents, indexes, and queries to be used as templates by developers.

TEXTML functions go beyond indexing XML documents. Documents in different formats (PDF, Office, etc.) can be ingested in the database, which is not restricted to XML. Full text and metadata indexing is available for those document types, and the tool supports Adobe's XMP metadata. At the document level, TEXTML provides functions for checking-out and checking-in documents so that users can avoid overwriting documents that are being edited by another colleague. When the author makes the check-out of one XML document it locks the document and author will be the only one with the capability of making changes in it. When the author finishes editing the content they will return the updated version to the repository by checking-in the XML document.

Content indexing is managed with the definition of indexes by the database designer. Indexes can be of one of these types: word, string, numeric, date, and time, depending on the values they hold. Indexes can be created using XML configuration files, and one index can be built for indexing several XML elements or attributes. This interesting function, called *conceptual indexing* in TEXTML documentation, is especially relevant when dealing with collections of XML documents based on different schemas: it provides the capability of building a single index for different XML elements that have the same meaning. For example, it would be possible to have a TITLE index that includes the `<unittitle>` elements of EAD documents, the `<dc:title>` of Dublin Core files and the 245 field of MARC records stored in XML format.

TEXTML Management Console (Fig. 4.12) also supports the creation of templates for queries. These are also defined using XML files. The development of XML solutions on top of the TEXTML repository can be made using the Java and .NET C# programing languages, or with any other alternative supporting COM. The API provides access to the different functionalities supported bythe tool, including the management security constraints.

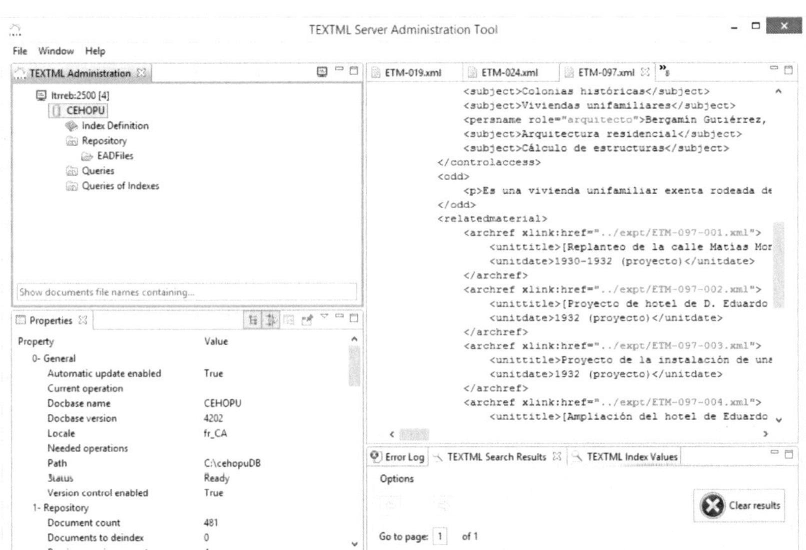

Figure 4.12 TEXTML—admininstration console.

The next code fragment, provided as an example with the product installation, shows how to run queries using VBScript:

```
Dim args
set args = wscript.Arguments
Dim totalDocs
Dim totalTime
totalDocs = 0
if (args.count = 4 Or args.count = 5) Then
      Dim server, docbaseName, path
      server = args.Item(0)
      docbaseName = args.Item(1)
      searchQueryFilename = args.Item(2)
      Dim cs, ss, dbs, ds
      set cs = CreateObject("TextmlServer.ClientServices.41")
      set ss = cs.ConnectServer(server)
      set dbs = ss.ConnectDocbase(docbaseName)
      set seas = dbs.SearchServices
      dim fso, f
      Set fso = CreateObject("Scripting.FileSystemObject")
      set f = fso.OpenTextFile(searchQueryFilename, 1, -1)
      content = f.ReadAll
      f.Close
      Dim rs
      seas.SearchDocuments content, rs
      RSCount = rs.Count
      wscript.Echo rs.Count & " documents found"
      For i = 0 to rs.Count - 1
            Dim document
            Set document = rs.ItemEx( i, hmtag)
            persist.Content = document.Content
      Next
else
      wscript.Echo "Usage: SearchDocuments <servername> <docbasename>
      <SearchQueryFileName> <directoryname> [<HitMarkerTag>]"
end if
```

DITACMS is another solution from IxiaSoft based on TEXTML, fully adapted to technical communicators working with DITA. Authors can interact with the content in TEXTML using XML editors based on

Eclipse, Oxygen, XMetal, and a web-based user interface that also supports the management of tasks and assignments. DITA content can be used to create publications in different output formats like PDF, XML, HTML, CHM, EclipseHelp, and WebHelp.

4.4 BASEX

BaseX is another native XML database offering functionalities similar to those described in the previous sections. One of the main features of BaseX is its graphical user interface (Fig. 4.13). Using this interface, administrators can create databases and query XML data using XQuery.

Database creation can be done by importing files available in any folder. Simple XQuery commands can be run using the query box available at the top of the window. The interface offers the possibility of displaying the results in tabular format, or in a visual map that highlights the documents in the collection that match the query (Fig. 4.14).

In the visual map it is possible to click on the highlighted items (small, red squares) to display the specific map for the selected document (Fig. 4.15).

BaseX user interface offers another section (called *Editor*) where more complex XQuery queries can be typed and run (Fig. 4.16).

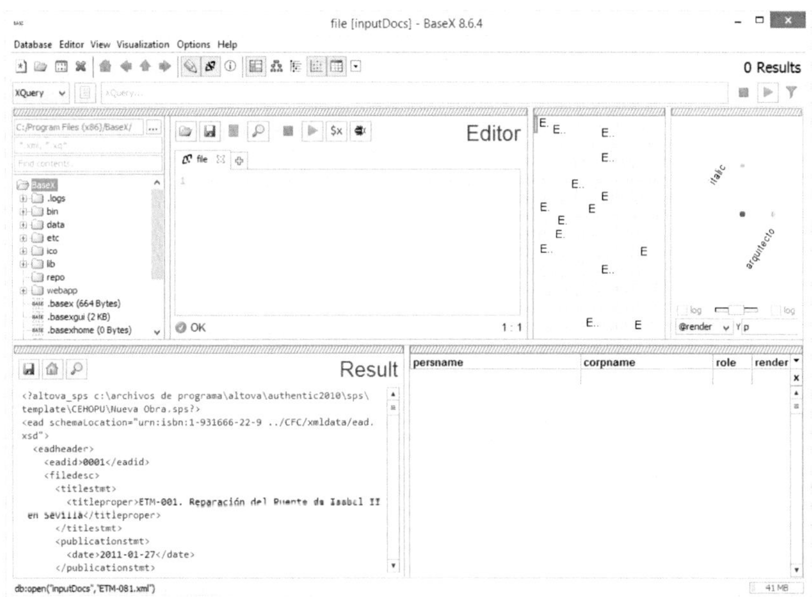

Figure 4.13 BaseX user interface.

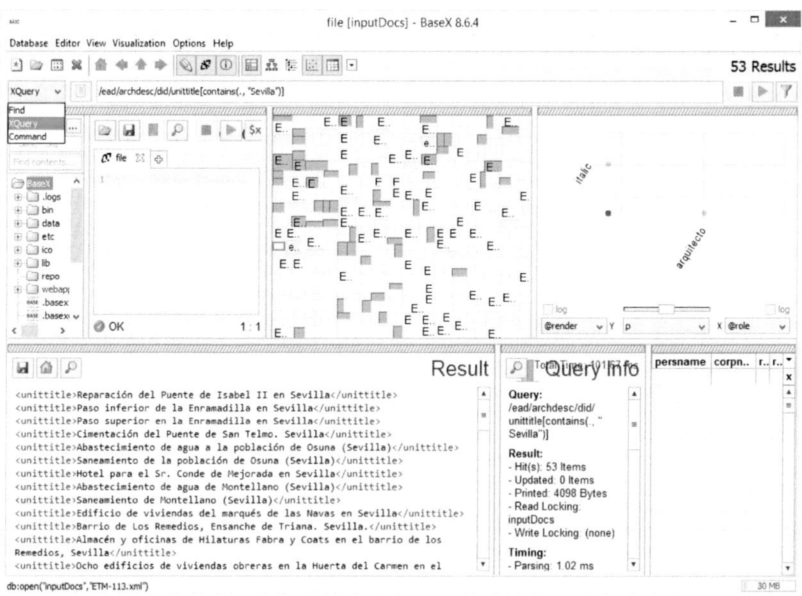

Figure 4.14 BASEX—search results.

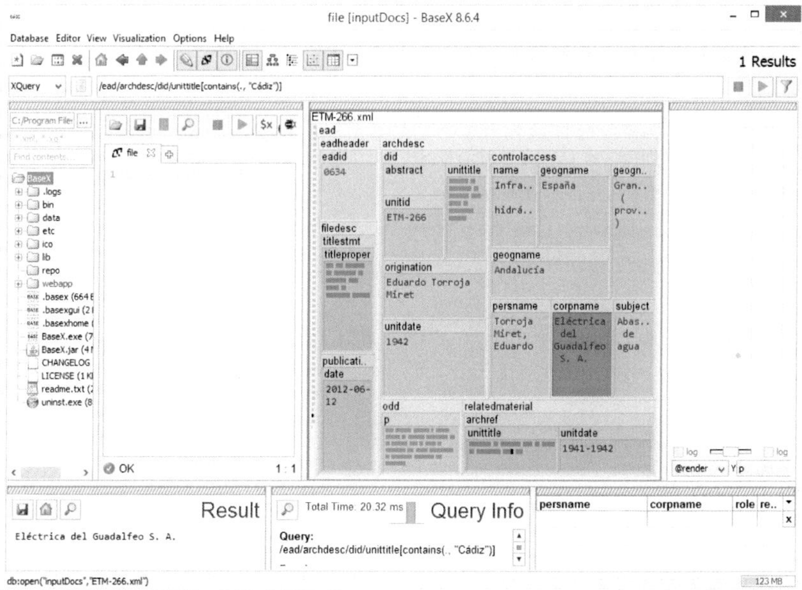

Figure 4.15 BASEX—document analysis.

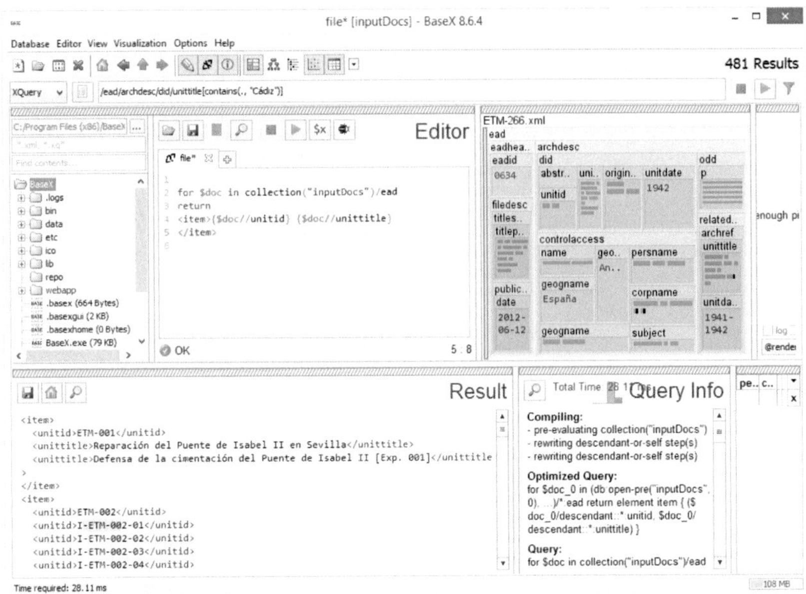

Figure 4.16 BASEX—XQuery.

This visual tool offers an excellent utility to build and text complex XQuery expressions that can be later reused in the design of the software applications that will interact with the XML database.

In addition to the visual interface, BaseX also offers a command-line utility and an HTTP server that runs on port 8984 (Fig. 4.17). The http server also gives access to administration functions (it can be reached using one browser, at the URL `http://localhost:8984`).

BaseX HTTP server offers a REST interface (Fig. 4.18) that permits running queries that return results in XML format. Complex queries can be stored in separate files with `.xq` extension. These query files must must be stored in the `/webapp` subfolder of the BaseX installation folder, so users can run them using the `.xq` files URL. For example, the next query can be saved in one file with name `myquery.xq`:

```
declare variable $keyword as xs:string external;
<result>
{

   for $doc in collection("inputDocs")/ead
   where matches($doc/archdesc/did/unittitle,$keyword,'i')

return
```

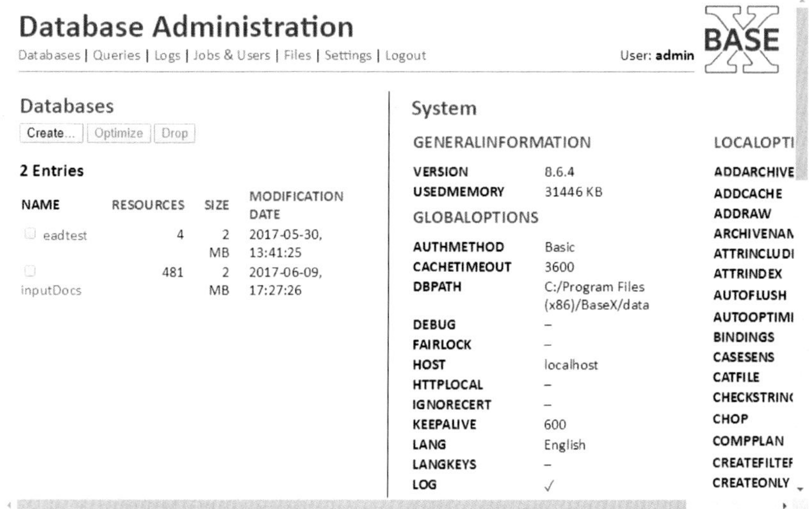

Figure 4.17 BASEX—web Interface.

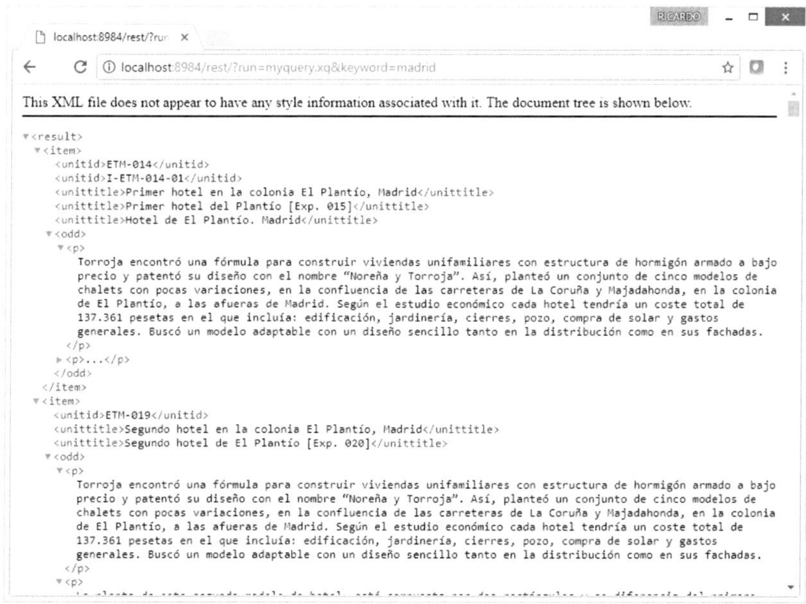

Figure 4.18 BASEX—Web REST interface.

```
<item>{$doc//unitid} {$doc//unittitle} {$doc//odd}
</item>
}
</result>
```

It receives the keyword parameter and then searches all the XML documents in the inputDocs database whose element <unittitle> contains the keyword passed as an argument. The results will show the values of the <unitid>, <unittitle>, and <odd> elements.

The query can be tested from any browser by calling it through REST, using this URL:

```
http://localhost:8984/rest/?run=myquery.xq&keyword=madrid
```

BaseX will return the results in XML format for all the documents matching the query.

4.5 NOSQL DATABASES

NoSQL dabases have become recently popular. These databases do not follow the relational model based on tables, rows, and columns. NoSQL databases offer higher performance, better synchronization capabilities in distributed environments, and can deal with larger volumes of data. Another difference with the relational databases is that they do not enforce the use of predefined schemas, and data can have an arbitrary structure of fields not fixed in advance. Due to this, data can be added at any time without updating the database structure first.

The term NoSQL was initially used in a meeting held in San Francisco in June 2011 (Sadalage and Fowler, 2013, p. 9). Pioneering tools that utilized NoSQL were BigTable from Google and Dynamo from Amazon. Today, within the NoSQL category, we can find products like MongDB, CouchDB, HBase, Apache Cassandra, Neo4j, and FlockDB. One interesting note is that these software products are not based on a common technology, and NoSQL databases are in turn classified into different groups: key/value stores, document, and graph databases.

Native XML databases share some characteristics of NoSQL databases because they are not based on the relational paradigm and on the SQL query language. But these similarities do not permit us to say that all the XML databases are NoSQL databases. Similarly, NoSQL databases are not necessarily XML databases because not all of them offer support to native XML storage and XML related standards like XSD or XQuery.

In fact, if we analyze the main features of NoSQL document databases like CloudDB or MongoDB we can find some differences. CouchDB was built in 2005 (three years later it became a project of the Apache Foundation). MongoDB was launched in 2007 by 10gen, company that was later renamed MongoDB. Both databases represent the document database paradigm: they store documents, give a unique ID, and index their data using a key-value structure (in fact, NoSQL document databases are sometimes considered a subcategory of key-value databases). Documents in the same collection can be based on different schemas, and the document structure does not need to be defined in advance. They use JSON as an input data format, and the conversion from XML to JSON is needed for data ingestions when working with XML. Document databases must be queried using proprietary command languages and do not support XQuery. These points make a big difference with respect to the native XML tools described in this chapter.

A different case is the MarkLogic NoSQL tool. Also defined as a NoSQL database, it offers direct support to XML data and XML standards. MarkLogic can store native XML data (alternative storage formats like JSON, PDF, Office, etc. are also supported), including RDF-encoded data for semantic web applications. MarkLogic also supports XQuery for searching XML data and SPARQL for RDF. Support to different data formats make MarkLogic an excellent candidate for organizations with data integration and aggregation requirements. Different kinds of data can be stored in a common repository with a common interface to access them. MarkLogic offers APIs and interfaces based on REST web services to interact with the repository using different languages: Java, JavaScript, Node.js, and a Query Console that can be used to build and test complex queries that can be saved as .xqy files for later reuse.

4.6 INTEGRATION OF DATABASES AND XML EDITORS

As part of the content management life cycle, XML authors need to open and store XML documents that are kept in controlled, secure repositories managed with XML databases. Companies developing XML editors have developed plug-ins that integrate their editors with different databases.

These integrations are found, among others, in the *Oxygen Author XML* editor developed by Syncro Soft. *Oxygen* provides interfaces with

BDB XML, *Documentum xDB*, *IBM DB2 Pure XML*, *MarkLogic* and *eXist*. Integration capabilities are also available for relational databases like Microsoft SQL-Server, Oracle, and for the Microsoft Sharepoint content management servers.

With these integrations, authors editing XML content can work with the data repository, browsing and searching documents, opening, saving, and updating the files stored in the database, etc. Fig. 4.19 shows how to open an XML document stored in *MarkLogic* from *Oxygen Author*.

Integrations also support running specific database commands, like managing indexes in the case of the BDBXML.

This integration capability is built in most of the XML editors available in the market.

4.7 THE XML QUERY LANGUAGE

The distinctive features of the tools described in the previous sections include the storage of the XML files in their native format (sometimes applying some optimization), and the support to XQuery. XQuery is a W3C recommendation based on XPath, which gives us the possibility of searching and updating XML data.

This section describes the main characteristics of this language, as the development of XML-based solutions heavily depends on its use. This section introduces the XPath syntax, which is used to identify nodes

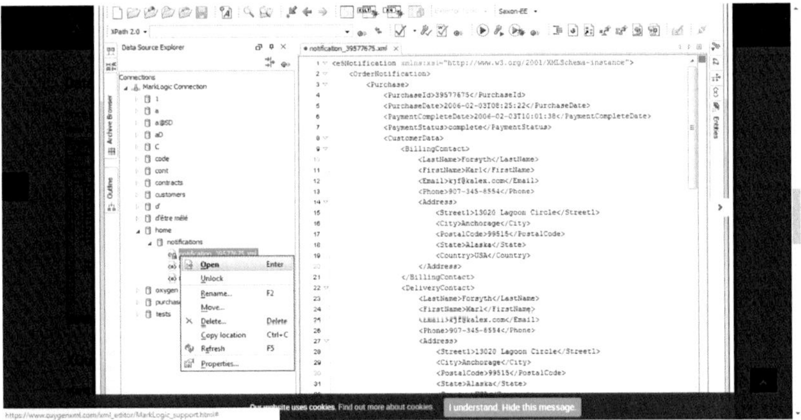

Figure 4.19 Integration of Oxygen with XML databases.

within the XML documents, and the structure of complex queries based on the FLWOR model.

XQuery is more than a query language for XML: using XQuery it is possible to create statements of adding, removing, or updating the nodes in XML documents. But these features are not described because document updates will usually be managed using XML editors.

The examples used in this section are based on a sample XML document that uses a subset of EAD:

```
<?xml version="1.0" encoding="utf-8"?>
<ead>

  <eadheader>
    <eadid>0009</eadid>
    <filedesc>
      <titlestmt>
        <titleproper>ETM-005. Paso inferior de la Enramadilla en
Sevilla</titleproper>
      </titlestmt>
      <publicationstmt>
        <date>2011-02-07</date>
      </publicationstmt>
    </filedesc>
  </eadheader>
  <archdesc level="collection">
    <did>
      <abstract />
      <unitid>ETM-005</unitid>
      <unittitle>Paso inferior de la Enramadilla en Sevilla</unittitle>
      <originationlabel="ingeniero">EduardoTorrojaMiret</origination>
      <origination label="arquitecto">Ricardo Magdalena Galliga</
      origination>
      <unitdate normal="1927" label="anteproyecto">1927 (anteproyecto)
      </unitdate>
      </did>
      <controlaccess>
      <name>Infraestructuras urbanas</name>
      <persname role="ingeniero">Torroja Miret, Eduardo</persname>
      <corpname role="propietario">Sevilla, Ayuntamiento</corpname>
```

```
      <geogname role="pais">España</geogname>
      <geogname role="ccaa">Andalucía</geogname>
      <geogname role="provincia">Sevilla (provincia)</geogname>
      <geogname role="localidad">Sevilla</geogname>
      <subject>Pasos subterráneos</subject>
      <subject>Estructuras de hormigón armado</subject>
      <persname>Magdalena Gallifa, Ricardo</persname>
    </controlaccess>
    <odd>
        <p>Es un anteproyecto de paso a nivel inferior en la línea de
    ferrocarril Sevilla a Cádiz. Eduardo Torroja presentó dos
    proyectos separados: uno para el paso inferior y otro para el
    superior para que el Ayuntamiento de Sevilla pudiera elegir la
    solución y el trazado más conveniente. Esta solución presenta una
    complicación mayor por la excesiva longitud: 42,50 m y por la
    fuerte y obligada oblicuidad de ambas líneas de las vías, para
    conseguir un paso de 22,50 m de ancho. El paso se subdivide en tres
    luces de 6 m entre ejes, reservando el central para el paso de
    tranvías, a ambos lados los carruajes y al extremo los peatones
    con un andén de 2,5 m de ancho útil. Como el ancho de la calle que
    se proyecta es inferior a la del Prado de San Sebastián, se ensan-
    cha con una curva la rampa, en ese lado, para disimular la irregu-
    laridad. La estructura es de hormigón armado: cada tramo está
    formado por ocho vigas paralelas a las vías y oblicuas a la calle,
    separadas 1,60 m entre ejes y con una luz de 10,40 m, sobre
    columnas </p>
    </odd>
    <relatedmaterial>
        <archref xlink:href="../expt/ETM-005-001.xml">
          <unittitle>Proyecto de paso inferior en la Enramadilla del
          ferrocarril de Sevilla a Cádiz</unittitle>
          <unitdate>1927 (anteproyecto)</unitdate>
        </archref>
    </relatedmaterial>
  </archdesc>
</ead>
```

4.7.1 XPath Expressions

XPath is used in XQuery to select nodes (elements or attributes) from the XML documents. In fact, only one query can consist on one XPath expression. Most common expressions are the following:

- Use of the node path to select one element or attribute.

  This expression starts from the root node, separating the elements in the hierarchy with the / character. Attribute names are preceeded by the @ character.

  For example, to get the `<unittitle>` element in the sample document, we should write the expression:

  ```
  /ead/archdesc/did/unittitle
  ```

  To reach the `@level` attribute of the `<archdesc>`, we should use the XPath expression:

  ```
  /ead/archdesc/@level
  ```

- Use `string()`to get the content of the selected nodes, removing the tags.

  The previous expressions can also include the `/string()` node to get the content of the selected nodes (without the open and end tags), e.g.:

  ```
  /ead/archdesc/did/unittitle/string()
  /ead/archdesc/@level/string()
  ```

- Use of the `//` character to get the element's descendents.

  The`//` character can be used to reach any descendant (in any level of the document hierarchy). For example, the XPath expression `//unittitle` will reach all the `<unittitle>` elements in the document, regardless of their position in the document hierarchy. To get all the `<bibref>` elements that are descendants of a specific element it is possible to use the `/ead//bibref` expression.

- Use the * to refer to all the elements.

  XPath expressions can use the * to refer to all the elements. The `//*` expression gets all the nodes in the document. The expression `//bibliography/*` returns all the elements that are children of `<bibliography>`, and `//bibliography//*` returns all the elements that are descendents of `<bibliography>`.

- Reaching the nodes that match specific conditions.

  The expressions above can include conditions or *predicates* to filter only those nodes that match them. Conditions are written within square brackets [ ]. Typical conditions are:
  - Getting the elements that have a specific child or descendant (element or attribute)
  - Getting those nodes (elements or attributes) whose value contains, starts, or ends with a specific string, or has a specific value.

For example, to get the `<unittitle>` of the EAD documents that contain a bibliography (element `<bibliography>`), we could use:

```
/ead/archdesc/did/unittitle[//bibliography]
```

To get the EAD documents whose `<archdesc>` element has a `@level` attribute with the value "collection", we run:

```
/ead[archdesc/@level='collection']
```

The document hierarchy can be used to make additional combinations, e.g., to the the `<unittitle>` element of the documents whose `<archdesc>` element has a `@level` attribute with a specific value, e.g.:

```
/ead/archdesc/did/unittitle[./../../../archdesc/@level="collection"]
```

In this example, the condition within square brakets contain the `../` characters to indicate that we want to move one level up in the document hierarchy (starting at the position of the `<unittitle>` element, until we reach the ancestor `<archdesc>` element). An abbreviated form to do the same is:

```
/ead/archdesc/did/unittitle[ancestor::archdesc/@level="collection"]
```

To apply content filters the condition can include the starts-with(), ends-with(), contains(), or matches() functions, for example:

```
/ead/archdesc/did[contains(.unittitle, 'Madrid')]
```

This expression reaches the <did> elements whose child <unittitle> contains "Madrid".

```
/ead/archdesc/did[starts-with(unittitle,'Proyecto')]
```

In this case we are getting the `<did>` element for the documents whose `<unittitle>` starts with the word "Proyecto".

The `match()` function is similar, however it can include regular expressions, and it can include the 'i' argument to avoid case-sensitive results:

```
/ead/archdesc/did[matches(unittitle,'Project','i')]
```

4.7.2 FLWOR Complex Queries

In some cases it is necessary to define more complex queries. For example, it may be needed to assemble the data of different elements and attributes, apply complex filters, or sort the list of results using different criteria.

XQuery define a syntax that makes use of XPath expressions and support these additional features. These are called FLWOR queries, as they are included different parts or clauses: For, Let, Where, Order, and Return.

- The For clause is used to differentiate between the various elements in the document collection.
- Let is used to assign the values of XML nodes to variables that can be used later in other clauses of the query.
- Where permits adding filters to select or discard data.
- Order is used to sort the list of results.
- Return is used to build the rows or triplets that are returned as part of the search results. The Return part of the query will refer to variables used in the previous parts (those used in the Let and For parts).

For example, the next query gets the values of the `<unitid>`, `<unititle>`, and `<unitdate>` elements of the XML documents in the `inputDocs` collection, ordered by the value of the `<unitid>` element. Those items whose titles contain the word *Madrid* are discarded. The returned tuples are enclosed within the `<results>` element.

```
<results>
{
    for $doc in collection("inputDocs")/ead
    let $id:=$doc/archdesc/did/unitid
    let $title:=$doc/archdesc/did/unittitle
    let $date:=$doc/archdesc/did/unitdate
    where not (matches($title,'Madrid','i'))
    order by $title
    return <document>{$id}{$title}{$date}</document>
}
</results>
```

In the example, the For clause fixes the context of the query. The query is evaluated for all the documents in the database having the `<ead>` element as a root. Then, the Let clauses get the elements we want to show in the list of results – `<unitid>`, `<unittitle>` and `<unitdate>` are assigned to three variables: `$id`, `$title`, and · `$date`.

The Where clause filters the rows whose title does not include Madrid. Order by sorts the tuples by title, and Return defines the **tuple** with the retrieved data (each tuple will be enclosed in one `<document>` element). To ensure that the result of the query is well-formed, the open and end tags of the `<results>` element are added at the beginning and end of the query. It must be observed that, in the Return clause, the names of the variables are written between the {and} characters.

XQuery let us change the order of the tuples (using the `ascending` and `descending` reserved words after the name of the variable used to sort the results).

Using XQuery, it is also possible to combine data from different XML documents that have common data. For example, the data of one document stored in EAD format could be combined with data taken from EAC-CPF documents that contain information about the originator of the archival materials. This function is similar to the join capabilities of SQL for relational databases, for example:

```
For $eadDoc in collection("ead.dbxml")//ead,
    $eacDoc in collection("eac.dbxml")//eac-cpf
    Where $eadDoc//origination/@id = $eacDoc//persname/@id
    Return <results>.... </results>
```

4.8 CONCLUSIONS

The development and management of XML based solutions and repositories require the use of a technical solution for data storage and retrieval. Different alternatives are possible: a) document indexers that can index the content of XML documents to support retrieval using full text and qualified queries, b) native XML databases that store the XML files in their original format and support both full text and XQuery based searching, and c) NoSQL databases. Relational databases also offer functions that work with XML data, although their use may require the distribution of the document content into several tables and columns.

This chapter has provided an overview of the typical functionalities offered by these tools, illustrating their common functionalities through different examples of commercial and open source tools.

The chapter also provides a summary of the standard XQuery language. This language, published as a W3C recommendation, is a standard supported by most of the tools and can be used to query and manage XML data using a syntax similar to the SQL language.

CHAPTER 5

Life Cycle of XML Publication

5.1 THE LIFE CYCLE OF XML CONTENT

This section provides an overview of the different tasks that are part of the life cycle of XML content. The description of these tasks refers to other concepts already explained in the previous chapters of the book, such as XML schemas, DTD, or XSLT stylesheets.

A general process for XML content management and life cycle is made up of the following activities:

- Definition of document types and adoption of XML schemas.
- Generation of content, using two different, complementary approaches:
  - Content creation from scratch, using manual or semi-automatic tagging.
  - Conversion of existing content available in other documents or structured data repositories like relational databases.
- XML document storage and management.
- Publication and distribution of XML content. This includes:
  - Generation of information products for end users.
  - Generation of information products for external software applications, with the aim of integrating XML content into other applications.
- Archiving of XML content for preservation purposes.

These phases and activities may require the use and deployment of different standards and tools, some of them have already been discussed in the previous chapters. The following subsections describe these activities in detail.

5.1.1 Definition of Document Types and Adoption of Schemas

One of the most important advantages of XML is the defining of tags and markup that are used for different types of content. The production of XML content starts with the identification of the document types to be produced, and the definition of their structure. Document structure includes the main sections of the document and the data that needs to be

XML-based Content Management
DOI: http://dx.doi.org/10.1016/B978-0-08-100204-9.00005-6

explicitly tagged to support business needs. Consequently, document analysis must be based on analysis of business specific requirements and on the envisioned future use that end users and external parties will make of the content. Analysis methodologies like UML use cases or BPMN (business process modeling notation) are good candidates to support the initial identification and analysis of business needs.

Once the document types are identified and their purpose and context of utilization is clearly defined, we can proceed on the definition of the document types' structure and markup. For each document type it is necessary to define in advance its elements and attributes; the way they will be grouped and nested; the need to follow a specific order; and their repeatability, mandatory, or optional characters. The structure of the document types shall be declared in the XML schemas (although alternatives like DTD are feasible, XML schemas provide more flexibility and accuracy for the definition of document types). The XML schemas establish the structure of each document type. They provide an abstract representation of all the documents with a common purpose and structure. The creation of XML schemas will result in XSD files, and they can be managed with tools like Oxygen, StylusStudio, or Altova XML Spy.

Besides creating a new schema from scratch, it must be noted that in most of the cases it is possible to reuse an existing schema. XML schemas are available for different scenarios: technical communication, description of archival materials, encoding of text, user guides, and operation manuals, etc. (refer to Chapter 2, Scenarios for Structured Data Management, for the description of the most relevant). A place to start identifying existing schemas candidates to reuse is the Organization for the Advancement of Structured Information Standards (OASIS (See https://www.oasis-open.org/standards.)). This is a not-for-profit, international consortium with members from the private sector and public administrations that works for the development, convergence, and adoption of open standards for the information society; popular XML document types like AMQP, CAP, DITA, DocBook, OpenDocument Format (ISO 26300), and OSLC are the result of its activities.

Another organization giving access to document types and XML schemas is the US Library of Congress (See http://www.loc.gov/standards/). Standards published the the Library of Congress include the EAD, MARCXML, METS, MODS, and VRA Core, among others.

5.1.2 Generation of XML Content

Once the document types and XML schemas are defined or adopted, it is possible to start the creation of documents. XML content must be compliant with the constraints established by the schemas used as a reference. In other words, they must be valid documents.

The use of XML editing tools for document creation, like *XMetal, Altova Authentic, Oxygen, XML Writer, StylusStudio*, etc., help authors create valid content, avoiding mistakes and errors in the use of the markup. But authors and people editing content must be familiar with the structure of the XML schemas they apply, and the meaning and purpose of the different elements and attributes. As a result, authors need to be trained, not only on the use of a specific tool for authoring content, but on the expected use of the proposed XML schema.

In some cases, decisions must be made on the use of alternative ways of tagging the same content allowed by the schemas, to ensure the consistency between the authors in the team. The organization needs to develop data entry templates that, keeping compliance with the XML schema, enforce some additional rules when editing the content. This is the purpose of the Schematron standard. It is published as an international standard: ISO/IEC 19757—Document Schema Definition Languages (DSDL)—Part 3: "Rule-based validation—Schematron, and it provides the mechanisms to enforce data consistency beyond the constraints that can be imposed with the use of XML schemas.

Authoring of XML content will not always be made from scratch. In some cases, organizations may have documents available in electronic format that were born digital or that are the result of the digitization of paper-based documents later processed with OCR (optical character recognition) tools. In these cases, XML editors can also be used to add tags and markup to documents. This process can often be partially automated, depending on the target schema and desired granularity of the markup. Utilities available to automatically process the documents (like the VBA Microsoft Word programming language and macros) can be applied to generate XML representations of existing electronic documents. Word processing tools also offer the possibility of saving the documents in XML format—using schemas like Open Document—that can later be processed and converted to other document types with the help of XSLT stylesheets. Desktop publishing tools like Adobe InDesign also support the exporting of files to XML.

The third situation in XML content creation corresponds to the reuse of structured data stored in relational databases like MySql, Access, and Postgresql. Scripting and programming languages can be used with XML libraries like XML DOM (*Document Object Model*) or SAX to extract the data from the database and save them later to XML. Google Open Refine and Microsoft Excel can be used in these cases as intermediate tools to collect the data from relational databases tables and queries that can be later saved as XML.

Fig. 5.1 provides a summary of the different alternatives discussed in this section for XML content generation.

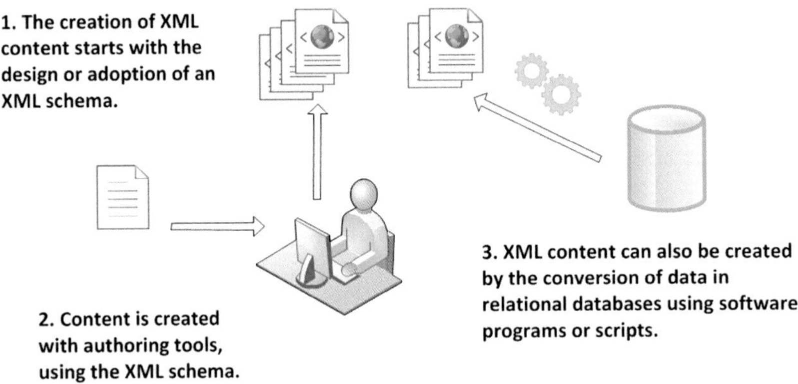

1. The creation of XML content starts with the design or adoption of an XML schema.
2. Content is created with authoring tools, using the XML schema.
3. XML content can also be created by the conversion of data in relational databases using software programs or scripts.

Figure 5.1 XML life cycle.

The result of the content generation process is a collection of well-formed, valid XML files, compliant with the XML schemas and rules used as a reference. In the case of XML content generated through a data conversion process, without the help of an XML editor, well-formedness and validation must be checked. Existing XML editors provide the capability of creating projects including large document sets and checking their validity against a specific schema.

5.1.3 Storage and Management of XML Content

XML content must be kept in a secure repository with the necessary access and security controls to avoid unauthorized changes in the documents' content. The controlled storage of XML files requires the use of a specialized software, like those described in Chapter 4, Databases for XML Data: Oracle BDB XML, TEXTML, OpenText Documentum xDB, etc. Generic document management tools or EDMS (electronic document management systems) like Microsoft Sharepoint can also be used for this purpose. In any case, one important functionality is the capability of accessing the document base from the XML content editors, and being able to open documents from the repository, save changes, new versions, etc., directly from the tools used to author the content.

Typical functionalities of content management tools include:

1. Logical organization of the documents in workspaces or folders defined by the administrator of the repository.
2. Management of users, user groups, and permissions to restrict the access to content and the possibility of updating the data according to the business requirements.
3. Version control, with the capability of keeping different versions for the same document as it evolves. Version control is usually linked to the check-out and check-in functionalities. When the user checks-out one document, they will reserve the right to update the document, and other users will not be able to update it. When the author completes the changes, they will check-in the document: the changes they made will be visible to other users, who will now be able to update the document (as long as they have been given permissions to do that).
4. Search and retrieval capabilities, to find documents in an easy way.

This minimum set of functionalities become more complex when dealing with XML data. A document or content management tool for XML needs to understand specific protocols and standards like XQuery and XML schemas, and they must also support the generation of complex work products as the result of the publication. In a typical, general purpose document management system, publication is usually restricted to PDF files: documents are converted to PDF and moved to a web site or the intranet. In XML, the publication of the content requires additional processing, like aggregating and merging data from different documents or doing transformations between XML schemas. In these cases, support to XSLT transformations is necessary. These XSLT files—as well as the XML schemas—should also be kept under control in the document base. The final work products generated with these transformations should also be stored in the document base, with a clear traceability between the source XML documents used to generate the product, the XSLT files, and the scripts used for doing the transformation and the final, resultant work products (like PDF, HTML, Word documents, etc.)

This is probably one of the more complex requirements for the management of XML documents. The system needs to support not only the storage, retrieval, control of versions, and secure access to the files, but it must also keep all the additional components that are needed and are a result of the publication process.

5.1.4 Publication and Distribution of XML Content

XML documents cannot be directly published, as tags and markup makes reading and understanding them difficult. Before publishing and distributing XML content, it is necessary to design stylesheets, assign them to the documents, and execute the transformations. These transformations will result on a visual representation of the content aimed for readers and end-users of the documentation, usually in the form of readable HTML or PDF files.

Stylesheets are external files saved with the .css, .xsl, or .xslt extension (depending on their type). They specify instructions on how to present the content of the elements and attributes of the XML documents, using reserved words to indicate the font family, size, color, margins, line height, etc. XML documents can be formatted using the same characteristics available in word processing and desktop publishing tools with stylesheets. A relevant difference is that XML stylesheets are written in a standard language, which is independent of any manufacturer or tool, so they can be easily reused.

The separation between content and its presentation is one of the main benefits of XML. Tags in XML documents are not used to indicate how data must be displayed on screen or printed. This feature makes information processing easier and gives the user the possibility to create different visualizations and outputs from the same content. This flexibility is a requirement in some business scenarios and is referred to as *single sourcing*. Single sourcing goes beyond the use of alternative formats to deliver content (e.g. PDF or HTML). For example, it may be necessary to present the information in different ways to registered and nonregistered users: nonregistered users will have access to basic metadata of the documents and registered users to the documents' full text. Or different outputs need to be generated depending on the devices (iphones, tablet PC, standard computers, etc.) that readers are using to open the documents. The physical characteristics of the devices may impose constraints on the layouts used to present the data, and the presentation of the content must be adapted.

In all these cases, the content provider must define different views and presentations for the same content. These requirements can be implemented with different stylesheets that are applied in the same documents in a dynamic way, depending on the users' permissions or on the devices they are working with. In any case, the content provider must keep a unique master copy of the XML documents, and apply different XSLT transformations to convert the data before delivering it to the user. A single instance of the content is kept, independently of the number of presentations that are needed now or in the future.

The XML content management life cycle requires the definition of custom XSLT stylesheets. This can be done with the help of dedicated tools like those described in Chapter 3, XML Authoring and Presentation Tools. Once the stylesheets are tested and defined, they must be applied to the XML documents. This can be done in two different ways:

1. XSLT stylesheets are simply linked to the XML files, by adding a declaration to the XML documents. By doing this, when the reader accesses one document using a standard browser, the browser will interpret the stylesheet and generate the desired presentation.
2. XSLT stylesheets are applied dynamically using an intermediate component before delivering the content to the user. The user will receive the output file generated by the XSLT transformation (usually an HTML document).
3. XSLT stylesheets are applied offline, in batch mode, on the collection of XML documents. These documents will be converted to an output format (HTML if working with XSLT or PDF when working with XSL-FO). The resulting HTML or PDF files can be published in a dedicated space (e.g. a web site), where they can be reached by end users. In this case, the readers will not receive the XML data, but instead the HTML or PDF files based on their content.

In the three scenarios above, the XML files or the HTML files obtained with the XSLT transformations can be published on a standard web server. They can also be indexed using content tools like Solr to make information retrieval easier.

Fig. 5.2 provides an overview of the main components in the publication process: XML schemas, authoring tools used to edit the XML documents, and the stylesheets.

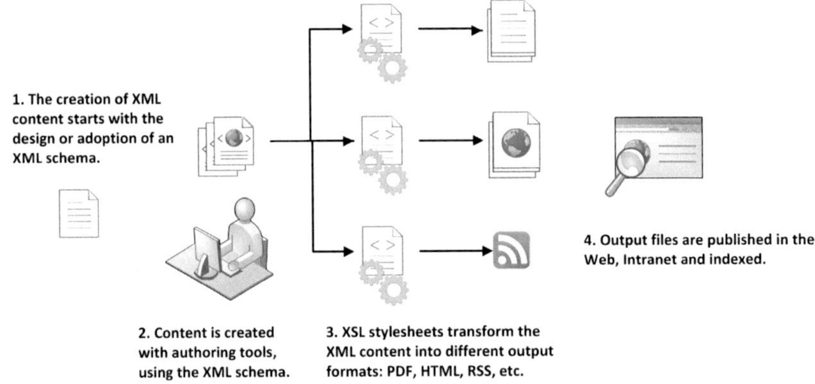
1. The creation of XML content starts with the design or adoption of an XML schema.
2. Content is created with authoring tools, using the XML schema.
3. XSL stylesheets transform the XML content into different output formats: PDF, HTML, RSS, etc.
4. Output files are published in the Web, Intranet and indexed.

Figure 5.2 XML Publishing life cycle.

5.1.5 Dynamic Delivery of Non-XML Data as XML

The previous section described a scenario where XML content was created using XML editing tools and stored in XML format. The delivery of this content required conversion to HTML, PDF, or other forms of XML using XSLT.

But information technology solutions and information systems using web services architectures use XML simply as a delivery format for data stored in relational databases. Web services use XML for data exchange only. The persistent storage of the XML documents are not necessary, and the tagged XML data only exist during their transfer to the target system: XML provides a means to send information between heterogeneous systems.

Using XML for data exchange only requires the capability of collecting the data from relational databases, converting them to XML, and sending the XML stream through the network using standard protocols like HTTP. The target organization or information system that receives the XML data must complete the same actions, but in the opposite order: data must be extracted from the XML data stream, which is possible thanks to the markup that distinguishes the information, and then they must be uploaded in the target database. This is the approach followed by one of the technical standardized protocols described later in this chapter: the OAI-PMH (Open Archives Initiative—Protocol for Metadata Harvesting).

There are standards and tools that provide the basis for doing this kind of data processing: W3C XML DOM (*Document Object Model*) and SAX (*Simple API for XML*). Both of them describe a model and programming interface for processing XML documents. These interfaces—implemented and available for different programming languages—define commands for opening and saving the documents, filtering elements and attributes, identifying child nodes, ancestors, and descendants of any element, getting their values, applying stylesheets, etc. Today, software developers can use the XML DOM from languages like *Java, Visual Basic.NET, C, C++,* etc. The main benefit of these specifications is that software developers can process XML data following a standard, common approach and reusing existing libraries.

5.1.6 Publication and Management of XML Content

The publication of XML content can be made by following the same routines that are followed with other files (HTML, PDF, etc.). To give access to XML content through the web we need to copy the XML files and their attached stylesheets to one of folders in our web server. If we opt for the publication of the HTML files that are the result of transforming the XML documents, the HTML files can be directly published.

Synchronization is needed between the published copies of the documents and the source XML files maintained by the authors. A common practice is to do the staging of the content. Staging is a process that loads the final versions of the documents (or their renditions in a different format best suited for publication), to a target web site. When the source XML documents are updated, the full or incremental staging process must be relaunched to update the content provided to the end users. The content staging process should be automated to be run on a regular basis or whenever XML content is updated (the selection of one method or another will depend on how critical it is to keep the content updated and on the requirements for the delivery time).

The XML content life cycle includes all the previous activities, starting with the identification and design of document types, their formal representation in XML schemas, the design of stylesheets for content delivery, the creation and tagging of content, its conversion to the target delivery formats by means of XSLT stylesheets, and their publication and indexing using standard web servers. The archival of XML data that have a value and must be preserved in the long term is an additional tasks that may be needed in specific contexts.

This life cycle should be supported by software tools for document authoring and tagging, schemas, and stylesheet creation, document transformation to HTML, PDF or other delivery formats, and databases to store the content and web servers.

This process can be observed in multiple cases and is part of the business practices of companies and institutions working with XML. Although there is not a specific standard that describes the typical XML content management process, one standard has been elaborated for the management of content in the area of technical communication. It is described in the next section of this chapter.

5.2 THE ISO/IEC 26531:2014 STANDARD

ISO/IEC 26531:2014—*Software and System Engineering—Content Management for product life-cycle, user, and service management documentation*, is an international standard created by the Joint Technical Committee ISO/IEC JTC 1, Information Technology, Subcommittee SC 7, Systems and Software Engineering in cooperation with the Systems and Software Engineering Standards Committee of the IEEE Computer Society. The purpose of the standard is to "provide requirements for the management of the content used in product life-cycle, software, and service management system documentation."

Although it focuses on technical content related to system and software engineering and operation (user guides, online manuals, policies and procedures, etc.), this standard defines a process, activities, and requirements for content management that are valid in other contexts (Hackos, 2016). The standard makes use of the term *Component Content Management System* (CCMS) to refer to the content management system "that supports the entire document- or information-development life cycle from authoring through review and publishing, including the reuse of modular content."

Content modularity and reuse in different publications and outputs, using the single-sourcing approach, is the philosophy behind this standard. Modularity is used at different levels: the term *component* is used to refer to "a discrete information type that is stored in the CCMS, such as topic, prerequisite, section, image or video." Different levels of granularity are identified in the concepts like *content units, content objects,* and components. Content units refer to "content encompassed by an XML element", while components correspond to "reusable definition of settings for storage, metadata, workflow, and behavior".

5.2.1 Process and Activities

Chapter 6, Case Study and Methodology of the standard establishes a set of processes that cover the definition, planning, and operation of the content management activities. It includes five major activities or subprocesses:

- *Project initiation*: the aim of this activity is to develop a business case to identify the benefits of deploying a CCMS for content management. This activity will define the requirements for this tool/database.

  The development of the business case shall consider the current situation of the company and its processes, and the opportunities and risks of moving to a new process, as well as the costs related to the acquisition and implementation of the new process, and its expected savings.

  The definition of requirements does not focus on the requirements for the tools that will support the new process. It must have a wider scope covering the methods to create content, the ability to find and reuse content, the identification and removal of duplicated information, traceability and auditing. Requirements are classified into different groups: output, storage and retrieval, assembly and linking, authoring and workflow.
- *Project planning*: this activity includes the tasks needed to plan content authoring, revision, publication, and reuse. As part of this activity, the organization must develop an information model, authoring guidelines, metadata schemas, workflows (for content editing and proofreading, technical review, testing, approval, translation, publication, and archival), stylesheets, the reuse strategy and a training program to ensure that the staff acquires the necessary skills and competences to work according to the new process.

  The definition of the information model shall specify the document types, information types, and content units to be managed; their definition, structure; and shall decide on the adoption of existing standards like DITA, DocBook, or tailored subsets of these specifications. The information model is defined at different levels:
  - Information items, which are equivalent to document types,
  - Information types such as tasks, reference information, concepts, etc.,
  - Content units: sections, lists, paragraphs, tables, illustrations, etc.,
  - Elements,
  - Terms to be used as metadata, and
  - Reuse of variables and file naming conventions.

The last point refers to the use of variables in the text instead of names or strings that are unknown at the time of authoring the document. These variables can be later replaced—e.g., at the time of generating the outputs for publication—with the final text to be used.

The standard makes a distinction between administrative, descriptive, and processing metadata. Administrative metadata includes: authors, contributors, dates associated to events, rights management, content validation status, etc. Descriptive metadata are the keywords and classification codes, product names, audience, platforms supported by the product, etc. Processing metadata refer to the rules to apply when processing content and generating outputs.

The planning phase includes the development of a pilot project to validate the new process and – in case of success – the deployment of the pilot project's conclusions to the whole organization.

- *Information development*: once the process is defined and deployed, the organization can start developing content according to the new guidelines and tools. Information development corresponds to the use of the new approach for authoring new content or converting existing content to the new information model. One of the activities requested by the standard is the inspection or review of the code, which can be made with the help of Schematron rules.
- *Publication*: This activity refers to the publication of content and releases. It is managed as a separate process that may require repurposing and merging of existing content to generate different information products.
- *Management and control*: this activity includes six tasks: quality management, review and approval, search and retrieval, localization and translation, content deletion, and content archiving.

Quality checks are controls that must be defined and executed at different points in the process. They include: checking the conformance of the documents with the structure defined in the information model, consistent use of style guides and terminology, completion of technical review by subject-matter experts, revisions of the translations, and the review of the final publication before its release.

When discussing content archiving the standard refers to another standard also presented in this chapter: ISO 14721:2012 "*Space data and information transfer systems—Open archival information system (OAIS)—Reference model*", and includes specific requirements like those for the format used to store the components or rules to limit access to the archived content, with attention to the legal requirements related to compliance and business continuity.

5.2.2 CCMS Requirements

In addition to this process, Chapter 12 of the standard also provides a list of requirements for the CCMS. They are independent of particular software solutions and technologies. The CCM may be based on relational, XML, object-oriented, or mixed database technologies, although there is one requirement for managing XML components in any case. The requirements listed in this section correspond to general storage requirements (e.g., all the components must have a unique identifier, a descriptive name, content type, and metadata), management of content types and metadata structures, and support to activities like component creation and updates using check-out and check-in, import and export capabilities, and support to archiving.

The CCMS requirements also request keeping the integrity between the different content items in the database and information about their dependencies. For example, content archiving should maintain the unity between the source content, their translations, and the published versions. Once the content is archived, the CCMS should restrict the possibility of modifying their metadata.

Requirements in Chapter 12 of the standard are grouped in eleven groups:

- General requirements.
- CCMS framework, which includes storage requirements, content type, metadata structures, and organizational structures.
- CCMS system management, which refers to import and export functionalities, component creation, and modification.
- Content object management: check-out and check-ín, link management, search, versioning, and release management.
- Graphics and multimedia management.
- CCMS administration: user administration, security, and auditing.
- Content authoring, including native authoring, authoring integration, and acquisition of content.
- Workflow management.
- Content publication, including exports and publishing interfaces with XML pipelines.
- Localization and translation management. In this section the support to the XLIFF (XML Localisation Interchange File Format) standard is included. XLIFF, standardized by OASIS in 2002, is an XML-based format created to standardize the way localizable data are exchanged between tools during a localization process.
- CCMS interoperabilitiy via APIs, libraries, and web services.

As an example of these requirements, we include below three requirements extracted from the standard:

> *The CCMS shall store digital images, including graphics and other media types. Appropriate graphic formats that are widely used and are recognized industry standards, such as JPG, GIF, BMP, PG, SVG and others should be supported.*
>
> *The CCMS shall allow an administrator to view the workflow status of each content objects in the CCMS sorted by status, content type, or date of the last change.*
>
> *CCMS shall produce output for the publication of content outside of the working content CCMS, typically to multiple media including PDF, web and mobile. The organization shall define the output types needed by their users and establish a publishing process to enable authors to select and implement a site of output types through the functionality of the CCMS.*

The requirements in this chapter of the standard are a useful tool for those organizations defining the functional scope of content management applications, or for those interested in evaluating different alternatives to support their content management process.

5.3 CONTENT EXCHANGE AND DELIVERY

Content delivery is one of the main sub-processes in the XML content life cycle. This process must answer the needs and requirements of human end users that access the repository by searching or browsing or define alerts to get notified whenever a new piece of content of their interest is added to the repository.

But content exchange and delivery in XML-based solutions must consider the capability to answer requests coming from nonhuman users, that is to say, by other software applications and information systems that interact with the content database. Different standards and technical protocols have been defined with this purpose, being the most relevant RSS, OAI-PMH, and RDF (the latter for exchanging data between semantic web applications). This section describes these protocols and discusses their role in the content life cycle.

5.3.1 RSS

RSS is a popular XML-based vocabulary widely used in web sites. Its scope and purpose is slightly different to OAI-PMH and RDF, as it was designed as an XML vocabulary to facilitate the aggregation of news headlines. The meaning of the RSS acronym has evolved over time, and we can find references to *Really Simple Syndication*, *Rich Site Summary*, and

RDF Site Summary. Its origin goes back to 1995 when *Ramanthan V. Gotha* developed a system called *Meta Content Framework* to describe web sites. *Gotha* moved from Apple to Netscape in 1997, where he developed the versions 0.9 and 0.91 of the language. After the collapse of Netscape, the maintenance of RSS 0.91 fell under the responsibility of *User land Software. In December 2000, O'Reilly* published a revised version of RSS, v1.0, and later on the v2.0 (Hammersley, 2003).

The objective of RSS is to automatically exchange the information about the contents available in a web site, giving other web sites the possibility of adding references or links to that content. The links are updated in an unattended way, with no intervention of the web masters. This is a general practice today on most web sites: links are automatically collected, displayed, and updated using RSS channels. When the user clicks on one of these links, they are redirected to the site hosting the full text of the target content. This functionality is based on *scripts* that download the XML RSS file from the remote site in a regular basis, process the file, and extract the headlines to be shown in a specific location of the pages.

In the information domain, libraries are making use of RSS to publish news about acquisitions coming from their integrated library management system (see Fig. 5.3).

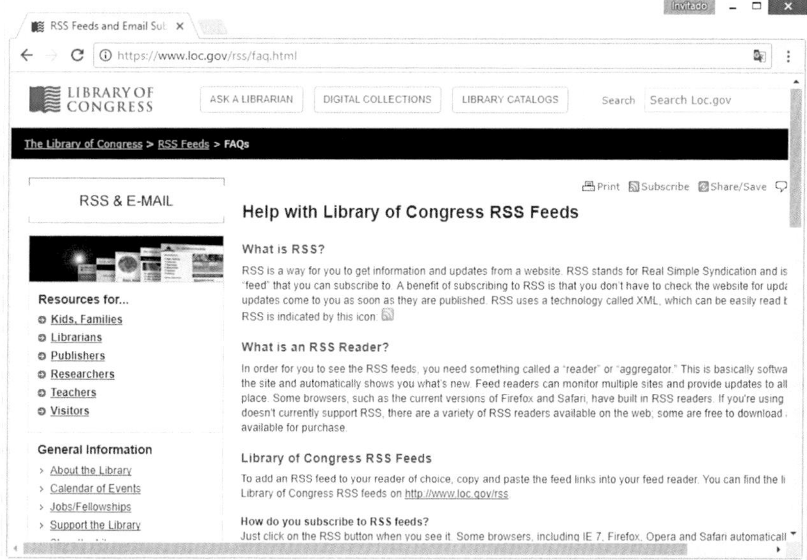

Figure 5.3 Integration of RSS data.

The description of the structure of one RSS channel is based on version 2.0 of the specification. One RSS channel or feed is a document or data stream that groups one or more items. Each item will have a title, a brief description, and the URL where we can access its full text. Additional elements that can be used, for example, to link items with binary files, assign them to categories, or indicate the provenance of the item. The RSS channel will have one `<rises>` root element followed by one `<channel>` element. The children of <channel> are described below:

Element	Description
`<title>`	Title of the channel.
`<link>`	URL of the web site linked to the channel.
`<description>`	Description of the channel.
`<language>`	Language of the content in the channel.
`<copyright>`	Information about the copyright for the items.
`<managingEditor>`	Email and name of the editor of the channel.
`<webMaster>`	Email of the administrator of the web site publishing the channel.
`<rating>`	PICS code used to indicate if the channel has content related to violence, pornography, etc.
`<pubDate>`	Publication date of the channel.
`<docs>`	URL pointing to the version of the RSS specification used to create the file.
`<skipDays>` `<skipHours>`	These elements are used to indicate if the RSS file must not be downloaded in a specific number of days or hours. Once the RSS file is downloaded, the consumer must request the file in the future to get an updated version. With this parameter it is possible to indicate that the update must not be requested at least *n* days or *n* hours since the last download.
`<category>`	Category of the information.
`<generador>`	Software application used to generate the RSS file.
`<image>`	Image or logo for the RSS channel.
`<ttl>`	Time period that the consumer must wait before sending a new request for new or updated content.
`<textInput>`	This element can be used to link one RSS file with one URL in the web site of the provider. This URL is used to point to a web page where users can search previous versions of the RSS files.

(*Continued*)

Element	Description
`<item>`	The <channel> element will contain one or more `<item>`. Each item will contain, in turn, the title, description, and URL of the target item. Its child elements include: `<title>` title of the item. `<link>` URL with the full text of the item. `<description>` description or abstract. `<source>` title of the web site and RSS channel name origin of the item. `<enclosure>` this is an empty element to link the item to a file in binary format: audio, video, etc. `<category>` this element is used to classify the item into categories. `<author>` email address of the author of the item. `<comments>` URL of one web page where the user can add comments about the item. `<guid>` unique ID of the item. `<pubDate>` publication date.

The fragment below shows a sample RSS file:

```
<?xml version="1.0"?>
<rises version="0.92">
<channel>
  <title>Novedades biblioteca</title>
  <description>Novedades semanales</description>
  <language>es</language>
  <copyright>Mi biblioteca</copyright>
  <managingEditor>ejemplo@correo.com</managingEditor>
  <pubDate>03 Apr 07</pubDate>
  <item>
    <title>La noche de los libros</title>
    <link>http://www.servidor.com/item01.html</link>
    <description>Ven a conocer los servicios...</description>
    <category>Noticias internas</category>
  </item>
  <item>
    <title>Exposición Don Quijote</title>
    <link> http://www.servidor.com/item02.html </link>
    <description>Exposición bibliográfica...</description>
  </item>
</channel>
</rises>
```

Today, the use of RSS as a method to distribute information about content is supported by most software applications managing documents and content, and these channels or feeds can be easily reused in target sites. Tools like DSpace for managing institutional repositories support different versions of RSS to distribute information about new items added to the collections.

5.3.2 OAI-PMH

OAI-PMH is another protocol based on XML for metadata exchange. It must be included within the alternative methods to distribute content to external applications and information systems from our content repository.

This technical protocol is linked to institutional repositories and open archives (Hirwade and Bherwani, 2009; Houssos et al., 2014).

Institutional repositories are databases where institutions and companies publish the content generated by their internal staff. They became popular within the last ten years, especially in universities and research centers, as they offer an effective way to control the content items produced by their researchers and teams. Institutional repositories are controlled databases of indexed documents where external users can search and retrieve items, and authors can publish items and give visibility to their research efforts. One factor that has contributed to the popularity of institutional repositories is the availability of free, open source tools that can be easily deployed and customized, like DSpace or ePrints. Although these tools do not store the content in native XML format (although they can store XML files), they make extensive use of XML with different purposes. Content is stored directly as files in any format (PDF, Microsoft Office, multimedia, etc.) attached to a record that contains the document's metadata (by default, the Dublin Core metadata schema is adopted, although the tool administrator can define additional or alternative metadata). Metadata are stored in relational databases like Oracle or Postgresql.

Open archives are larger databases that collect metadata about resources provided by other institutions or data providers. Data providers build a network of contributors that regularly send the metadata of open archive using Internet protocols. The term *open archive* highlights two of the characteristics of these databases:

- They are repositories of documents and information, but they are not related to the traditional concept of *archive*.
- Open means that there are technical mechanisms to publish content and to ensure the availability of content from different providers. It

does not mean, necessarily, that the access to the documents is granted for free, with no costs, although this is in fact the most common situation (most of the open archives follow the open access guidelines).

Open Archives had their origin in the world of *e-prints*. This term referred to repositories of academic documents that were published in electronic format directly by their authors (self-archiving). The first archives of *e-prints* were created at the beginning of the 1990s (Lagoze and van de Sompel, 2001, 2003), and open archives inherited these characteristics:

1. Faster transmission of knowledge, avoiding the costs and time needed by the review process applied by the scientific and academic journals.
2. Researchers are able to exchange preliminary results of their research, before they are formally published in academic journals or conference proceedings.
3. They tend to adopt the open access model and offer access to the content for free.
4. Researchers in academic institutions can give visibility to their research on the Internet, with minimum costs and without delay.

OAI (Open Archives Initiative) is the most relevant initiative toward the standardization and development of technical standards for open archives. It was created at a meeting held in Santa Fe (New Mexico) in October 1999 and organized by three researchers from Los Alamos Nacional Laboratory (United States): Paul Ginsparg, Rick Luce, and Herbert Van de Sompel (Sompel and Lagoze, 2000). It defines itself as "an initiative that develops and promotes interoperability standards that aim to facilitate the efficient dissemination of content." The initiative has defined two related technical protocols to help repositories interoperate and share metadata.

OAI was created with the purpose of analyzing the possibilities of integrating the data stored in different repositories. Having the capability to aggregate metadata gives higher visibility to the content stored in those archives, and end users would not need to visit each archive to get exhaustive search results (Arms, 2003). In response to evolving needs, one technical protocol for exchanging metadata using XML was released in January 2001, and subsequent versions in July 2001 and 2002. The protocol was named OAI-PMH (where PMH stands for *Protocol for Metadata Harvesting*).

5.3.2.1 OAI Principles

During the Santa Fe meeting, two different approaches for metadata integration were discussed: (1) one model based on distributed queries, similar to the Z39.50 protocol, and (2) another one based on the automatic harvesting of metadata and their subsequent aggregation in a centralized database. A harvester is a software application that—at defined time intervals—establishes a connection with a remote web site, searches some files and downloads them through the web. No human intervention is needed and the process is totally automated. The files collected by the harvester can be processed for any purpose. In the case of the open archives, metadata about the documents are extracted and loaded in the central database that keeps the metadata for all the aggregated resources.

OAI opted for the automatic harvesting of metadata because it guaranteed a higher scalability. Distributed queries may be impacted by the servers providing a slower answer because all the servers running queries must be available at the time the query is run. Other constraints of distributed queries refer to the problems derived from the use of different query languages, metadata, and algorithms to sort the results at the different repositories. In the harvesting model, the organization giving access to the central database will publish a single point of access where users can search the aggregated metadata.

OAI-PMH makes a distinction between data providers and service providers:

- Data providers are the entities that create the documents and expose their metadata to the harvester in a standard, easy to process format. Metadata shall include the URL—or an alternative persistent identifier—where the full text of the item can be reached.
- Service providers are the entities that run the harvesting process and aggregate the metadata in a centralized database. They manage the web site where end users can search and browse the content.

Data providers can expose their metadata to several service providers, and one service provider can harvest metadata from different data providers. In some cases, a third agent—called the *aggregator*—may be present. This agent mediates between data and service providers adding additional value with activities like content filtering, reviews, comments, etc.

5.3.2.2 The OAI-PMH Technical Protocol

OAI-PMH is the technical protocol that governs the interaction between data providers and harvesters. The harvester interacts with the data providers by sending requests through HTTP. These requests have arguments or parameters that tell the data provider which operation is being requested and the criteria to apply. The data provider must be able to understand these requests and their parameters, build the necessary queries in their databases to get the requested metadata, convert the results to XML, and send the resulting XML DataStream back to the harvester (Requests can be sent through HTTP GET. In this case, parameters are added to the URL of the data provider. Each parameter has a name and a value, separated by the=sign. If the request includes more than one parameter, they will be separated by the & character.).

OAI-PMH uses the term verbs to refer to the different requests that the harvester can send to the data providers. Six verbs are defined in the protocol: `Identify`, `ListMetadataFormats`, `ListSet`, `ListIdentifiers`, `ListRecords`, and `GetRecord`. In the HTTP request sent by the harvester, the verb argument will indicate the type of the request and each request will include different arguments. For example, `ListRecords` is used to get the metadata for items matching the specified filter criteria, or `GetRecord` to get the metadata of one particular document.

OAI-PMH supports two criteria for filtering metadata: dates and sets. With the dates it is possible to request the records created or updates since a specific date and time. As the harvester will repeat the requests in defined time intervals, the next request will ask for those records that were created or updated since the last executed request. Sets are used to organize and group together those items having common characteristics that will be harvested as a separate group (e.g. by topic or subject, provenance, etc.). Set and dates can be combined in the same OAI-PMH request.

The following is an example of a ListRecords requests:

```
http://www.mysite.com/oai-script?
verb=ListRecords&metadataPrefix=oai_dc&set=biology
```

And the corresponding answer:

```
<?xml version="1.0" encoding="UTF-8"?>
<OAI-PMH xmlns="http://www.openarchives.org/OAI/2.0/"
     xsi:schemaLocation="http://www.openarchives.org/OAI/2.0/
     http://www.openarchives.org/OAI/2.0/OAI-PMH.xsd">
<responseDate>2002-06-01T19:20:30Z</responseDate>
<request verb="ListRecords" from="1998-01-15"
metadataPrefix="oai_rfc1807">
</request>
<ListRecords>
```

```
  <record>
    <header>
      <identifier>oai:arXiv.org:hep-th/9901001</identifier>
      <datestamp>1999-12-25</datestamp>
      <setSpec>physics:hep</setSpec>
      <setSpec>math</setSpec>
  </header>
  <metadata>
    <rfc1807>
        <bib-version>v2</bib-version>
        <id>hep-th/9901001</id>
        <entry>January 1, 1999</entry>
        <title>Investigations of Radioactivity</title>
        <author>Ernest Rutherford</author>
        <date>March 30, 1999</date>
      </rfc1807>
    </metadata>
  </record>
  <record>
    ..........................................................................
    ..........................................................................
  </record>
</ListRecords>
</OAI-PMH>
```

OAI-PMH uses XML to encode and transfer the answers that the data provider sends to the harvester in response to the requests. The structure of the XML answers is defined in one schema that includes all the answers for the six requests in the protocol (The schema is available at: http://www.openarchives.org/OAI/2.0/OAI-PMH.xsd). The root element is `<OAI-PMH>`. This element will contain these elements:

- `<oai:responseDate>`–date and time when the answer is sent.
- `<oai:request>`–requests for which the response is generated.
- One of the following elements, depending on the requests being answered:
  - `<oai:Error>`
  - `<oai:Identify>`
  - `<oai:ListMetadataFormats>`
  - `<oai:ListSets>`
  - `<oai:GetRecord>`
  - `<oai:ListIdentifiers>`
  - `<oai:ListRecords>`

The answers to the `ListIdentifiers` and `ListRecords` requests must contain the items' metadata. For each harvested item, the answer will have one <oai:header> element acting as header, one <oai:metadata>, and one optional <oai:about>. <oai:metadata> is the metadata container. Metadata are encoded in *Dublin Core*, although this is not the only choice supported by the protocol (*rfc1807*, MARC XML or *oai_marc* are also possible). OAI has published an XML schema for encoding the Dublin Core metadata (The schema is available at: http://www.openarchives.org/OAI/2.0/oai_dc.xsd). Fig. 5.4 shows the proposed schema.

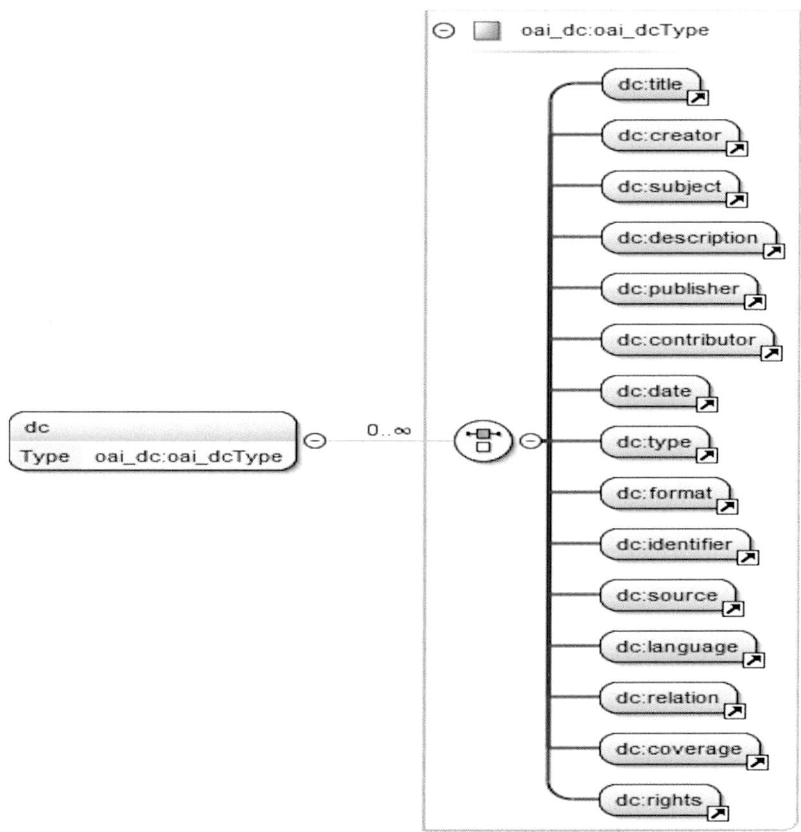

Figure 5.4 XML schema used by OAI-PMH.

Dublin Core metadata are grouped together within the <dc> element. According to the rules of the Dublin Core metadata schema, all the metadata are optional, repeatable, and can appear in any order. @xml:lang attribute can be used to indicate the language in which their values are written.

The fragment below shows an example including *Dublin Core* metadata in the XML answer to the OAI-PMH request:

```
<oai:metadata>
  <oai_dc:dc
  xmlns:oai_dc="http://www.openarchives.org/OAI/2.0/oai_dc/"
    xmlns:dc="http://purl.org/dc/elements/1.1/"
    xmlns:xsi="http://www.w3.org/2001/XMLSchema-instance"
    xsi:schemaLocation="http://www.openarchives.org/OAI/2.0/
oai_dc/
    http://www.openarchives.org/OAI/2.0/oai_dc.xsd">
      <dc:title>Descripción de recursos en la web</dc:title>
      <dc:creator>Smith, John</dc:creator>
      <dc:subject>Catalogación en Internet</dc:subject>
      <dc:date>2006-12-07</dc:date>
  </oai_dc:dc>
</oai:metadata>
```

5.3.2.3 Recommendations to Implement the OAI-PMH Protocol

OAI has published some recommendations for data and service providers to help in the implementation of the technical protocol.

Data providers must consider the metadata they want to expose or publish, as well as the harvesters or data providers they want to work with. Another decision is the metadata schema to be used, although current practice is the use of Dublin Core. They must also deploy a software solution with the capability of answering OAI-PMH requests, extract the requested metadata from their repositories, format them in XML format, and send them back to the harvester. A web server must be set up to receive and process the OAI-PMH requests through HTTP. Tools like DSpace, eprints, etc., offer built-in support to the OAI-PMH protocol and its variant OAI-ORE, and their users can benefit from these functions to satisfy content distribution and publication requirements.

To ensure that our data repositories are known by other service providers—who can aggregate them into their centralized databases—OAI maintains an online register of data providers (It is available at: http://www.openarchives.org/data/registerasprovider.html). When you register as a data provider with this site, a set of checks is completed to verify the capability of answering to the different requests defined in the OAI-PMH protocol.

Service providers must consider:

- The execution and maintenance of the harvester software, to automatically collect and harvest metadata from the data providers in a regular basis
- The set up of a database where the harvested metadata shall be stored and a web-based interface where users can browse items and run queries.

OAI also maintains an online register of service providers.

From the perspective of the XML content life cycle, organizations involved in the deployment of XML-based solutions must consider the requirements derived from the need to participate in this type of initiative (either as data or service providers) and the possibilities offered by the protocol. Because XML is used as the format for data exchange in the OAI-PMH protocol, conversions between the format of the XML source documents and the OAI-PMH XML metadata streams can be easily implemented with XSLT transformations.

5.3.3 RDF (Resource Description Format)

This standard, developed by the W3C, is one of the pillars of the Semantic Web initiative. It is briefly defined as a language for representing information about resources on the World Wide Web. Its initial version was proposed in 1997 as a means to codify and transfer metadata about resources across the web. RDF establishes a model for declaring metadata about resources. RDF metadata are expected to be processed by other software applications, which will act as consumers of the metadata and will process them for any application specific purpose.

5.3.3.1 Encoding Metadata in RDF

In RDF, metadata records consist of triples, each triple having a subject, a predicate, and an object. The subject refers to the resource for which metadata are provided, the predicate to one property of this resource, and the object to the value assigned to that property. RDF also uses the term statements to refer to triples, so this language is sometimes described as a means to formalize statements about resources. The specification is roughly related to a graphic representation, where triples are displayed as graphs where resources (subjects) and property values (objects) are displayed as nodes (drawn as ovals or squares) and predicates (properties) are displayed as arcs (directed arrows going from the resource to the property value). The object (property value) of RDF statements may be a literal (string, integer, etc.) or a reference to another resource. In the first case, a distinction is made between typed literals (those having one datatype defined in the XML schema specification like xsd:integer, xsd:string, etc.) and plain literals (those for which no data type is indicated). The value of a predicate can also consist of an XML fragment. In the case of predicates having a resource as their value, the graph will show the property's value as an oval and additional statements can be declared for it.

RDF makes use of URIs to identify both resources (the subjects of statements) and resource properties (the predicates of the statements). As previously stated, URIs ensure the uniqueness of resources and properties, and avoid issues due to name collisions if two organizations use the same name for different properties in their metadata schemas.

RDF does not declare specific metadata elements to describe resources, but a framework that can be used to declare and codify any kind of metadata, possibly taken from other schemas. This raises some questions about RDF: How are resources and properties identified? Which kind of properties and metadata elements can be used in RDF triples? How are these RDF triples/statements serialized for storage, transport, etc.?

W3C specifications for RDF include the serialization of statements as XML documents, to support their storage, transfer, and processing. The selection of XML as serialization method was a natural choice, when we consider the role of RDF in the transfer and exchange of metadata across the Web and the treatment that software agents are expected to conduct from these metadata in the Semantic Web scenario.

As a summary, RDF statements in XML—from now on RDF/XML—are enclosed in XML documents having a root element called `<rdf:RDF>`. This root element will contain the set of statements or triples. There will be one or more `<rdf:Description>` elements, one for each resource that is being described (this resource is the subject of the statements).

The `<rdf:Description>` element is accompanied by an about attribute that takes as a value the URI identifying the resource (except in the case of the anonymous ones); this element will also contain, within its open and closing tags, one XML element for each property or metadata element. The name of these XML elements will be the qualified name (or

URI) of the properties, and will be different depending on the metadata system being used, as shown in the example below:

```
<?xml version="1.0"?>
<rdf:RDF xmlns:rdf="http://www.w3.org/1999/02/22-rdf-syntax-ns#"
xmlns:contact="http://www.w3.org/2000/10/swap/pim/contact#">

  <contact:Person rdf:about="http://www.w3.org/People/EM/contact#me">
    <contact:fullName>Eric Miller</contact:fullName>
    <contact:mailbox rdf:resource="mailto:em@w3.org"/>
    <contact:personalTitle>Dr.</contact:personalTitle>
  </contact:Person>

</rdf:RDF>
```

The serialization of the RDF statements in XML must make use of XML namespaces, as the resulting documents combine tags from different vocabularies:

- elements and attributes taken from the RDF vocabulary like `<rdf:RDF>`, `<rdf:Description>`, etc., that are qualified by the `http://www.w3.org/1999/02/22-rdf-syntax-ns#` prefix (abbreviated with the `rdf` alias) and
- elements that refer to resource properties, that are taken from other metadata schemas.

Properties (or predicates) that takes a text string (literal) as a value, will contain this literal between their start and ending tags; it is possible to add an `@xml:lang` attribute to indicate the language of the text. When the properties take an URIRef as a value, the element corresponding to the predicate shall be empty and include an `@rdf:resource` attribute. The value of this attribute will be the URI of the resource (see example below).

```
<?xml version="1.0"?>
<rdf:RDF xmlns:rdf="http://www.w3.org/1999/02/22-rdf-syntax-ns#"

      xmlns:dc="http://purl.org/dc/elements/1.1/"
      xmlns:exterms="http://www.example.org/terms/">
  <rdf:Description rdf:about="http://www.example.org/index.html">
    <exterms:creation-date>August 16, 1999</exterms:creation-date>
    <dc:language>en</dc:language>
    <dc:creator rdf:resource="http://www.example.org/staffid/85740"/>
  </rdf:Description>

</rdf:RDF>
```

5.3.3.2 RDF Schemas

RDF schemas provide the capability of fixing the vocabulary and the terms that can be used in RDF statements. The XML elements used when serializing RDF in XML are taken from one of these schemas. RDF schemas specification explains how to declare these vocabularies.

The main construct in RDF schemas are the classes. One class corresponds to an abstraction representing instances of the same type and are characterized by a common set of properties. This is a similar concept to the classes used in object-oriented programming, with the difference that just properties (and no methods or operations) are defined in RDF schemas.

Classes can be hierarchically arranged, and one class can be declared as a subclass of an existing one. The subclass shall inherit the properties assigned to its parent class.

Besides defining classes, RDF schemas shall define properties. Properties will have a name, a range, and a domain. The domain of one property corresponds to the classes that can make use of this property. Domain indicates which properties or metadata elements can be used when describing particular types of resources. The range of the properties indicates which values can be assigned to the property. The range can be an XML schema data type or an existing class.

The following fragment from an RDF schema shows the definition of three classes (book, author, publisher) and three properties assigned to the book class: written_by, published_by, isbn. The values for the first two properties must be instances of author and publisher classes. The value of the isbn property can be any string.

```
<?xml version="1.0"?>
<!DOCTYPE rdf:RDF [<!ENTITY xsd "http://www.w3.org/2001/
XMLSchema#">]>
<rdf:RDF

   xmlns:rdf="http://www.w3.org/1999/02/22-rdf-syntax-ns#"
   xmlns:rdfs="http://www.w3.org/2000/01/rdf-schema#"
   xml:base="http://example.org/schemas/vehicles">

<rdfs:Class rdf:ID="MotorVehicle"/>
<rdfs:Class rdf:ID="PassengerVehicle">

   <rdfs:subClassOf rdf:resource="#MotorVehicle"/>

</rdfs:Class>
<rdfs:Class rdf:ID="Truck">

   <rdfs:subClassOf rdf:resource="#MotorVehicle"/>
```

```
</rdfs:Class>
<rdfs:Class rdf:ID="Van">

   <rdfs:subClassOf rdf:resource="#MotorVehicle"/>

</rdfs:Class>
<rdfs:Class rdf:ID="MiniVan">

   <rdfs:subClassOf rdf:resource="#Van"/>
   <rdfs:subClassOf rdf:resource="#PassengerVehicle"/>

</rdfs:Class>
<rdf:Property rdf:ID="registeredTo">

   <rdfs:domain rdf:resource="#MotorVehicle"/>
   <rdfs:range rdf:resource="#Person"/>

</rdf:Property>
<rdf:Property rdf:ID="rearSeatLegRoom">

   <rdfs:domain rdf:resource="#PassengerVehicle"/>
   <rdfs:range rdf:resource="&xsd;integer"/>

</rdf:Property>
<rdfs:Class rdf:ID="Person"/>
</rdf:RDF>
```

One point to note, before completing this summary, is the differences between RDF schemas and XML schemas. Despite their expected similarity, RDF statements are not based on the elements and attributes defined in XML Schemas, and they are totally independent specifications. The main purpose of XML Schemas is to declare the allowed tags for a specific document type, their order, and how they must be nested. RDF schemas declare types of resources and the properties that are applicable to them.

When using RDF as a format for delivering metadata about a collection of XML resources, it is possible to process an XML Schema or document collection, extract the contents of elements or attributes and build RDF statements into a separate RDF/XML document. These transformations can be done with XSLT stylesheets.

5.3.3.3 Querying RDF Data

RDF has a specific query language—SPARQL—also published as a W3C recommendation. This language is independent of XQuery because it focuses on searching and transversing a network of nodes built from a set of RDF statements.

SPARQL has been developed by the RDF Data Access Working Group (DAWG) within W3C. This specification provides a query language for RDF, open access protocol to transport queries and an XML-based format for sending the results of queries.

Several "query modes" are supported:

- SELECT—returns data from the RDF statements bounded or associated to specific variables. It is possible to say that this query mode returns the results in the form of a "table of variables".
- CONSTRUCT—returns an RDF graph as a result, with the subset of statements matching the query conditions. Results for CONSTRUCT queries are serialized as RDF/XML documents.
- ASK—returns a boolean value indicating whether there is at least one statement within the RDF repository matching the query.
- DESCRIBE—returns an RDF graph that describes the resources matching the query.

SPARQL's SELECT mode presents strong similarities with the SQL language designed for accessing relational databases. As an example, an SPARQL query includes the SELECT, FROM, and WHERE parts that are also found in SQL queries. A basic example is given below:

```
SELECT ?title
WHERE
{
<http://www.uc3m.es /text1> <http://purl.org/dc/elements/1.1/
title> ?title .
}
```

This query is requesting the value assigned to the `http://purl.org/dc/elements/1.1/title` property for the resource identified by the `http://www.uc3m.es/text1` URI.

There are different tools dedicated to RDF data management. These tools offer RDF data storage and SPARQL end-points where data can be queried using this standard. RDF data management tools differ from native XML databases, although some tools—like MarkLogic—provide the capability of storing both RDF and XML data, and offer support to both XQuery and SPARQL. In the scope of this book, RDF is treated as another means to distribute metadata derived from the XML content repository. As RDF is also based on XML, transformation of selected metadata or content from XML files to RDF statements can be managed with XSLT transformations.

5.3.4 EPUB

EPUB is an XML-based format for the distribution of electronic books. The latest version available is 3.1 (published in January 2017), and its development is under the responsibility of the *International Digital Publishing Forum*. Numerous publishers have given support to this format: Penguin, HarperCollins, Cambridge University Press, John Wiley & Sons, Hachette, Oxford University Press, Random House, etc., as well as devices manufacturers (Sony, Apple) and providers of tools like Adobe. The Association of American Publishers (AAP) embraced the format and recommended its affiliates to distribute their materials using EPUB. The DAISY Consortium also adopted EPUB in 2010 for audiobooks. Before 2010, most of the books in electronic format were published in PDF. After that year, the situation changed and a greater number of publishers start delivering content in EPUB.

The advantages of EPUB include: accessibility (text-to-speech capabilities, rendering of video as text), adaptability of the text and font to the screen size and fixed-layout, independence of suppliers and openess. The format is also a recommended alternative for digital preservation. In the report *Preserving eBooks* published in the *DPC Technology Watch Report* (June 2014) of the *Digital Preservation Coalition*, Kirchhoff and Morrissey indicated that:

> *There is a growing consensus for the desirability of converging on standard open preservation formats for eBooks: in particular EPUB3 and NCBI BTS... EPUB meets many of the requirements for a preservation-robust format.*

From a technical perspective, EPUB inherits the characteristics of a previous format, OEB (Open EBook), published in September 1999 and prepared with the collaboration of companies like Adobe, Andersen Consulting, Microsoft, Palm, Nuvomedia, IBM, IDB, McGrawHill, Time Warner, EveyBook, Barnes & Noble, Softbook Press, etc. OEB was also used by Microsoft to create the .lit format (.lit files were compiled OEB files).

OEB used HTML, XML, Dublin Core metadata, JPEG and PNG images and CSS stylesheets. OEB ebooks had an XML file with .opf extension (Open eBook Package) that included a list of all the HTML files that composed the book, their sequence, the list of multimedia files and the descriptive metadata (identifier, title, author, subject, editor, publication date, etc.)

The text below shows the typical content of an OPF XML file:

```
<package unique-identifier="84-5455-111-32">
<metadata xmlns:dc="http://purl.org/dc/elements/1.0/"
xmlns:oebpackage="http://openebook.org/namespaces/oeb-
package/1.0/">

    <dc-metadata>
        <dc:Title>Hamlet</dc:Title>
        <dc:Identifier>84-5455-111-32</dc:Identifier>
    <dc-metadata>
    <x-metadata>
        <meta name="code" content="34CELcam">
        <meta name="access" content="open">
    </x-metadata>

</metadata>
</manifest>

    <item id="chap1" href="chapter_1.htm" type="text/x-oeb1-
document" />
    <item id="chap2" href="chapter_2.htm" type="text/x-oeb1-
document" />
    <item id="chap3" href="chapter_3.htm" type="text/x-oeb1-
document" />
    <item id="chap1il1" href="img/img1.png" type="image/png" />
    <item id="chap1il2" href="img/img2.png" type="image/png" />
    <item id="chap2il1" href="img/img3.png" type="image/png" />

</manifest>

    <spine>
        <itemref idref="chap1" />
        <itemref idref="chap2" />
    </spine>

</package>
```

OPF also included an optional element, <guide>, which contained the cover, glossary, index, list of tables, list of images, bibliography, colophon, copyright page, etc.

In addition to this XML file, the content of the OEB ebooks consisted of XHTML files.

EPUB inherited these characteristics of OEB. EPUB books also consist of a set of XHTML files, multimedia content (SVG) and CSS stylesheets, and their organization and metadata is recorded in XML files. All these files are saved in a compressed zip format. This zip file will include a META-INF folder containing the XML files: container.xml, manifest.xml, encryption.xml, metadata.xml, rights.xml, and signatures.xml.

When defining an XML-based content management program, the EPUB format should be considered as a complementary of additional format for delivering content, in addition to PDF. As EPUB is built on XHTML and XML, the conversion of existing XML content into EPUB is a feasible activity that can be easily achieved with XSLT stylesheets.

5.4 CONTENT ARCHIVING. THE OAIS REFERENCE MODEL

OAIS (*Open Archival Information System*) is a reference model for digital preservation published by the *Consultative Committee for Space Data Systems* (CCSDS). It defines the concept of an *archival information system*, defined in the glossary of the standard as "an organization, which may be part of a larger organization, of people and systems that has accepted the responsibility to preserve information and make it available for a Designated Community" (CCSDS, 2012, 1-1). OAIS proposes a conceptual model that is independent of particular technical implementations and that can be used as a reference to develop standards and to understand the concept of an archive of digital information.

Since 2003, OAIS has been available as an ISO standard: ISO 14721:2003, and was reviewed in 2012. But it was created for the aerospace sector: The *Consultative Committee for Space Data Systems* (CCSDS) is an entity that groups the different national space agencies to coordinate the development of standards for managing aerospace data. The origin of OAIS dates back to 1990, when CCSDS started a joint project with the ISO TC20/SC13 to develop a standard for the preservation of digital information. The result of this work was published in January 2002 with the title: *Reference Model for an Open Archival Information System (Blue Book Version)*.

OAIS is a reference model that can be used to plan and assess the activity of the systems dedicated to the preservation of digital data. It defines the concept of archive, their functions, and the services that must be offered to their users.

The lack of a similar model in the context of libraries, archives, and documentation centers led information professionals to the adoption of

OAIS as a reference for their activities. Today, OAIS is used beyond the context of aerospace data, and it has become a generic model that is valid for any entity with responsibilities for the preservation of digital information.

5.4.1 Responsibilities of OAIS

OAIS responsibilities include the following:

1. Establish the criteria for the selection of the materials to be preserved. Some aspects to consider include how to make authors interested in depositing content in the archive and the protection of the authors' interests.
2. Accept the information provided by the data providers, as long as it meets the rules defined for its ingestion in the archive.
3. Ensure that the information being preserved can be understood by the target community. Users should not need any assistance to understand the information. This responsibility means that the archived data leads to specialized user communities with technical knowledge on how to interpret the preserved data.
4. Make the preserved information accessible to the users.
5. Apply documented policies and procedures to ensure the preservation of the data against reasonable contingencies and the diffusion of authentic copies. This responsibility includes monitoring the user community and how users are making use of the archive.

5.4.1.1 Structure of the OAIS

The reference model also provides a description of the OAIS environment, its functional components, and an information model. It is remarked that OAIS does not specify or enforce a specific implementation for the model and does not mention software, technologies, or database solutions: it just describes a generic model that can be used as a reference when designing and implementing archives focused on the long term preservation of data.

5.4.1.2 Environment of the OAIS

The OAIS environment includes three external entities that interact with the archive: the information producers, the community of users who access the data, and those in charge of managing the archive.

1. Producers will create the information to be preserved in the archive. OAIS must provide interfaces to transfer and send the data to the

archive. The transfer of data between producers and the OAIS will be governed by a formal *submission agreement* that describes the guidelines to follow when submitting content to the archive.

2. The users or consumers are the people, organizations, or information systems that search and access the data preserved in the archive. The interests of the user community and the information being preserved must be aligned.

   The interaction between consumers and the OAIS includes: searching documents and data, requesting documents, asking for support and assistance, etc. OAIS makes a distinction between ad hoc queries and event-based queries. Ad hoc queries are those that end users can run at any time, and event-based are those that are linked to events or time intervals (e.g., whenever the producer adds a new object to the archive: every day, on a weekly basis, etc.). Event-based queries may result in the delivery of data to the users by email or any alternative dissemination channel.

3. The managers of the OAIS will be in charge of defining the policies, managing financial aspects, setting up the prices and conditions for the services, assessing the performance of the archive, and solving conflicts between producers and users. The specification remarks that this group is not responsible for the regular, day-to-day operation and maintenance of the archive.

5.4.1.3 OAIS Functional Model

This refers to the internal organization of the archive and the units or functions that support its operation. The functional model includes six services, functions, or components:

1. *Ingest*: this is the function in charge of the reception of the digital objects and data sent by the producers. It includes validation activities, like checking that documents meet the requirements agreed between the OAIS and the producers, the transformation or conversion of data to the format used for archiving, and their transfer to the OAIS.
2. *Archival storage*: this function consists on the preservation of the digital objects and data, including the actions to ensure their long-term preservation with techniques like the migration of formats, refreshing, etc., and the retrieval of objects from the repository for delivery.
3. *Data management*: this function consists of the maintenance of the metadata used to search and manage objects and data in the archive. It

maintains the databases used to answer the end user queries, and includes statistical data, data related to users, and subscriptions, access conditions, etc.

4. *Preservation planning*: this function is in charge of monitoring the external environment to identify the influence and impact of new technologies, formats, and innovations on the archive. The definition of a separate function to monitor and manage this information demonstrates how important the continuous evolution of techniques and technologies for preservation are.
5. *Access*: includes the services used by the users to access the materials preserved in the archive, request them, and make and obtain copies. This function interacts with the Data Management and Storage functions.
6. *Administration*: this function covers all the aspects related to the day-to-day management and operation of the archive: maintenance of the infrastructure, assistance to end-users, control of the system, monitoring of work procedures, etc.

Fig. 5.5 shows the modules described in the previous paragraphs.

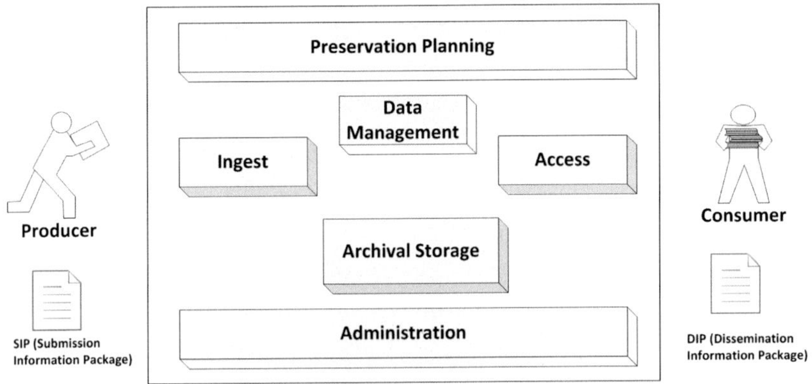

Figure 5.5 OAIS structure.

CCSDS (2012) provides additional details for these functions, and a more detailed decomposition that distinguishes activities and the processing to be done with the data. In addition to the six services described above, OAIS also defines a set of common services that include functions related to security (access keys, user authentication, etc.), network services, etc.

5.4.1.4 OAIS Information Model

OAIS also defines an information model. The model proposes managing both the digital objects and data, and the metadata needed for their long-term preservation. The term *information package* or IP is used to refer to the entity composed by the digital object and its metadata.

The information model makes a distinction between three types of IPs:

- IP used by the producers to send the data to the archive, called *Submission Information Package* (SIP);
- IP used to store and preserve the data, called *Archival Information Package* (AIP); and
- IP used to deliver the data to the end user, called *Dissemination Information Package* (DIP).

This distinction gives flexibility to all the involved parties when maintaining and using the archive. Organizations and users may opt to use different metadata or file formats that will be later processed and converted to other formats better suited for different purposes. In addition, the producer may not have preserved all the data needed by the end users. In addition, not all the data that are needed to ensure preservation are provided by the producer or needed by the consumers. The relationships between the different types of IPs are not 1-1. For example, several AIPs can be created from a single SIP, and the DIP can be the result of combining data from more than one AIP, or several DIPs could be derived from a single AIP.

The relationship between the IPs and the external entities of the OAIS are shown in Fig. 5.6.

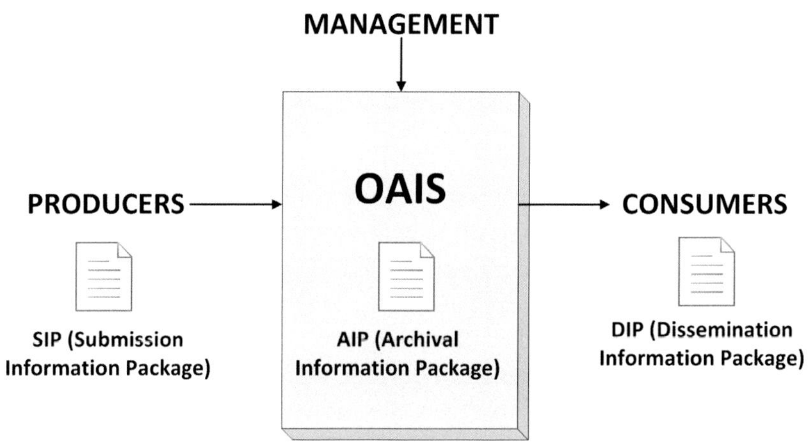

Figure 5.6 OAIS information model.

OAIS also defines the structure of the IPs. They will have these sections or parts:

1. *Content Information* or *CI*: this is the content to be preserved and the information that end users need to understand it. CI includes two components:
   a. *Content Data Object* or *CDO*, which is the file or files to be preserved.
   b. *Representation Information* or *RI*, which is additional information that users need to understand the CDO (provenance, history, meaning, etc.).
2. *Preservation Description Information* or *PDI*, which contains additional metadata, divided into four groups:
   a. *Reference Information*—the identifiers of the object in the archive, or external identifiers like the ISBN, DOI, etc. This group also includes information that describes the methods used to assign these identifiers to the object.
   b. *Context Information*—metadata that represents the relationships between the object and its environment with other objects (versions, copies in alternative formats, etc.)
   c. *Provenance Information*—metadata that corresponds to information about the creation of the object, preservation activities completed on it, changes in its custody, etc.
   d. *Fixity Information*—metadata that checks the authenticity and integrity of the data: digital marks, timestamps, *check sums*, *hash*, etc.
3. *Packaging Information*—these data are used to group the CI with the PDI in a single entity. The example provided in the specification refers to the data about the folders used in an optical disk that act as a container of the CI and the PDI.
4. *Descriptive Information*—metadata that supports the searching and retrieval of the objects.

5.4.1.5 Strategies for Preservation and Interoperability

The OAIS specification identifies the need to apply different strategies to ensure the preservation of archived data. These strategies are defined in response to the risks related to the obsolescence of the storage media, formats, and computer equipment. The user community may also require new services and methods to access the information, in response to the evolution of technologies and changes in their requirements. OAIS mentions strategies like refreshing, migration, emulation, and the preservation of hardware and software.

The interoperability between different OAIS is also described in the specification, with requirements like searching data from different OAIS. The classification of the OAIS according to their capabilities to interact with other archives distinguishes between:

- Independence, when there is no interaction with other OAIS; the archive can only answer the requests coming from its community of users.
- Cooperation: when one instance OAIS can act as a user of another OAIS, with technical interfaces between the two systems.
- Shared resources: when there are formal agreements between several OAIS to share resources.
- Federated: when several OAIS provide their services to a global community with common search tools. This model includes a common catalog where it is possible to search the objects managed by all the OAIS. Alternative implementation is possible: a central site where the metadata are exported, or a query system based on distributed metasearch (queries are distributed to the different OAIS and the results are consolidated in a single list of results).

ISO has adopted an additional CCSDS standard to support the interaction with the OAIS: ISO 20652:2006 "Space data and information transfer systems—Producer-archive interface—Methodology abstract standard" and ISO 20104:2015 "Space data and information transfer systems—Producer-Archive Interface Specification (PAIS)" (CCSDS, 2014).

ISO 20652:2006 defines the relationships and interactions between information producers and an OAIS during the ingestion process. ISO 20104:2015 provides a standard method for defining how the digital information objects should be transferred by producers to the OAIS and how these data must be packaged in a SIP. This second standard makes use of XFDU (XML Formatted Data Unit) (CCSDS, 2008), an XML-based schema for packaging data. XFDU is also defined as an ISO standard: ISO 13527:2010.

5.6 CONCLUSIONS

This chapter presents the life cycle of XML content. A general view of the process is provided at the first part of the chapter. The process starts with the definition and identification of specific requirements using business analysis techniques. This task will led to the identification of document types and its representation through XML schemas. It is likely that the organization can reuse existing schemas. The next activities in the process are the content creation and tagging, the preparation of stylesheets for publishing, the storage of the content and its delivery according to the user requirements. Content archiving for future preservation is also one of the latter stages of the process.

Organizations can use existing standards to identify requirements, guidelines and recommendations for the different stages of the process. Standards that should be used as a reference include ISO/IEC 26531 and ISO 14721. The first one provides a model process for content management, and a set of requirements for content management software tools. Although this standard was created for technical documentation (user manuals, services guides, procedures, etc.), it proposes a set of activities and requirements that can be applied in any structured-content management project. ISO 14721 focuses on the organization of the long-term preservation activities, and its application is restricted to those cases where the future preservation of the digital assets is needed.

The chapter also discusses other standards and technical protocols that can be used for the distribution of the digital content. XML content can be delivered to both human users and external software applications that will do something with it: from data aggregation to value-added services. The automated exchange of data between content management applications is supported by standards like RSS, OAI-PMH, or RDF/SPARQL. All these cases require the conversion of the data into XML data formatted according to another schema. As discussed in different sections of this book, XML technologies and in particular XSLT, offer the capability of repurposing the same content in different formats. This characteristic of XML allows organizations to deliver the same content and data in different formats, suitable for different reuse needs.

CHAPTER 6

Case Study and Methodology

6.1 SCHEMA SELECTION AND INPUT DATA

The aim of the project was the digitisation of the documents that compose the personal fond of two Spanish civil engineers: Carlos Fernández Casado and Eduardo Torroja Miret, and their publication in electronic format.

The analysis of the documents led to the selection of the EAD XML schema for encoding the description of the different records and files. The fonds also included a large collection of image files. These images were related to the files with the technical documents generated by the engineers during the design and the construction activities of their works. The archive had a relational database with metadata of the images, and documents written with a word processing tool describing records and files.

The reasons to select EAD and XML for authoring, storing, and archiving the content included:

- Content could be stored in an independent, easy to process format. If, in the future, the archive needs to migrate the content to a different platform or software application, this will be feasible as all the content is kept in a standard format that does not depend on particular tools or suppliers.
- EAD is a standard format widely used in archives to describe records. The use of this standard makes possible the involvement in other activities, projects and programs at the national and international levels, as EAD content can be easily shared and repurposed using standards like OAI-PMH and RDF.
- There are different mature work to work with XML content, and the adoption of XML does not imply any risk from a technical perspective.
- EAD is compatible with ISAD(G)

The first activity completed in the project was an analysis to verify the feasibility of EAD to describe the different holdings. The outputs of the document analysis task included a mapping between the fields in the database and the EAD elements. The same mapping was done for the sections

XML-based Content Management
DOI: http://dx.doi.org/10.1016/B978-0-08-100204-9.00006-8

used in the existing unstructured documents. The mapping is summarized as follows:

- Engineering Works were described in separate EAD XML documents.
- The set of documents related to each engineering work were also described in independent EAD documents.
- For the digitised images and photographs, separate XML files were created containing the image description and its technical characteristics.

As EAD supports multilevel descriptions and hyperlinks between the different documents, links were created between the EAD documents describing the records and files, those that describe the engineering works, and those that describe the graphic materials. In addition to the links, multilevel description was implemented with the EAD <dsc> and <c> elements, which allow nesting the descriptions at the different levels. Naming conventions were also applied to keep the relationship between the different types of EAD and XML documents in the repository.

The EAD document below contains the description of an engineering work.

```
<?xml version="1.0" encoding="utf-8" ?>
<ead xmlns="urn:isbn:1-931666-22-9" xmlns:xlink="http://www.w3.
org/1999/xlink" xmlns:xsi="http://www.w3.org/2001/XMLSchema-
instance" xsi:schemaLocation="urn:isbn:1-931666-22-9 C:/CEHOPU/
xmldata/ead.xsd">

      <eadheader>
        <eadid>cfc582</eadid>
      <filedesc>
        <titlestmt>
          <titleproper>FC-012. Paso sobre ferrocarril en Alcalá de
          Henares</titleproper>
        </titlestmt>
      </filedesc>
    </eadheader>

  <archdesc level="collection">

    <did>
      <origination label="ingeniero">Carlos Fernández Casado
      </origination>
      <unitdate label="obra" normal="1942">1942 (O)</unitdate>
      <unitid>FC-012</unitid>
```

```
        <unittitle>Paso sobre ferrocarril en Alcalá de Henares</unittitle>
</did>
<controlaccess>
        <corpname role="propietario">Dirección General de Aeropuertos
        </corpname>
        <geogname role="provincia">Madrid</geogname>
        <geogname>Acceso al Aeródromo de Alcalá, Alcalá de Henares
        (Madrid)</geogname>
        <geogname role="localidad">Alcalá de Henares (Madrid)</geogname>
        <geogname role="pais">España</geogname>
        <geogname role="ccaa">Comunidad de Madrid</geogname>
        <subject>Puente de altura estricta</subject>
</controlaccess>
    <odd>
        <p>El tramo principal es un modelo de la serie III, con tres vanos
            de 7,50+10+7,50 m. Los tramos de acceso, simétricos a ambos
            lados del principal, son palizadas de 5 m de luz y pendiente
            del 5,5%. Tiene 7,50 m de ancho y la cimentación es directa.
            </p>
    </odd>
<dsc>
    <c level="item">
        <did>
                <abstract>Vista del paso</abstract>
            <physdesc>
                    <dimensions>23 x 35 mm</dimensions>
                    <physfacet type="estado.conservacion">B</physfacet>
                    <physfacet type="diapositiva">1</physfacet>
                    <physfacet type="positivo">0</physfacet>
                    <physfacet type="digital">1</physfacet>
                    <physfacet type="negativos">0</physfacet>
                    <physfacet type="color">1</physfacet>
                    <physfacet type="b_n">0</physfacet>
                    <physfacet type="sepia">0</physfacet>
                    <physfacet type="no_copias">1</physfacet>
            </physdesc>
            <unitid>I/FC-012/001</unitid>
```

```
        <unittitle>Paso sobre ferrocarril en Alcalá de Henares. Vista
        del paso</unittitle>
      </did>
    <note>
        <p>Anotación manuscrita al dorso: "Sobre el FFCC cerca de
          Alcalá de Henares"</p>
    </note>
    <note>
      <p>Sello en relieve en el anverso: "Kodachrome diapositiva -
        revelado por Kodak"</p>
    </note>
    <daogrp>
      <extrefloc xlink:href="img_lr/I-FC012-001.jpg" xlink:role="img" />
      <extrefloc xlink:href="thumbnail/I-FC012-001.jpg"
      xlink:role="thumbnail" />
    </daogrp>
   </c>
  </dsc>
 </archdesc>
</ead>
```

The next example shows an XML document with the description of a file componsed of several records.

```
<?xml version="1.0" encoding="utf-8" ?>
<ead xmlns="urn:isbn:1-931666-22-9" xmlns:xlink="http://www.w3.
    org/1999/xlink" xmlns:xsi="http://www.w3.org/2001/XMLSchema-
    instance" xsi:schemaLocation="CEHOPU\xmldata\ead.xsd">

    <eadheader>
      <eadid>FC-015-001</eadid>
    <filedesc>
      <titlestmt>
        <titleproper>Puente en Salobreña sobre el río Guadalfeo
        </titleproper>
      </titlestmt>
    </filedesc>

</eadheader>
<archdesc level="file">

    <did>
      <unitid>FC-015-001</unitid>
```

```
      <unittitle>Puente en Salobreña sobre el río Guadalfeo
      </unittitle>
      <unitdate>(P) 1943</unitdate>
      <physloc>Archivador 49</physloc>
    <origination>
      <persname>Fernández Casado, Carlos</persname>
    </origination>
    </did>
<odd>
      <p>No se conserva el proyecto original. Es documentación prepar-
         atoria del proyecto. Incompleta.</p>
</odd>
<scopecontent>
      <p>
        <emph>Planos</emph>
        : incompletos. Copias del proyecto "Puente de hormigón armado
          sobre el río Fluviá. Gerona. Carretera Nacional de Madrid a
          Francia por La Junquera". Sin firmar ni sellar. Madrid, 1940.
      </p>
    <p>
      <emph>Croquis</emph>
      : dibujos a lápiz negro con anotaciones y correcciones en rojo y
        azul sobre papel milimetrado. Sin fecha ni firma.
    </p>
</scopecontent>
- <controlaccess>
        <geogname>Guadalfeo (río)</geogname>
        <geogname>Salobreña</geogname>
        <geogname role="geogprov">Granada</geogname>
        <geogname role="geogccaa">Andalucía</geogname>
        <subject>Puentes de altura estricta</subject>
        <title>Puente en Salobreña sobre el río Guadalfeo</title>
      </controlaccess>
    </archdesc>
</ead>
```

The conversion of existing data—stored in a relational database—into XML was done with the help of several XSLT stylesheets. The database tool supported the conversion of records to XML (a single XML file could be generated with all the records in the database). This XML file was processed with an XSLT to split the file into several files (a separate file per image or photograph). Finally, another XLST was run to convert the markup used by the database tool to EAD tags.

The code below shows the XSLT stylesheet used to split the XML file generated by the relational database tool:

```
<?xml version="1.0" encoding="UTF-8" ?>

<xsl:stylesheet version="2.0" xmlns:xsl="http://www.w3.org/1999/
    XSL/Transform" xmlns:fo="http://www.w3.org/1999/XSL/Format"
    xmlns:xs="http://www.w3.org/2001/XMLSchema" xmlns:fn="http://
    www.w3.org/2005/xpath-functions" xmlns:xdt="http://www.w3.
    org/2005/xpath-datatypes">

  <xsl:template match="/">
    <xsl:for-each select="//Base_x0020_obra">
      <xsl:variable name="filename0"
          select="replace(./Número_x0020_de_x0020_obra,'/','-')"/>
      <xsl:variable name="filepath" select="concat('c:\cehopu
          \xmldata\obras\',$filename0,'.xml')" />
      <xsl:result-document href="{$filepath}" method="xml" omit-
          xml-declaration="no" indent="yes">
        <img.root>
          <xsl:copy-of select="." />
        </img.root>
      </xsl:result-document>
    </xsl:for-each>
  </xsl:template>
</xsl:stylesheet>
```

The next code shows a fragment of the XSLT stylesheet that converts the database markup to EAD:

```
<?xml version="1.0" encoding="UTF-8" ?>

<xsl:stylesheet version="2.0" xmlns:xsl="http://www.w3.org/1999/
    XSL/Transform" xmlns:xsi="http://www.w3.org/2001/
    XMLSchema-instance" xmlns:xs="http://www.w3.org/2001/
    XMLSchema" xmlns:od="urn:schemas-microsoft-com:officedata"
    xmlns:xlink="http://www.w3.org/1999/xlink"
    xmlns="urn:isbn:1-931666-22-9" xmlns:fn="http://www.w3.org/
    2005/xpath-functions" exclude-result-prefixes="xs od fn">

  <xsl:output method="xml" encoding="UTF-8" indent="yes" />
```

```
<xsl:template match="/img.root">
      <ead>
        <xsl:attribute name="xsi:schemaLocation">urn:isbn:1-931666-22-9
            C:/CEHOPU/xmldata/ead.xsd</xsl:attribute>
      <eadheader>
        <xsl:variable name="Vvar3_CONST" select="'cfc'" />
      <xsl:for-each select="Base_x0020_obra">
        <xsl:for-each select="Id">
          <xsl:variable name="Vvar6_Id" select="xs:int( . )" />
          <xsl:variable name="Vvar7_RESULTOF_concat"
              select="fn:concat($Vvar3_CONST,
              xs:string($Vvar6_Id))" />
          <eadid>
              <xsl:value-of select="$Vvar7_RESULTOF_concat" />
          </eadid>
        </xsl:for-each>
      </xsl:for-each>
    </eadheader>
<archdesc>
      <xsl:variable name="Vvar18_CONST" select="'collection'" />
      <xsl:attribute name="level">
          <xsl:value-of select="$Vvar18_CONST" />
      </xsl:attribute>
    <did>
      <xsl:for-each select="Base_x0020_obra">
        <xsl:for-each select="Autores">
          <origination>
                <xsl:value-of select="." />
              </origination>
            </xsl:for-each>
          </xsl:for-each>
        ...............
        </archdesc>
      </ead>
    </xsl:template>
</xsl:stylesheet>
```

The design of these XSLT stylesheets was done with the Altova MapForce tool. This software application supports the visual creation of

XSLT. The designer must select a source and a target XML schema, and the equivalences between their elements can be established by linking or connecting the elements and attributes in those schemas. The tool also includes the possibility of using XSLT functions to transform the data to be copied to the target documents. The visual mapping done by the designer is automatically converted into a standard XSLT stylesheet that can be used from any other tool to execute the transformations (see Fig. 6.1).

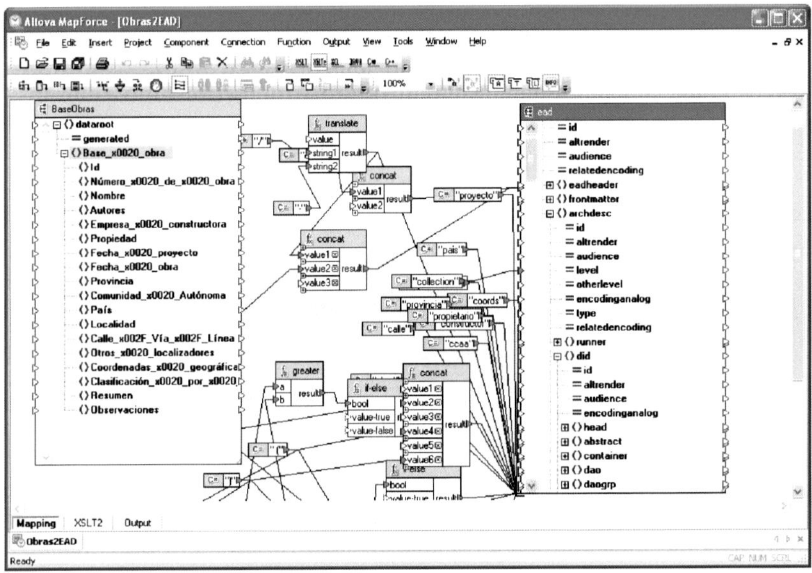

Figure 6.1 XML Schema mappings.

Additional processing of the EAD documents was needed to link the EAD documents that described related ítems: engineering works, files and records, graphic materials, etc. This processing was automated with a Visual Basic.NET program that uses XML-DOM to read, create and update XML documents. For example, the next fragment of code shows the program used to link the EAD files of the engineering works with the XML files of their pictures:

```
Private Sub linkImagestoEngWorks_Click(ByVal sender As System.
Object, ByVal e As System.EventArgs) Handles Button4.Click

  Dim xmlExpDoc, xmlImgDoc As XDocument
  Dim xmlElement, xmlDscElement, xmlCElement As XElement
```

```
Dim xmlAttLevel As XAttribute
Dim xmlArchDescElement, xmlDumpElement As XElement
Dim strXMLOutputFile As String

Dim inputExpFolder, inputImgFolder As System.IO.DirectoryInfo
Dim inputExpFile, inputImgFile As System.IO.FileInfo
Dim intcounter As Integer
xmlExpDoc = New XDocument
xmlImgDoc = New XDocument

inputExpFolder = New System.IO.DirectoryInfo("C:\CEHOPU\xmldata\obras")
For Each inputExpFile In inputExpFolder.GetFiles()
  Debug.Print(inputExpFile.FullName & " " & inputExpFile.Extension)
  If inputExpFile.Extension = ".xml" Then
    xmlExpDoc = xmlExpDoc.Load(inputExpFile.FullName)
    intcounter = 1
    For Each xmlElement In xmlExpDoc.Descendants
      If xmlElement.Name.LocalName = "archdesc" Then
        xmlArchDescElement = xmlElement
      End If
  Next
  inputImgFolder=New System.IO.DirectoryInfo("C:\CEHOPU\xmldata\pict")
    For Each inputImgFile In inputImgFolder.GetFiles()
      If inputImgFile.Name <> "Thumbs.db" Then
        If inputImgFile.Name.Substring(4, 3) = inputExpFile.Name.
        Substring(3, 3) Then
          If intcounter = 1 Then
            xmlDscElement = New XElement("{urn:isbn:1-931666-22-9}dsc")
            xmlArchDescElement.Add(xmlDscElement)
            intcounter = 0
        End If
        xmlCElement = New XElement("{urn:isbn:1-931666-22-9}c")
        xmlAttLevel = New XAttribute("level", "item")
        xmlCElement.Add(xmlAttLevel)
        xmlDscElement.Add(xmlCElement)
          If inputImgFile.Extension = ".xml" Then
            xmlImgDoc = xmlImgDoc.Load(inputImgFile.FullName)
            For Each xmlElement In xmlImgDoc.Descendants
            If xmlElement.Name.LocalName = "archdesc" Then
              For Each xmlDumpElement In xmlElement.Elements
                If xmlDumpElement.Name.LocalName <> "controlaccess" Then
                  xmlCElement.Add(xmlDumpElement)
                End If
              Next
            End If
          Next
        End If
      End If
    End If
```

```
        Next
        strXMLOutputFile = "C:\CEHOPU\xmldata\obras2\" & inputExpFile.Name
        xmlExpDoc.Save(strXMLOutputFile)
        End If
      Next
      MsgBox("final")

    End Sub
```

Once these documents are generated from the data in the database, they can be stored in a controlled repository.

6.2 STORAGE OF EAD/XML DOCUMENTS

The storage of the XML files in the repository (EAD documents and other files used to manage the indexes, stylesheets, etc.) was implemented with a native database tool. A separate work space was created for the publication process. This work space consisted of several folders in a common storage server where the XML documents could be checked-out from the database before running their transformation into HTML and PDF via XSLT stylesheets. According to the principles of the single sourcing approach, output documents (HTML files) should never be directly updated: any change in the content of the documents must be done in the XML documents, and then the corresponding HTML or PDF documents must be regenerated using the defined transformation process.

6.3 HOME PAGE AND INDEXES

In addition to the XML documents describing the different files and records, graphic materials and engineering works, EAD documents containing the description of the fonds as a whole were created. This XML document was used to generate the home page of the final publication, as it gives access to the rest of the content in the repository.

The look and feel of the HTML page generated from this EAD document is shown in Fig. 6.2 (the conversion of XML content into HTML pages ready for publication was done with XSLT stylesheets).

Another tool used to improve access to the content were the indexes. Four different indexes were created: topographic index for locations,

Figure 6.2 Web site homepage.

names of persons and entities, type of engineering works, and the chronological index.

Indexes were created by extracting the index terms from the EAD documents using an automatic process implemented in Visual Basic.NET. The entries for the topographic index are collected from the EAD <geogname> element; the index of persons and entities is created from the <corpname> and <persname> elements. The index for the types of work with <subject> and the chronological index with the @normal attribute fo the <unitdate> element.

The index were also stored in XML format (not base don EAD). Fig. 6.3 shows the partial content of the topographical index.

The creation of the indexes was fully automated, with a two step process. First, the content of the <geogname>, <persname>, etc., elements was extracted from the EAD documents and added to a temporary XML file containing the index entries. The Visual Basic.NET code below shows the code used to create the topographical index:

```
Private Sub Button3_Click(ByVal sender As System.Object, ByVal e As
System.EventArgs) Handles Button3.Click
  Dim xmlExpDoc, xmlImgDoc As XDocument
```

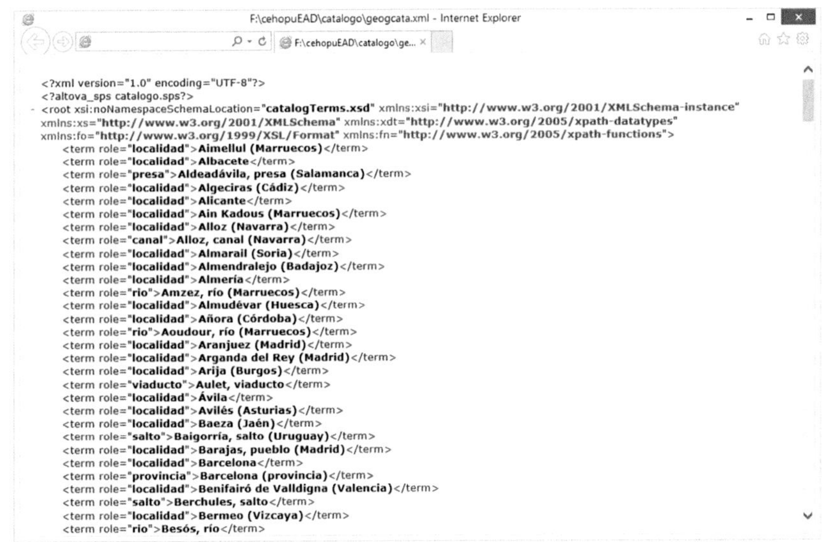

Figure 6.3 XML index.

```
Dim xmlElement, xElement0, xmlDscElement, xmlCElement As XElement
Dim xmlAttLevel As XAttribute
Dim xmlArchDescElement, xmlDumpElement As XElement
Dim strXMLOutputFile As String
Dim inputExpFolder, inputImgFolder As System.IO.DirectoryInfo
Dim inputExpFile, inputImgFile As System.IO.FileInfo
Dim intcounter As Integer
xmlExpDoc = New XDocument
xmlImgDoc = New XDocument
Dim strFilePath As String
Dim strIndexKey As String
Dim strFileName As String
Dim xIndexKey, xIndexDoc, xIndexEntry, xIndex, xFather As XElement
Dim xgeogindx As XDocument
Dim xIndexPath As XAttribute
xgeogindx = New XDocument
xIndex = New XElement("index")
xgeogindx.Add(xIndex)
inputExpFolder=New System.IO.DirectoryInfo("C:\CEHOPU\xmldata\obras")
For Each inputExpFile In inputExpFolder.GetFiles()
  If inputExpFile.Extension = ".xml" Then
    strFilePath = inputExpFile.Name
    xmlExpDoc = xmlExpDoc.Load(inputExpFile.FullName)
```

```
      For Each xmlElement0 In xmlExpDoc.Descendants
        If xmlElement0.Name.LocalName = "unittitle" Then
          xFather = xmlElement0.Parent.Parent
          If xFather.Name.LocalName = "archdesc" Then
            strFileName = xmlElement0.Value
          End If
        End If
      Next
      For Each xmlElement In xmlExpDoc.Descendants
        If xmlElement.Name.LocalName = "geogname" And xmlElement.Value
        <> "España" Then
          strIndexKey = xmlElement.Value
          xIndexEntry = New XElement("index.entry")
          xIndexKey = New XElement("term")
          xIndexKey.Value = strIndexKey
          xIndexDoc = New XElement("doc")
          xIndexDoc.Value = strFileName
          xIndexPath = New XAttribute("href", "../obras/" & strFilePath)
          xIndexDoc.Add(xIndexPath)
          xIndexEntry.Add(xIndexKey)
          xIndexEntry.Add(xIndexDoc)
          xIndex.Add(xIndexEntry)
          xIndexEntry = Nothing
          xIndexKey = Nothing
          xIndexDoc = Nothing
          xIndexPath = Nothing
        End If
      Next
    End If
  Next
  strXMLOutputFile = "C:\CEHOPU_FINAL\xmldata\indices\geogindx.xml"
  xgeogindx.Save(strXMLOutputFile)
  End Sub
```

The entries in the index file were sorted by calling this XSLT stylesheet:

```
<?xml version="1.0" encoding="UTF-8" ?>
<xsl:stylesheet version="2.0" xmlns:xsl="http://www.w3.org/1999/
    XSL/Transform" xmlns:fo="http://www.w3.org/1999/XSL/Format"
    xmlns:xs="http://www.w3.org/2001/XMLSchema" xmlns:fn="http://
    www.w3.org/2005/xpath-functions" xmlns:xdt="http://www.w3.
    org/2005/xpath-datatypes">
  <xsl:output method="xml" />
<xsl:template match="/">
```

```
    <root>
      <xsl:call-template name="index" />
    </root>
  </xsl:template>
  <xsl:template name="index">
    <xsl:for-each select="//index.entry">
      <xsl:sort select="term" order="ascending" />
      <xsl:sort select="doc" order="ascending" />
     <index.entry>
        <xsl:copy-of select="./term" />
        <xsl:copy-of select="./doc" />
     </index.entry>
    </xsl:for-each>
  </xsl:template>
</xsl:stylesheet>
```

6.4 PUBLISHING THE CONTENT

The publication of the EAD/XML documents was done by converting the XML files to HTML and PDF documents using XSLT. Different XSLT stylesheets were created for the different types of ítems: engineering works, records and files, graphical materials, indexes and the fonds description or home page.

The execution of the XSLT created separate HTML pages, and converted the links in the XML documents into HTML hyperlinks, keeping the consistency of the whole publication. The XSLT also included both static and dynamic content (document headers and footers, logos, menus, etc.) Fig. 6.4 shows the HTML page generated for one EAD document that describes an engineering work.

The publication of the indexes was also managed with XSLT: each XML index file was converted to an HTML document (Fig. 6.5).

The HTML and PDF files created by the XSLT transformation process were published in an Apache Web server. It is noted that the HTML pages are just a method to distribute the content, and that the source files are the XML files stored in the native XML database.

6.5 AUTHORING AND EDITING CONTENT

To support the creation of new content and the modification of existing files (with the exception of the indexes that are updated automatically), an XML editor was adopted. Data entry templates were created to make content

Figure 6.4 Web page generated for a EAD document.

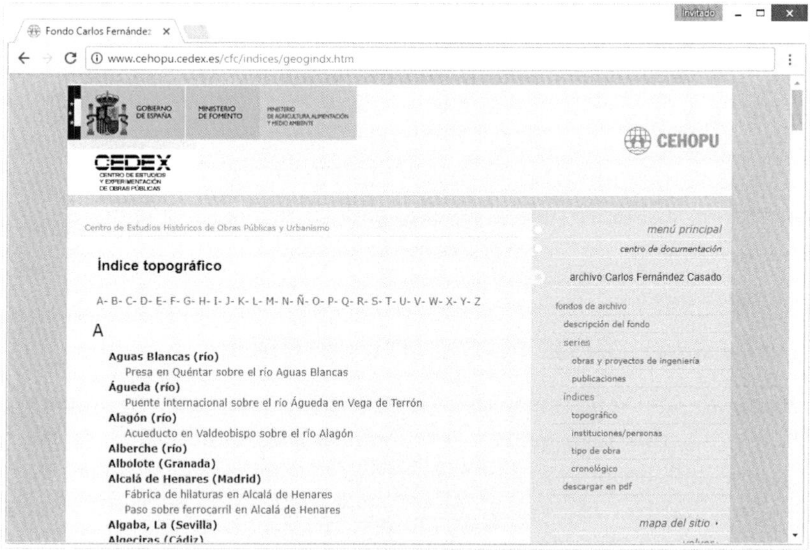

Figure 6.5 Web page generated for an XML index.

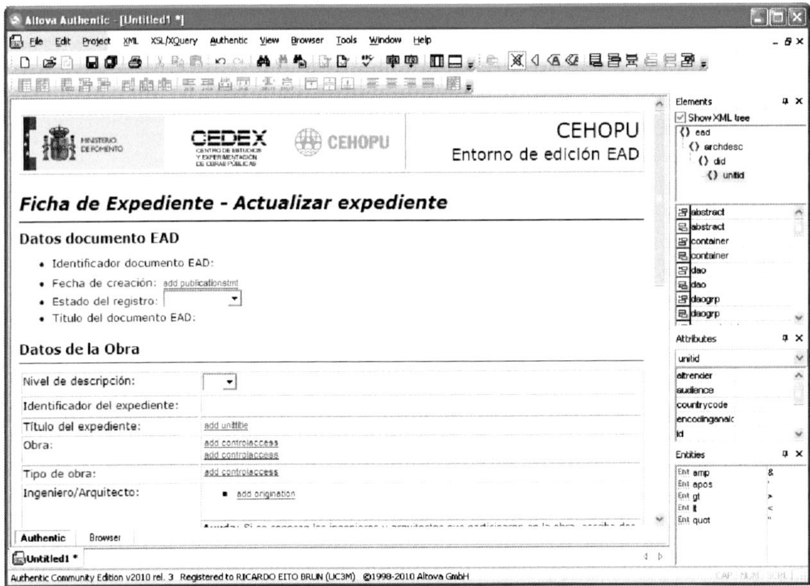

Figure 6.6 Editor for XML documents

creation easier. The templates limited the number of the EAD elements to those actually used in the proposed tailoring. Fig. 6.6 shows the template used to edit the XML content. Besides the limit in the number of elements and attributes that are shown to the user, the template hides the XML tags (users see literals they are familiar with instead of the EAD tag names).

The functions provided by the XML editors (document validation, spellchecker, assistance when adding new elements or attributes, etc.) ensure that documents and well-formed and valid.

6.6 INTEGRATION OF AUTHORITY CONTROL

Organization and representation of knowledge is a key activity in centers dedicated to the management of documentation. Libraries, archives, museums, and documentation centers have systematically applied controlled vocabularies and classification schemas for the intellectual control and arrangement of materials and to make easier the access to their collections. The amount of materials that these centers hold has been increased with the addition of digital resources; this has resulted in a greater complexity, and the need of working with additional metadata schemas for the description and management of materials and descriptive records. Metadata schemas like MODS, EAD, METS, or PREMIS are now part of the standard professional practices of librarians and archivists.

In the scope of the knowledge organization techniques, SKOS (Simple Knowledge Organization System) is the most relevant proposal for encoding, transfer and exchange *thesauri*. SKOS is closely related and based on the Semantic Web W3C initiative, and is a bridge between the current tendencies in Web engineering and the traditional practices of libraries and archives for vocabulary control and organization of indexing languages. Published as a W3C recommendation in 2009 by the *Semantic Web Deployment Working Group* of W3C, SKOS offers a model to represent the structure and content of conceptual schemas like thesauri, classification systems, lists of subject headings, or even taxonomies (Cantara, 2006). A detailed description of SKOS is provided in Pastor-Sanchez et al. (2009); this author also mention different initiatives developed before SKOS with the same objective (to facilitate the encoding and exchange of controlled vocabularies): LIMBER (*Language Independent Metadata Browsing of European Resources*), CERES (*California Environmental Resources Evaluation System*), GEM (*Gateway to Educational Materials*), CALL (*Center for Army Lessons Learned*) Thesaurus, ETT (*European Treasury Browser*, or KAON/AGROVOC.

In SKOS, controlled vocabularies are encoded in XML format. SKOS is also proposed as an economic alternative to migrate existing vocabularies to the Semantic Web. One important point to remark is that SKOS should not be considered just as a tool to publish vocabularies, but as a tool to represent the relationships between different conceptual schemas, as the specification gives the choice of establishing equivalences between concepts from different controlled vocabularies. The W3C recommendation remarks on the need for taking advantage of the experience of librarians and documentation specialists in knowledge organization in the development of the Semantic Web. We can find recommendations on how to use SKOS to encode different types of controlled vocabularies (thesauri, classification systems, and taxonomies) in Miles and Pérez-Agüera (2007).

SKOS is based on RDF. The concepts in the indexing language correspond to instances of one class, and the relationships between concepts and their descriptions are managed as declarations about those instances. One important feature of SKOS is that controlled vocabularies encoded in SKOS are not intended to represent a shared vision of reality (as happens with formal ontologies); the representation that we find in an SKOS-based vocabulary is restricted to the terms and descriptors taken from specific controlled vocabularies developed with a clear purpose and intended for a specific practical usage.

SKOS's main characteristics may be summarized as follows:

- Concepts (defined as "units of thought") are identified by means of URIs, and different labels, in one or more language, can be assigned to them.
- Concepts are grouped in "concept schemas".
- It is possible to add annotations to concepts.
- It is possible to create relationships between concepts, using the hierarchical and associative relationships used in indexing languages.

In addition, one feature especially relevant in our practical application of SKOS is the possibility of linking and relating concepts from different vocabularies. SKOS incorporates properties like exactMatch and closeMatch to indicate the different level of semantic similarity between concepts. Other properties like broadMatch, narrowMatch, and relatedMatch may be used for those cases in which one concept has a meaning more or less generic or specific than another concept taken from a different vocabulary. The available options to establish equivalences between different vocabularies have been said to be insufficient by authors like McCulloch and McGregor (2008), who attempted to analyze the compatibility between different vocabularies (DDC, AAT, LCSH, MeSH) based on the different types of semantic correspondencies proposed in 1995 by M.A. Chaplan.

SKOS does not indicate how concepts must be linked or related to the information resources to which they are assigned. We have the possibility of using SKOS descriptors from any metadata schema like Dublin Core, MODS or EAD, using the metadata and elements that these schemas incorporate to indicate the subject of the documents.

This section summarizes the development of a software tool based on SKOS for accesing and searching thesauri developed by the Spanish Ministry of Civil Engineering (Ministerio de Fomento) from an EAD/ISAD(G) editor. Archivists cataloguing and describing archival materials (documents, photographs, manuscripts, etc.) are given the choice of creating and editing EAD/ISAD(G) finding aids as well as EAC-CPF authority records. When editing these finding aids, they can interact with remote SKOS repositories to locate and assign the descriptors they want to use as access points for their records (see Fig. 6.7).

The SKOS repository is a DBXML database. The interaction and communication between the EAD/ISAD(G) editor and the DBXML

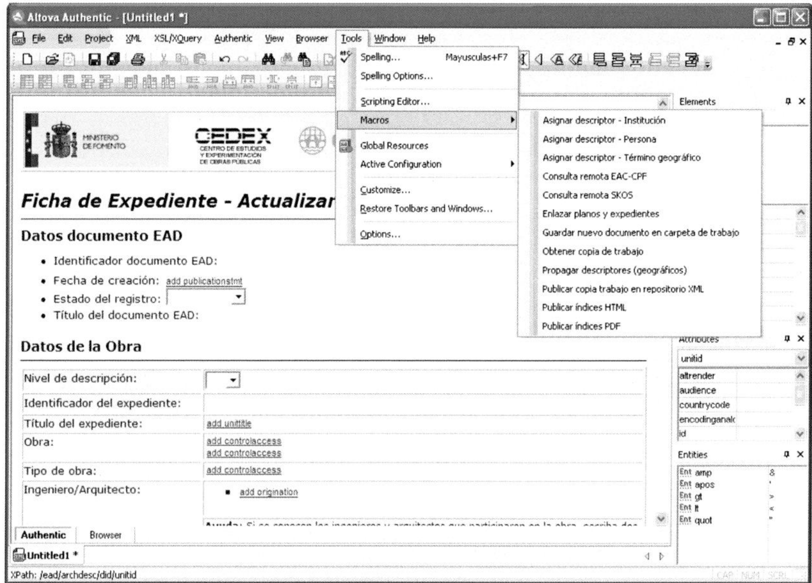

Figure 6.7 Access to SKOS index terms.

database is implemented by means of XML web services implemented on PHP, VBScript and compliant with the SRU technical protocol. Using the services and messages defined in this technical protocol, archivists who are cataloguing materials can select the controlled vocabulary they want to search, enter the terms, and restrict the search to different choices (e.g., just preferred terms, any term in the vocabulary, terms with a meaning more specific than the proposed one, etc.). To this end, an SRU/CQL profile has been defined as part of this project.

Once the search criteria are entered, the local system (EAD editor) creates an SRU request that is directed to the database that corresponds to the chosen controlled vocabulary (see Fig. 6.8). After the execution of the search by the remote server, the client computer receives an SRU/XML response with the terms that meet the search criteria. The list of retrieved terms (Fig. 6.9) are shown to the archivists/cataloguer (preferred and non-preferred terms are displayed with different types, and the system does not allow to assign non-preferred terms).

From the list of results, the user can:

- Select one preferred term and assign it to the finding aid or IAD(G) description. The selected term shall be added to the EAD document in a new <subject> element. The attribute @source shall take as a

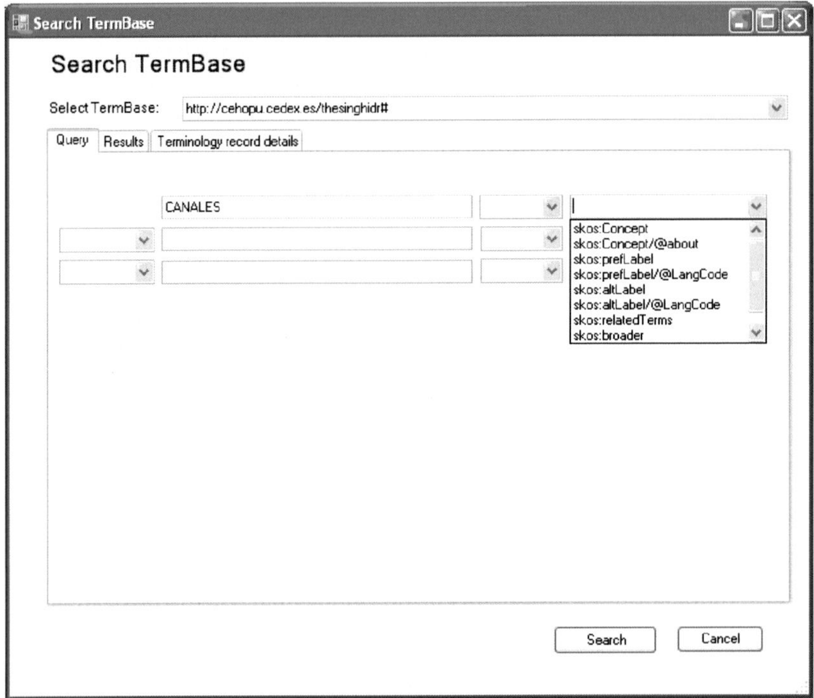

Figure 6.8 Searching the SKOS thesauri.

value the URI of the controlled vocabulary. If the user is creating an authority record based on EAC-CPF, he/she may indicate to which EAC-CPF element the term must be assigned, and the source of the term shall be recorded in the @vocabularySource EAC-CPF attribute.

- Select one term from the list (Fig. 6.10) and request to the remote server the list of its related terms and the full information for this term (scope notes, etc.) available in the thesauri.

Regarding the selected method of storage for the SKOS thesauri within the DBXML database, each term in the controlled vocabulary—with all its relationships—is kept in a separate XML file. The full set of XML files (one per term) have been ingested in the DBXML database. This gives the choice of editing and updating each term, and its relationships, one by one, and improves the capability of managing semantic relationships between terms from different vocabularies.

The interaction between the client application (the EAD/ISAD(G) editor) and the SKOS repository has been implemented by means of the messages defined in the SRU technical protocol. As an example,

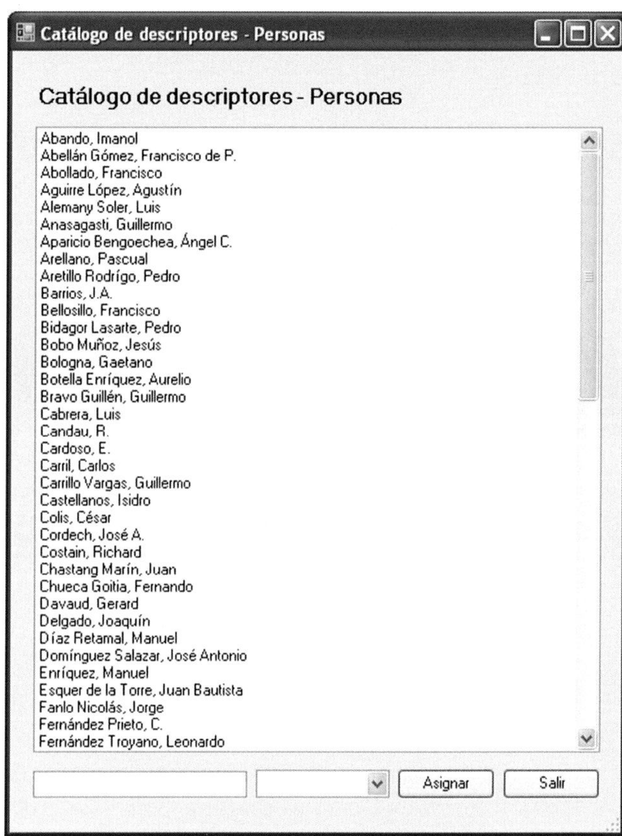

Figure 6.9 List of terms retrieved from the SKOS thesauri

this is a sample requests sent by the client to retrieve terms from the vocabulary:

```
http://server.es/sruSrvr/skos_processRequest.php?
version=1.2&operation=searchRetrieve&
query=CONSULTA_CQL&maximumRecords=100&recordSchema=skos_summary
```

The response from the remote server shall be also SRU-compliant, and shall include all the terms / descriptors matching the search criteria. It is an XML message similar to this one:

```
<?xml version="1.0" encoding="UTF-8" ?>
<SRU:searchRetrieveResponse xmlns:SRU="http://www.loc.gov/zing/srw/">
<SRU:version>1.2</SRU:version>
<SRU:numberOfRecords>5</SRU:numberOfRecords>
```

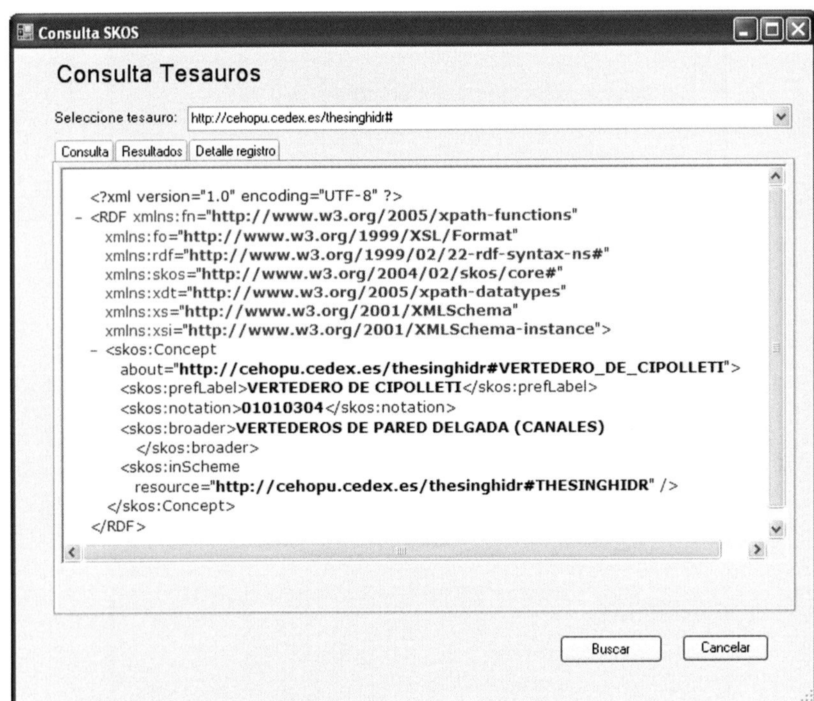

Figure 6.10 SKOS display of a term.

```
<SRU:records xmlns:skos="http://www.w3c.org/2004/02/skos/core#">
  <SRU:record>
    <SRU:recordSchema>info:srw/schema/1/skos-v1.0
    </SRU:recordSchema>
    <SRU:recordPacking>xml</SRU:recordPacking>
    <SRU:recordData>
      <skos:Concept rdf:about="http://cehopu.cedex.es/thes#1002">
        <skos:prefLabel>Obras hidráulicas</skos:prefLabel>
      </skos:Concept>
    </SRU:recordData>
  </SRU:record>
  <SRU:record>
    <SRU:recordSchema>info:srw/schema/1/skos-v1.0</SRU:recordSchema>
    <SRU:recordPacking>xml</SRU:recordPacking>
    <SRU:recordData>
      <skos:Concept rdf:about="http://cehopu.cedex.es/thes#0350">
```

```
            <skos:altLabel>Drenaje hidráulico</skos:altLabel>
            <skos:prefLabel>Drenajes</skos:prefLabel>
          </skos:Concept>
        </SRU:recordData>
      </SRU:record>
      <!—REST OF THE RECORDS -->
    </SRU:records>
    </SRU:searchRetrieveResponse>
```

6.7 CONCLUSIONS

The previous process describes the steps completed to develop a content management system based on the XML language, format and standards. The key elements to be considered in the applied methodology include:

- Artifacts and work products. These include the XML schemas, the XML documents, the transformations (via XSLT), and other output formats (HTML, PDF, or other XML document types like RDF, OAI, Dublin Core, RSS, etc.)
- Roles. They include the stylesheet designers, the authors, and editors of the content, and software applications and scripts used to complete tasks according to a defined schedule or on demand.
- Activities and tasks. These are the different activities to be done during the content life cycle: document type analysis, content authoring, conversion, publication, indexing, etc.

The provided example demonstrates that complex XML repositories, based on different document types and schemas, can be developed with the aim of giving access to the content in electronic format and keeping our assets in a controlled environment. The example also shows how the different standards, tools, and techniques described in the previous chapters of the book can be combined to provide a work environment where authors and editors can contribute to the creation of content, and end users can search and browse digital collections based on different schema.

BIBLIOGRAPHY

Arms, C.R., 2003. Available and useful: OAI at the Library of Congress. Library Hi Tech 21 (2), 129−139.

Burnard, L., Sperberg-McQueen C.M., 2012. TEI Lite: Encoding for Interchange: an introduction to the TEI Final revised edition for TEI P5. The TEI Consortium. <http://www.tei-c.org/Guidelines/Customization/Lite/>.

Candela, P., 2003. W3C Glossary and Dictionary. <http://www.w3.org/2003/glossary/>.

Cantara, L., 2006. Encoding controlled vocabularies for the Semantic Web using SKOS Core. OCLC Syst. Serv. 22 (2), 111−114.

CCSDS, 2008. Recommended StandardBlue Book XML Formatted Data Unit (XFDU) Structure and Construction Rules. Consultative Committee for Space Data Systems (Recommendation for Space Data System Standards).

CCSDS, 2012. Reference Model for an Open Archival Information System (OAIS): Recommended Practice CCSDS 650.0-M-2. Consultative Committee for Space Data Systems (Recommendation for Space Data System Standards).

CCSDS, 2014. Producer-Archive Interface Specification (PAIS): Recommended Standard CCSDS 651.1-B-1. Consultative Committee for Space Data Systems (Recommendation for Space Data System Standards).

Cornish, A., 2004. Using a native XML database for encoded archival description search and retrieval. Inform. Technol. Libraries 23 (4), 181−184.

Cundiff, M.V., 2004. An introduction to the metadata encoding and transmission standard (METS). Library Hi Tech 22 (1), 52−64.

Desantes, B., 2005. The Encoded Archival Guide (EAG), DTD, and the Censo-Guía de los Archivos de España e Iberoamérica Project: An Electronic Guide to Spanish and Iberian American Archives. J. Arch. Organ. 3 (2/3), 23−38.

Devarrewaere, A., Roelly, A., 2005. Using a software package to publish EAD encoded finding aids: a practical approach and gradual implementation at the archives Départementales de la Côte-d'Or, France. J. Arch. Organ. 3 (2/3), 171−181.

Di Monte, L., Serafin, M., 2017. Drupal, TEI and XML: How to prototype a digital humanities tool? Library Hi Tech News 34 (4), 9−15.

Dooley, J.M. (Ed.), 1998. Encoded Archival Description: Context, Theory, and Case Studies: [also published in: American Archivist v. 60, no. 3−4]. Society of American Archivists, Chicago.

Erjavec, T., 2010. Text encoding initiative guidelines and their localisation. Infotheca J. Inform. Librarianship 11 (1), 3a−14a.

Evia, C., Tech, V., Priestley, M., 2016. Structured authoring without XML: Evaluating lightweight DITA for technical documentation. Tech. Commun. 63 (1), 23−37.

Goldfarb, C.F., Prescod, P., 2004. Charles F. Goldfarb's XML Handbook, fifth ed Prentice-Hall, Upper Saddle River, NJ, 1280 p.

Hackos, J.T., 2016. International standards for information development and content management. IEEE Trans. Professional Commun. 59 (1), 24−36.

Halsell, L.A., 2013. TEI and so can you: corpus linguistics and the text encoding initiative. PNLA Q. 77 (3), 63−70.

Hammersley, B., 2003. Content Syndication with RSS, 2003 xi. Prentice Hall PTR, Beijing [etc.], 208 p.

Hirwade, M.A., Bherwani, M.T., 2009. Facilitating searches in multiple bibliographical databases: metadata harvesting service providers. Liber Q. J. Eur. Res. Libraries 19 (2), 140−165.

Houssos, N., et al., 2014. Enhanced OAI-PMH services for metadata sharing in heterogeneous environments. Library Rev. 63 (6/7), 1.

International Council on Archives, 2000. ISAD(G): General International Standard Archival Description: Adopted by the Committee on Descriptive Standards Stockholm, Sweden, 19–22 September 1999, second ed. ICA, Ottawa, 91 p.

International Council on Archives, 2004. ISAAR(CPF): International Standard Archival Authority Record for Corporate Bodies, Persons and Families, second ed. ICA, Paris, 70 p. (ICA Standards).

ISO, 1986. Standard Generalized Markup Language (SGML). ISO 8879:1986. International Organization for Standardization (Information processing - Text and office systems), Geneva.

ISO, 1996. Document Style Semantics and Specification Language (DSSSL). ISO/IEC 10179:1996. International Organization for Standardization (Information technology - Processing languages), Geneva.

ISO, 2012. Open archival information system (OAIS) - Reference model. ISO 14721:2012. International Organization for Standardization (Space data and information transfer systems), Geneva.

ISO/IEC, 2006. Document Schema Definition Languages (DSDL) - Part 3: Rule-based validation – Schematron. ISO/IEC 19757-3:2006. Information Technology.

ISO/IEC/IEEE, 2015. Content management for product life-cycle, user and service management documentation. ISO/IEC/IEEE 26531:2015. Systems and software engineering.

Kelley, K., 2017. DITA: Past, Present, and Future. University of Minnesota Digital Conservancy. Available from: http://hdl.handle.net/11299/187929.

Lagoze, C., van de Sompel, H., 2001. The Open Archives Initiative: building a low-barrier interoperability framework. In: Proceedings on ACM/IEEE Joint Conference on Digital Libraries, pp. 54–62.

Lagoze, C., van de Sompel, H., 2003. The making of the open archives initiative protocol for metadata harvesting. Library Hi Tech 21 (2), 118–128.

Lu, E., et al., 2006. *An empirical* study of XML data management in business information systems. J. Syst. Softw. 79 (7), 984–1000.

McCallum, S.H., 2004. An introduction to the Metadata Object Description Schema (MODS). Library High Tech 22 (1), 82–88.

McCarthy, E., Welsh, A., Wheale, S., 2012. Early modern Oxford bindings in twenty-first century markup. Library Rev. 61 (8/9), 561–576.

McCulloch, E., McGregor, G., 2008. Analysis of equivalence mapping for terminology services. J. Inform. Sci. 34 (1), 70–92.

Miles, A., Pérez-Agüera, J.R., 2007. SKOS: Simple Knowledge Organization for the Web. Cat. Classif. Q. 43 (3/4), 69–83.

Nicholson, D., 2006. Interpretive journeys and METS: Determining requirements for the effective management of complex digital objects in a National Park. J. Document. 62 (2), 271–290.

OAI, 2015. The Open Archives Initiative Protocol for Metadata Harvesting: Protocol Version 2.0. Open Archives Initiative. Available from: http://www.openarchives.org/OAI/openarchivesprotocol.html.

Pastor-Sánchez, J.A., Martínez, J.F., Rodríguez-Muñoz, J.V., 2009. Advantages of thesaurus representation using the Simple Knowledge Organization System (SKOS) compared with other alternatives. Inf. Res. 14 (4), 19–20.

Pitti, D., 2004a. Creator description: encoded archival context. Int. Cat. Bibliogr. Control 33 (2), 32–38.

Pitti, D., 2004b. Creator description: encoded archival context. Cat. Classif. Q. 38 (3/4), 201–226.

Pitti, D., Duff, W.M. (Eds.), 2001. Encoded Archival Description on the Internet. Haworth Press, New York [etc.], 241 p.

Sadalage, P.J., Fowler, M., 2013. NoSQL Distilled: a Brief Guide to the Emerging World of Polyglot Persistence, vol. XIX. Addison-Wesley, Upper Saddle River, NJ, 164 p.

Seadle, M., 2002. METS and the metadata marketplace. Library Hi Tech 20 (3), 255–257.

Sompel, H.V.D., Lagoze, C., 2000. The Santa Fe Convention of the Open Archives Initiative. D-Lib Mag. 6 (2). Available from: http://www.dlib.org/dlib/february00/vandesompel-oai/02vandesompel-oai.html.

Szary, R.V., 2005. Encoded Archival Context (EAC) and archival description: rationale and background. J. Arch. Organ. 3 (2/3), 217–227.

Thurman, A.C., 2005. *Metadata Standards* for archival control: an introduction to EAD and EAC. Cat. Classif. Q. 40 (3/4), 183–212.

Travis, B.E., Waldt, D.C., 1996. The SGML Implementation Guide: a blueprint for SGML migration, vol. xxv. Springer, Berlin [etc.], 522 p.

W3C, 2004a. XML Schema Part 0 Primer Second edition: W3C Recommendation 28-10-2004. <https://www.w3.org/TR/xmlschema-0/>.

W3C, 2004b. XML Schema Part 1 Structures: Second Edition: W3C Recommendation 28 October2004. <http://www.w3.org/TR/xmlschema-1/>.

W3C, 2006a. Extensible Markup Language (XML) 1.1: W3C Recommendation 16-08-2006. second ed. <https://www.w3.org/TR/xml11/>.

W3C, 2006b. Extensible Stylesheet Language (XSL) Version 1.1: W3C Recommendation 05 December 2006. <https://www.w3.org/TR/xsl11/>.

W3C, 2007a. SOAP Version 1.2 Part 0: Primer: W3C Recommendation 27 April 2007. <http://www.w3.org/TR/soap12-part0/>.

W3C, 2007b. SOAP Version 1.2 Part 2: Adjuncts: W3C Recommendation 27 April 2007. <http://www.w3.org/TR/soap12-part2/>.

W3C, 2008. Extensible Markup Language (XML) 1.0 (Fifth Edition): W3C Recommendation 26 November 2008. <https://www.w3.org/TR/xml/>.

W3C, 2009. Namespaces in XML 1.0 (Third Edition): W3C Recommendation 8 December2009. <https://www.w3.org/TR/xml-names/>.

W3C, 2010. Associating Style Sheets with XML documents 1.0: Second edition: W3C Recommendation28-10-2010. <https://www.w3.org/TR/xml-stylesheet/>.

W3C, 2017. XSL Transformations (XSLT) Version 3: W3C Recommendation 8 June 2017. <https://www.w3.org/TR/xslt-30/>.

INDEX

Note: Page numbers followed by "*f*" and "*t*" refer to figures and tables, respectively.

D

Printed in the United States
By Bookmasters